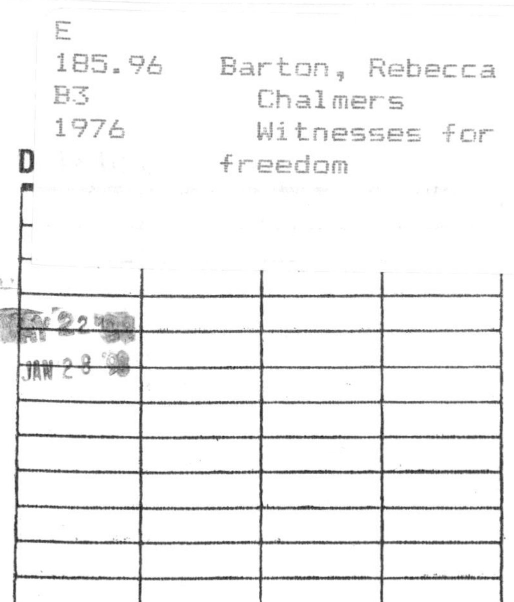

LENDING POLICY

IF YOU DAMAGE OR LOSE LIBRARY MATERIALS, THEN YOU WILL BE CHARGED FOR REPLACEMENT. FAILURE TO PAY AFFECTS LIBRARY PRIVILEGES, GRADES, TRANSCRIPTS, DIPLOMAS, AND REGISTRATION PRIVILEGES OR ANY COMBINATION THEREOF.

". . . an important contribution to the expanding faith of the American Negro race in its destiny."

Harrison Smith
Saturday Review

"*Witnesses for Freedom* opens up a previously closed but highly significant area of typical American social experience . . . it affords an unsentimental and therefore sobering and enlightening journey into the psychological heart of the American race problem . . . In a day of enlarging perspectives in group relations, Rebecca Barton has performed a real service toward enlarged social understanding and dynamic democratic thought and action."

Dr. Alain Locke
Professor of Philosophy
Howard University

"I have borrowed this phrase, 'witnesses for freedom,' from Rebecca Chalmers Barton to say many times over, to Negro American student audiences in particular, that this is an aspect of our heritage which our country and the world needs in a particular sense in these times. Our nation is called upon by its place of leadership in the world to bear witness for freedom; Negro Americans are called upon to bear witness for freedom now as they have done all during our history in this land."

Carleton L. Lee
Tuskegee, Alabama
Saturday Review

Witnesses for Freedom

Negro Americans in Autobiography

Rebecca Chalmers Barton

Author of

Black Voices in American Fiction 1900-1930

and

Our Human Rights

Dowling College Press
Oakdale, New York 11769

For further information, contact

Dowling College Press
Oakdale, New York 11769

Library of Congress Catalog Card Number: 76-29575

ISBN: 0-917428-02-1

Printed in the United States of America

FOR

ELOISE

AND

NORMAN

and all the like-minded
of their generation

CONTENTS

FOREWORD

by Alain Locke

Professor of Philosophy, Howard University

Many a liberal, resolved to break through the barriers of racial prejudice, is dismayed and discouraged to find that there are two sets of barriers to be surmounted instead of just one. He is well aware of the traditional outer wall — the intrenched bulwark of majority group pride and prejudice. But he is surprised to discover beyond that another — the minority group's inner barricade of defensive self-protection, which with the generations may have piled itself up into a spite-wall of stubborn and resentful alienation.

It is this second wall which Mrs. Barton attempts to breach in her revealing study of Negro American autobiography; and she does so with considerable success and pioneering skill. As a careful digest and interpretative comparison of twenty-three such autobiographies from the late Reconstruction days of Booker Washington to the contemporary experiences of Richard Wright and Langston Hughes, *Witnesses for Freedom* opens up a previously closed but highly significant area of typical American social experience. For the general reader, it affords an unsentimental and therefore sobering and enlightening journey into the psychological heart of the American race problem. Yet primarily, the book is a study of progressively maturing Negro self-interpretation.

Negro self-portraiture, it is soon discovered, however, is not all uniformly candid and self revealing even when trying to record how it feels and fares to be a Negro and to live and work as a Negro. But Mrs. Barton is able to document over several decades a maturing recovery of confidence and objectivity and a gradual shedding of strategic reserve and protective compensation.

Hitherto, the only widely read Negro biography has been Booker Washington's *Up From Slavery,* with considerably fewer readers for Frederick Douglass's *Life and Times,* W. E. DuBois's *Souls of Black*

Folk and James Weldon Johnson's *Along This Way*. Now a panoramic survey of the whole field is made available, with the added virtue that instead of any one personal experience, however typical, we are presented with a composite and accordingly more balanced and representative picture of Negro life experience.

At the same time that characteristic common factors of Negro experience are revealed, they are found to have many facets and variations of personal reaction. This volume reveals no "Negro mind," no "minority temperament" or "personality." There is wide variation from high optimism to deep cynicism, from minority self-reliance to socialistic integration, from militant racialism to general social reformism, from Booker Washington's strategic but compromising gradualism to DuBois's militant and defiant equalitarianism, from escapist flight to inner spiritual culture to radical revolutionary class struggle, from doctrines of individual success to programs of group solidarity and mass progress.

Indeed this most salutary and, to the general reader, most unexpected discovery and documentation of variety de-stereotypes the Negro more convincingly and effectively than volumes of abstract analysis of the sins and injustices of "stereotyping." No careful reader should hereafter be the psychological victim of the psychological pitfalls of race group stereotypes, whether malign or beneficent. For, unfortunately, friends as well as foes of the Negro too often overgeneralize and fall prey to them. This should now be completely outmoded with the opportunity to see more of the human side of the Negro in his infinite human variety.

Both accomplishments — the documentation of Negro experience far beyond a general formula and the rescuing of the human side of the Negro from popular over-simplification — make this book a substantive and substantial contribution to interracial understanding. In a day of enlarging perspectives in group relations, Rebecca Barton has performed a real service toward enlarged social understanding and dynamic democratic thought and action.

INTRODUCTION

✓ ✓ ✓

THIS is a study of the autobiographies of Negro Americans written during the last half century. The autobiography has always been a welcome means of enlarging our knowledge of our fellow human beings. It can be particularly useful for all of us who are separated from first-hand acquaintance with each other by the thousand and one barriers attendant on race.

In our American culture the Negro has been a fruitful subject for a many-sided investigation. The controversial nature of his status has attracted the attention of both Negro and white scholars, and has resulted in the data furnished by laboratory experiment and intelligence test, by class-caste and acculturation studies. In the process the old concepts of race purity and of innate difference between racial groups have received some jolts all along the line, from political science to cultural anthropology.

Enlightening as this research has been, we need to supplement its sane conclusions by turning to the human equation at the same time. We cannot expect social worker or participant-observer, psychoanalyst or statistician always to transmit the touch and feel of actual life. Even the social scientist does not pretend to deal in those unique clusters of feeling which identify each individuality. Rather, he wisely concedes jurisdiction to the arts and literature. It is here that we glimpse most intimately man's aspirations and despair, whether battled out in a hostile world or measured against the stars.

Negro autobiographies thus serve as human documents of the highest importance. Each writer is directly concerned with translating the essentials of his own life pattern. Taken as a whole, this collection of personal histories offers to Negro Americans a fund of information about outstanding men and women who have many problems in common with them. To white Americans it holds forth a key to those still unlocked doors waiting to reveal the Negro point of view.

Outsiders who study the Negro may indeed more successfully grasp the slippery tool of objectivity, but who else can so quickly add flesh and blood to the skeletal framework of fact as the insiders themselves? Too many generations of readers have missed an acquaintance with Negro Americans through the pages of their rich and varied autobiographical writing. Introductions are now in order.

Admittedly, the autobiography has limitations as a vehicle of truth. Although so long an accepted technique towards understanding, the self-portrait often tends to be formal and posed, idealized or purposely exaggerated. The author is bound by his organized self. Even if he wishes, he is unable to remember the whole story or interpret the complete experience. Undoubtedly, the Negro autobiographer especially has layer upon layer of consciousness that he may or may not choose to expose to the casual reader, while his unconscious omissions and distortions further complicate the presentation of reality. He is often the first one to recognize this danger, as evidenced by the direct statements of writers like Dr. Du Bois. According to him, the autobiography assumes too much or too little: "too much in dreaming that one's own life has greatly influenced the world; too little in the reticences, repressions, and distortions which come because men do not dare to be absolutely frank."

It is not merely a question of the elusive nature of the self. There is the added difficulty of fixing that self in time. Any autobiography suffers the onus of being dated. It is written at one moment in an author's life span and can only approximate genuineness in that moment. It makes no allowances, except by inference, for future changes in point of view and feeling. Our Negro American autobiographers claim no exemption from this general limitation, as external evidence and the later writings of some of the same authors easily prove.

Yet, as long as the study of man remains a lodestar, the autobiography will play its role. With all our technical skills we have not discovered the final answers in human understanding. The autobiography is only one of many approaches. But often a sudden observation can illuminate more clearly than a dozen graphs. Like the chance clue of the detective, information which appears fragmentary turns out to have far-reaching significance.

In the case of the Negro, we have the opportunity to determine whether the total value systems which he reveals in his personal writing follow a pattern, conditioned negatively by the fact of discrimination and by his limited participation in American life. Does he really feel that he is an American in name rather than in fact? Does he believe that the attitudes of the dominant group will permanently freeze his status at a lower level? Does he anticipate that his destiny is forever entwined in the meshes of prejudice, that the poles of his existence are set by submission to or rebellion against the white man?

In the last analysis it is irrelevant to press for perfect sincerity or completeness of answer. Each autobiography is at least a reflection of one aspect of the writer's personality and one phase of his thought, and these contain their own validity. Certainly the expressed opinions and experiences in these books can provide us with intimate conscious data. With luck we can also hope to find in them high degrees of self-revelation and logical analysis.

In addition, we can expect implied or expressed criticism of our society, and specifically of white people. Just as the traditional assumption that the slave was an acquiescent and good-natured creature has long ago been replaced by the notion of a man of shrewd observation and secret reservations beneath his mask, so has curiosity about the modern Negro's estimate of the white man superseded the former indifference. It is salutary to remember that prejudice is a two-way track, that interaction has two starting points. To see ourselves as others see us has always been an incentive to study.

Instead of being the products of random sampling, the books chosen for study reflect all the major types of attitude about race prevalent in Negro American autobiography. Allowing for numerous deviations from each other, these examples fall into categories according to the manner in which they approach the question of race. In attempting to evaluate them in their setting, the present investigation cuts across various fields of knowledge towards a social-psychological view of literature.

In the conviction, then, that Negro Americans are their own best interpreters, the author has not only summarized the life events and main ideas recorded by these Negro autobiographers, but has relied frequently on direct quotation of their words. In this way it is hoped that the original flavor of their books will be preserved. Only if it first serves as a medium for the personalities and points of view of these men and women can this study presume to make interpretations and draw conclusions about the changing realities of the Negro's group experience.

ACKNOWLEDGMENT

The research for this publication was made possible by the kindness of the Rockefeller Foundation which provided me with a grant-in-aid. As a research associate of the University of Wisconsin, I was enabled to enjoy the facilities not only of the University of Wisconsin Library, but also of the New York Public Library, the Schomburg collection of Negro literature in Harlem, Howard University and the Library of Congress. My thanks are extended also to Arthur Spingarn for the use of his exhaustive collection and knowledge of books by and about the Negro.

From Alain Locke of Howard University, S. B. Liljegren of the University of Uppsala, Sweden, and Ruth Useem and Merle Curti of the University of Wisconsin I received not only friendly encouragement but also professional evaluation of the manuscript. The personal indebtedness to individuals who gave me the will and the way to complete this study is too great to record or repay. A special word of appreciation goes to John Marshall of the Rockefeller Foundation who strengthened my hand in attempting to pull values out of research. Finally, I owe most profound gratitude to my long-suffering husband, daughter, and son, who so cheerfully relinquished me, for the duration of the emergency, to the pursuit of understanding beyond the four walls of home.

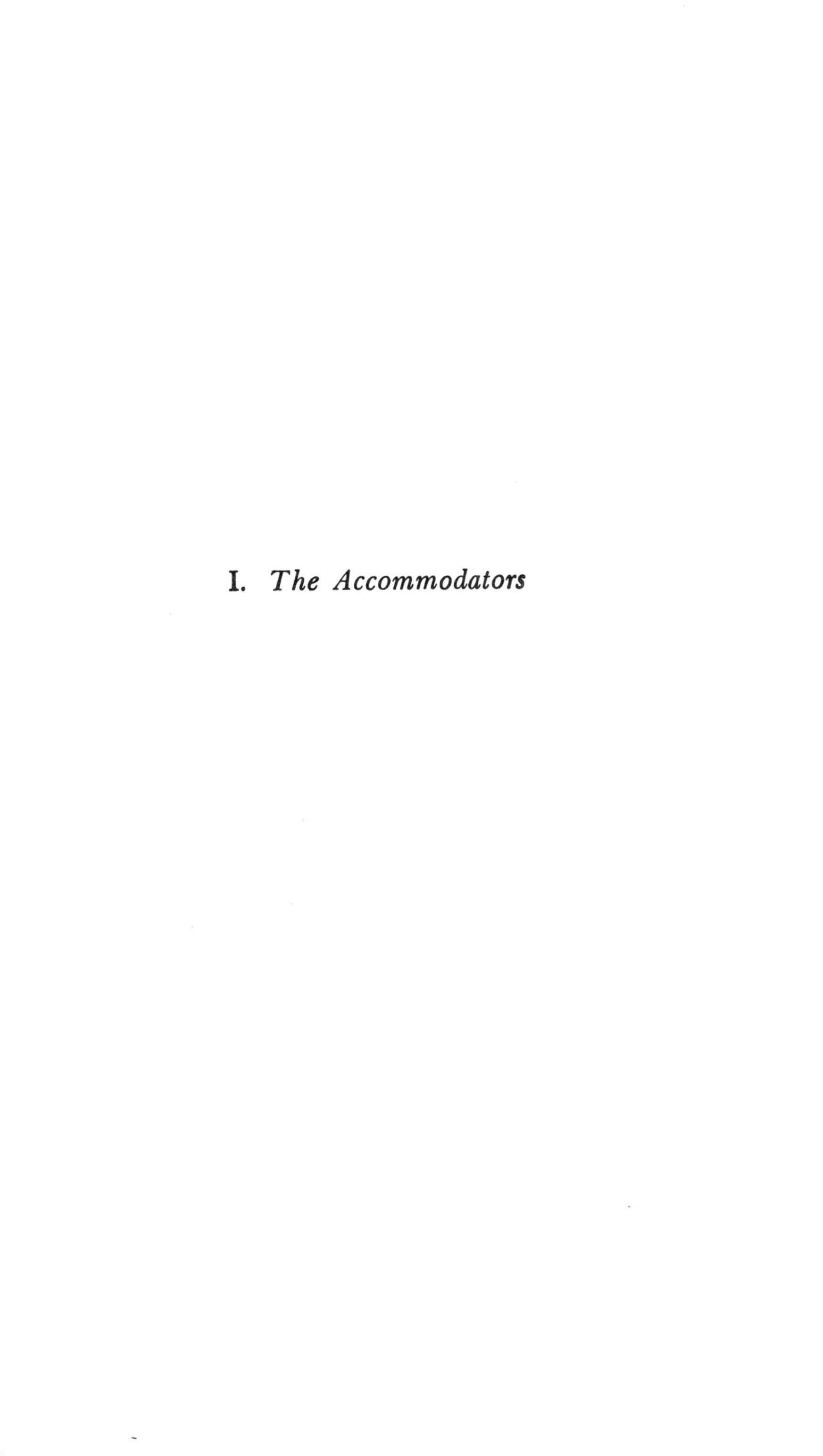

I. *The Accommodators*

Up from Slavery

BOOKER T. WASHINGTON

THERE is still magic in the name of Booker T. Washington. No Negro leader can lay stronger claim to Emerson's dictum that an institution is but the lengthened shadow of a great man. The development of agricultural and vocational education for Negroes is almost synonymous with his career. It will take more than the few decades since his death to dilute the influence of his thought and conduct on Negro-white relations. Even when the student of the subject decides that the tradition is at last dead, even as he consigns it to the dustbin of historical records, he will often be amazed to discover a flicker of life.

On second thought, he accepts this phoenix-like quality of Washington's philosophy as a recurring theme in group interaction. While some will deplore his "Uncle Tom" attitudes, others will admit their popular appeal. In the experience of the Negroes it has not been easy to slough off the slave mentality instilled over a long period of years. The metamorphosis from slave to man, with all the rapid demands for adjustment this involved, necessitated experiment in various directions. Advance and retreat, rebellion and compromise naturally characterize the Negroes' attempt to wrest a new status from a dominant white group. Any method which brought lush dividends won adherents.

Therefore a consideration of twentieth-century Negro autobiography can aptly begin with Booker T. Washington's *Up From Slavery*, written in 1900. As he gathered the material for the personal history the events of his life had already assumed symbolic importance. The views he promulgated, not only educational but also economic, political, and moral, had already established a norm. His book contains the raw materials of a legend, a solid, substantial legend which throve in both life and literature.

It is a temptation when dealing with such a figure to have recourse to his other writings, his public speeches, and journal articles. Yet, oddly enough, the flavor of the apple would be the same. Seldom has an autobiographer kept so true to form. Those who have previous knowledge of his public career find no surprises in his own story of his life. The opposite is equally valid. In fact, we can well claim as close an acquaintance with the man when we finish the last page, as he ever could or would let the outsider have.

Struggle Against Odds

Up From Slavery has the comprehensive quality of a "cradle to the grave" account. The author assumes that an eager public wishes to know the full story of his life struggle, for he is a classic example of the self-made man, so dear to an American public, with the success story only enhanced by the added handicap of race. The title of his book sets the tone, especially if we place the emphasis on the first word. *Up* connotes all the "bloody but unbowed" progress, all the noble aspiration and strong character clinging to the log cabin tradition.

Typically melancholy are the events of his childhood. There are the earthen floor of the slave cabin in Virginia, the pallet shared with a brother and sister, the uncomfortable flax shirts and handmade wooden shoes. Like dumb animals these children eat their scanty and unvaried diet of cornbread and fat pork. The dire necessity of poverty does not permit either playtime or schooling. That he starts from the very lowest rung of the ladder is indisputable. The young Booker has no knowledge of his birthyear, guessing later that it must have been 1857 or 1858; no information about his ancestry beyond his mother; and hardest of all, no last name.

Yet even in this gloom there is a groping upward. When he carries his mistress' books to school, the schoolhouse appears like "paradise" to him. Inarticulate and unaware, he at least responded to deprivation with longing. The vague connection between freedom and opportunity is given some substance by a mother who prayed for and rejoiced over Emancipation.

Urges toward a better life are implemented when the family moves to West Virginia. Although work still claims priority, there is room for the hope of education. His desire to read prompts him to memorize the number, eighteen, on his stepfather's barrel in the saltmines. Then he acquires a "blue-back" speller only to find no Negro equipped to help him. Finally a literate colored man, a Civil War veteran, arrives in town and forms the nucleus of a school. Booker meets the crisis of the roll call by choosing a last name on the spot—a name oddly in keeping with his ambition. Thus comes his initiation into the pursuit of education as a lifelong occupation.

Outer poverty matched by inner determination constitute a pattern for many years to come. In this small town of Malden, five miles from the State Capital of Charleston, he utilizes every resource. In order to gain a few hours of schooling each day, he works in the mines early and late. When this plan doesn't seem feasible, he studies at night. His first library is a drygoods box, with planks across it. His next goal is Hampton Institute, a school for Negroes five hundred miles away.

The fact that he arrives at Hampton after many days of work, hiking his way, with only fifty cents in his pocket and without any decent clothes, only adds a lustre to his "promised land." He approaches his first assigned task, the sweeping of a recitation room, as if it were a labor of Hercules. Three times he sweeps back and forth in order to impress the "Yankee" head teacher with his caliber. Always he regarded this as the best examination he ever passed, for she was quickly persuaded that this penniless boy could apply himself to his schoolwork.

After this steppingstone, the pace accelerates. Rather than a hindrance, his self-support becomes the setting for the gem of his school career. He is invited back to Hampton to give a postgraduate address, and, finally, to teach. Meanwhile his experience had been broadened by returning to his home town as a teacher, where he not only assumed extra duties such as starting a reading room and organizing a debating society, but also delighted in teaching those habits of cleanliness and manners to the Negro children which he had missed in his own life. The recognition that he now begins to win prompts him to remark: "I think I may say, without seeming egotism, that it is seldom that five years have wrought such a change in the life and aspirations of an individual." It is almost an anticlimax to learn that he is chosen to start the new Institute of Tuskegee on the grounds that he is more suited to the task than any available white man.

Achievements

The Tuskegee chapter is a long one, and keeps to the pattern. Started in a little shanty in 1881, against some community opposition, Tuskegee twenty years later can claim twenty-three hundred acres of land, much of it cultivated, forty buildings almost entirely erected by student labor, a property evaluation of $300,000, an endowment fund of $225,000, an $80,000 yearly budget, and eleven hundred students from twenty-seven states and territories. White enemies have been pacified. Booker T. Washington explains that they had feared education would take the Negro away from the farms and domestic service and cause an economic loss. But he demonstrates that he, too, believes farming is basic, since people must eat, and that all he aims to do is to make better farmers and defter servants and to provide a pool of skilled artisans. "We wanted to be careful not to educate our students out of sympathy with agricultural life, so that they would be attracted from the country to the cities, and yield to the temptation of trying to live by their wits."

To carry out such a program he and his small group of coworkers faced almost constant hardship, ranging from hunger to debts. But they bought land for a new site and raised money by suppers and the donations of friendly neighbors who often had only a half dozen eggs to offer. It was inevitable that suspicious observers would gradually relax in the presence of a man who could feel that "few things are more satisfactory to me than a high-grade Berkshire or Poland China pig." He was a hard worker but not a dangerous one. This leader who had never learned to play as a child passed on to his students the need for thrift, self-reliance, and skill in their given spheres. It was socially acceptable to the larger community that gardening was his preferred form of relaxation.

How pleased he is that his returning alumni exclaim over the new, beautiful buildings, fine furnishings, and prompt, nourishing meals embellished with vases of flowers and singing birds. So devoted is he to the values embedded in his life work that it is not surprising to find that his last two wives were his "Lady Principals" first, that his daughter learned dressmaking as well as music, his son brickmasonry as well as architecture. To him, it is the humble beginning, the useful task well learned which is the basis for the graces and higher skills of living. He regarded Lincoln as his "patron saint."

In his own case, hard work always brought its rewards. It was no light matter to spend six months of each year traveling, lecturing, raising money for his expanding Institute. But Northern philanthropists gave generous support, audiences expressed warm interest in the man and his school, and friends arranged a European trip when they detected signs of overwork after eighteen years of this strenuous regime.

The trip is almost a tour, and forms a convenient milestone on his road to fame. He protests that he doesn't know how to take a vacation, that "luxuries had always seemed to me to be something meant for white people, not for my race," and that he had regarded London and Paris as "heaven." Yet he does learn to relax, and the "dream" does come true. He is feted everywhere he goes. The man who has "never sought or cared for what the world calls fame," and who has looked on it only "as something to be used in accomplishing good," must have been in a strange state of mind as the guest of Queen Victoria at Windsor Castle.

Actually, according to his account, fame seems to seek him out persistently. There is the honorary degree which Harvard bestows. " 'Why you have called me from the Black Belt of the South, from among my humble people, to share in the honors of this occasion, is not for me to explain.' " President McKinley and his Cabinet officers visit Tuskegee. As departments pass in review, with floats showing the contrast between old and new methods in dairying, tilling the soil, and cooking, Booker T. Washington's educational emphases are given a magnificent demonstration, and the President is visibly impressed. Other Presidents also fall under the spell of this Negro's personality and message.

Opinions

At appropriate points in his autobiography, Booker T. Washington lays down the moral code which he hopes can serve others as it has him. Redundant as it may seem, after his life sketch, a summary quickly reveals a shrewd and practical idealism worthy of Benjamin Franklin.

1. Hard work, not luck, brings results.
2. Efficiency is a virtue.

   "Nothing must be slovenly or slipshod."

   "Even to this day I never see bits of paper scattered around a house or in the street that I do not want to pick them up at once."
3. Obstacles are often the best road to success.
4. Merit is eventually recognized and rewarded.
5. The dignity of labor is the foundation of democracy.
6. Individual initiative is a law of progress.

   "Learn to produce what the world wants, and produce it better than others."

> Learn to do a common thing in an uncommon way in order to become indispensable to society.

Supporting this moral view is a religious nature. He reads the Bible for spiritual help. He seeks God's blessing before his speeches. He pays tribute to the contribution of the churches and missions in "elevating" the Negro race from prisons and "dens of crime."

Even under difficulties, Booker T. Washington writes as a humanitarian and an optimist. His moral precepts are bound together in this framework. This whole attitude towards life is preserved instead of dissolved by the acid test of the race problem. Rather than wavering into bitterness or confusion before the raw details of prejudice he seems to rise to new heights of idealism.

For it is not obstacles in general that he has in mind as beneficial to an abstract man. In particular, the Negro boy's "birth and connection with an unpopular race is an advantage" which the white boy lacks. The law of merit, also, should give special consolation to the Negro since it operates "no matter under what skin found." Such reflections have led Washington to confess that he pities rather than envies or resents white people. He has learned that "great men cultivate love, and that only little men cherish a spirit of hatred." This attitude has enabled him to feel just as happy doing a service for the Southern white man as for a member of his own race.

In this spirit of bright friendliness he can hurdle the Ku Klux Klan. He refers to their cruelties in Reconstruction days, but "simply for the purpose of calling attention to the great change that has taken place. . . . Today there are no such organizations in the South, and the fact that such ever existed is almost forgotten by both races."

This best-of-all-possible-worlds motif reappears constantly. On one trans-Atlantic crossing he is struck by the contrast between the treatment accorded to Frederick Douglass on shipboard and his own. His rugged predecessor is confined to the decks whereas he is waited on by a committee of "ladies and gentlemen" who ask him to make an address. Without reference to possible intrinsic factors of explanation he comments: "And yet there are people who are bold enough to say that race feeling in America is not growing less intense."

With such homely virtues, willing cooperation, and mellow philosophy, it would be strange indeed if Booker T. Washington had not been accepted even by white Southerners. But he paves the way even further for a royal welcome. He publicizes in his autobiography specific views about slavery and about the comparative traits of Negroes and whites.

In his reminiscences, cause and effect lose their sharp contours. As he looks back on his childhood, in spite of the animal-like existence he describes, he does not feel that his owners were "especially cruel"; even his unknown white father was not to blame. "He was simply another unfortunate victim of the institution which the Nation unhappily had engrafted upon it at that time." The direct connection between the conduct of this father and his own sense of loss about name and ancestry is never drawn. In the same breath he has told us that his mother's addition to the slave family "attracted as much attention as the purchase of a new horse or cow." Thus does the individual gain convenient anonymity in the group.

It is all the fault of the callous system. And, within it, individuals still manage to have good relations. We are given the time-honored picture of slaves who feel no bitterness when their masters go off to fight against the Northerners, who sorrow when they are killed—"no sham sorrow, but real"—and who tenderly care for destitute masters after the war. Many are sad to be parted when Emancipation comes, and often choose to remain or to return to their former owners when they find that "freedom was a more serious thing" than they had expected. The author's emphasis on this picture conveys more to the reader than any historical information.

In addition, he points out certain good results stemming from the evil of slavery, for "Providence so often uses man and institutions to accomplish a purpose." Thus the whites who depended on black labor were robbed of self-reliance. The Negroes got "nearly as much out of slavery" because they could make a living more easily with their hands when the need arose. With the exception of education and property ownership, the slaves were more equipped than their masters to face a new life after the Civil War, and are now better off physically and spiritually than "an equal number of black people in any other portion of the globe."

As a precaution against misunderstanding, he warns his readers that he is not trying to justify slavery. Again, the fact that he feels called upon to do so is revealing. Always he seems conscious of two audiences, of two sets of interests that he must try to reconcile. He must walk the razor's edge between Negro pride and white prejudice.

With this dilemma in mind, he makes an appraisal of both groups. Starting with the Negroes, we note that he speaks of them always in general and in racial terms. As a race, they are loyal; in few instances have they betrayed a "specific trust." As a race, they lack bitterness, much as they longed for freedom in their patient way. As a race, they have an eager desire for education. They are by nature responsive to help: ". . . this is not more true of any race than of the Negro. Let them once understand that you are unselfishly interested in them, and you can lead them to any extent."

To his way of thinking, these characteristics are all to the good. He seems to feel that there is nothing here to offend the Negroes or to disturb the whites. So, to be truly objective, he must expose a more unfavorable side of his group.

This is accomplished with apparent ease. He pokes fun at their first foolish enthusiasms after Emancipation: their "craze for Greek and Latin learning," fondness for big titles, "desire to hold office." He bemoans the so-called educated Negro, "with a high hat, imitation gold eye-glasses, a showy walking-stick, kid gloves, fancy boots, and what not . . ." He tells anecdotes deprecating Negroid laziness and ignorance.

But what disturbs him most is the wrong set of values he observes. Money is often misused. In the cities he is shocked by the poor Negroes, who earn only $4.00 a week, spending $2.00 on a Sunday buggy-ride. On the other hand, the well-to-do Negroes are usually "spoiled." In the rural districts he visits, he discovers plenty of "conspicuous consumption." Families will have organs, sewing machines, and ornate clocks but no forks, vegetable gardens, or decent clothes.

This distorted judgment carries over to education. We are given a dismal picture of a young man studying a French grammar while sitting in a filthy one-room cabin with grease on his clothes and weeds in his garden. Similarly, the girl students at Tuskegee coming from these rural areas could often locate the Desert of Sahara on a map more easily than the proper place for forks and knives on a dinner table. There is a tendency to want to learn about cube roots before mastering the multiplication table. To reduce his point to the simplest denominator, he believes that teaching the use of the toothbrush brought about "a higher degree of civilization among the students."

We can almost chart the course of approval among many whites. As he confirms their stereotypes about a childlike, irresponsible, but good-natured group he must induce a state of glowing comfort. If they are doing the Negroes as well as themselves a service by restricting them to the sphere of manual skills, how much more pleasant for all concerned.

It seems to follow logically that white Southerners are justified in withholding higher political as well as higher educational rights from a backward group. Booker T. Washington states his opinions on this question. Voting is "a matter of natural, slow growth, not an overnight, gourd-vine affair." The Negro must first prove by his conduct and program that he is prepared for such a responsibility. It is the duty of the Negro "to deport himself modestly in regard to political claims, depending upon the slow but sure influences that proceed from the possession of property, intelligence, and high character for the full recognition of his political rights." Until this point is reached, presumably in some distant future, he should "more and more be influenced by those of intelligence and character who are his nextdoor neighbors." These white friends will show their goodwill gradually, if trusted to work things out in their own way. For the South must not be "forced by 'foreigners,' or 'aliens,' to do something which it does not want to do."

Again, Washington hastens to add that he believes in universal, free suffrage, in principle. But after all, there are "peculiar conditions that justify the protection of the ballot in many of the states, for a while at least, either by an educational test, a property test, or by both combined . . ." Since he, himself, has gone to considerable pains in his autobiography to describe the low level of Negro education and property ownership in the South, it would seem that this opinion is another and practical basis for postponing Negro enfranchisement indefinitely.

So characteristic is this slant on a controversial subject that we can almost anticipate his reactions in other fields. For instance, he is critical of labor. He objects to strikes as neither thrifty nor sensible. The miners are always worse off than before, and yet, in his experience, strikes occurred "whenever the men get two or three months ahead in their savings." Or, to go further afield, let us note his estimate of the British people. The nobility are "loved and respected by the masses" and give time and money to philanthropy. He has a "higher regard than ever before" for them. As for the servants, they are pleasingly deferential. The English servant expects to be nothing but a servant, "and so he perfects himself in the art to a degree that no class of servants has yet reached. In our country the servant expects to become, in a few years, a 'master' himself. Which system is preferable? I will not venture an answer." This hesitancy undoubtedly won him friends in high places.

Booker T. Washington's final credential for trust is his direct and unqualified praise of three groups of white Americans: the Southern whites, the Northern educators who came South to teach, and the Northern philanthropists. According to his own experience in the South, "the relations between the two races are pleasant." Often a colored and white man will own and operate the same store without trouble. Although he has been active in the Negro cause and widely known throughout the South, he can witness that "I have never received a single personal insult." He is tolerant of any prejudiced Southerner on the grounds that he has lacked "opportunity for the highest kind of growth."

The first white man with whom he came into real contact was a Northerner, General Armstrong, head of Hampton Institute. It did not take him long to idealize him and his "Yankee" coworkers. "I never saw a man who so completely lost sight of himself"; moreover, "the history of the world fails to show a higher, purer, and more unselfish class of men and women than those who found their way into those Northern schools."

However, his highest eulogy is reserved for those benefactors who support and finally endow his school. Their "fine and Christ-like spirit" makes them "the best people in the world." He is impressed with their attitude of stewardship towards their wealth: "more and more, rich people are coming to regard men and women who apply to them for help for worthy objects, not as beggars but as agents for doing their work . . ."

Promoted by this whole complex of thought, ovations become a commonplace in the meteoric rise of Booker T. Washington. His famous speech at the Atlantic Exposition in 1895 crowns his victories. The fact of a separate Negro exhibit does not cloud his day. It was an achievement to have an exhibit on any terms. Besides, segregation might exist in the market place but not on the speakers' platform. "I knew, too, that this was the first time in the entire history of the Negro that a member of my race had been asked to speak from the same platform with white Southern men and women on any important National occasion. I was asked now to speak to an audience composed of the wealth and culture of the white South, the representatives of my former masters." According to the press dispatches he quotes, the result was a "revelation" and a "sensation," and everywhere men wish to shake his hand for cementing race friendship.

Actually, the complete text, included in his autobiography, fails to disclose a single new idea. It is only a dramatic reinforcement and expansion of his previous views on race relations. For many years he has been building up towards this particular rejection of social equality which made history.

Once again he reminds his own people that, "It is at the bottom of life we must begin, and not at the top. Nor should we permit our grievances to overshadow our opportunities." Once again he reminds the white people that "in our humble way we shall stand by you with a devotion that no foreigner can approach . . ." The conclusion is almost automatic: "The wisest among my race understand that the agitation of questions of social equality is the extremist folly . . ." Just as the chance to earn a dollar in a factory is worth more than the right to spend it in the opera house, so is the preparation for political and legal privilege more important than the privilege itself.

Negro Opponents

One gathers, at first, that there were no dissenting voices. No foes would feel at home in the general mood of optimism which flows from this autobiography. Yet so strong were the repercussions of this Atlanta speech that he touches upon the matter in passing. According to his interpretation, the trouble seems to lie in his "too liberal" remarks about Southern whites. "For a while there was a reaction, so far as a certain element of my own race was concerned, but later these reactionary ones seemed to have been won over to my own way of believing and acting."

Such a light dismissal of historic opposition is suspicious. It forces us to digress from the autobiography long enough to mention a fact which it chooses to ignore. There were many keen-minded Negroes, especially in the North, who regarded his point of view as dangerous, as a betrayal of the race. So positive and articulate were they that they constituted a separate school of thought, spear-headed by Dr. W. E. B. Du Bois. In 1903 Du Bois summarized the disagreement in *The Souls of Black Folk:* "So far as Mr. Washington preaches Thrift, Patience, and Industrial Training for the masses, we must hold up his hands and strive with him, rejoicing in his honors and glorying in the strength of this Joshua called of God and of man to lead the headless host. But so far as Mr. Washington apologizes for injustice, North or South, does not rightly value the privilege and duty of voting, belittles the emasculating effects of caste distinctions, and opposes the higher training and ambition of our brighter minds—so far as he, the South, or the nation, does this,—we must unceasingly and firmly oppose them." Thus waged the battle of industrial-vocational versus cultural education, humble duties versus full-fledged rights. A critic of the mental acumen of Du Bois deserves the same serious attention which Du Bois, we shall see, later accords Washington in his own autobiography. Du Bois may admit that he is a gadfly, but certainly no ordinary fly to brush aside.

Psychological Flaws

Booker T. Washington's oversimplification on this score is the clue to the whole surface nature of his personal history. This busy, self-made man has evidently had no time to understand his own motives or no inclination to share them. Often, as we read, we suddenly become aware of a kind of double talk wherein this and that are both true and not true. Outer disagreements he irons out almost before they can occur. Inner conflicts he cushions with velvet motives. Criticism of his beliefs he silences by the solid achievements of his life.

Why could he not bear the thought of friction? Why did he learn to tread so carefully between the feelings of white and colored? Why did he align himself, in the last analysis, with the powerful, the wealthy, or the majority? Some of the implications in these questions he would not grant; to others he would have only one simple answer: for the sake of my people. Compromise and tact were effective tools in winning gradual gains for his group. They were whittling down prejudice from a giant to a pygmy.

He paid no heed to the personal ambition which also goaded him. He applied himself to his duties heroically. He left no stone unturned to set a lasting example of the respectable and respected Negro. The job was almost too perfect. There was so little of the sluggard in Booker T. Washington that we cannot ignore the possible role of overcompensation in his personality. Perhaps he felt compelled to assertion constantly in order to disprove his "inferior" origin and connections. The price in energy must have been exorbitant.

If the results brought him personal glory, he is free to consider it a by-product of the cause. His very stress on self-effacement enables him to accept this gift with a clear conscience. His doctrine of sweetness and light seems to induce a type of self-hypnosis which is almost contagious. Seldom has a writer enjoyed with such equanimity his double role of martyr and hero, servant and leader, egoist and benefactor. Pride and modesty are wedded. His humble origin can serve both to accentuate the height of his achievement and to retain the common touch.

Cloaked in an armor of personal immunity, he passes serenely along the path of racial plagues. His capacity to interpret the favorable acceptance of himself as a change for the better in American race relations suggests psychological explanations ranging from wishful thinking to struggle for status. His failure to analyze those underlying reasons for his personal triumph which nestle in the pages of his own life history suggests an "ostrich in the sand" technique. Whether inspired by fear, naïveté, or deliberate strategy, the result is satisfying to him. He is a master at accommodation to his environment. In this process the race problem becomes both the sword and the shining plume.

Taken as a personality sketch, then, the autobiography must be estimated in negative terms. It is not three dimensional. It has too many omissions and reservations about the self. The stress falls on activity, not on inner conflict. It is a chronicle of events and opinions, not of deep feelings. Those that the author does express crystallize into such conventional phrasing that they do not ring true across half a century. This can be explained partly by his natural conformity to the literary styles of the day. But there is still a false note which persists beneath all the pious phrasing, as if the perfection of this success story were strained to the limit.

Social Conditioning

This very condemnation leads to a measure of exoneration. For it forces us, in a search for understanding, to consider the man in relation to his times. Just as surely as the social pressures of his day influenced Washington to become the champion of vocational education for Negroes, so did they prompt him to write a story of his life which would conform to the white demand for safe and sane Negroes. Booker T. Washington's young manhood was spent in the bitter aftermath of the double humiliation of Civil War defeat and of the Reconstruction regime. The Negro was the bone of contention, and it was much more convenient for the South to turn its wrath on the bone rather than on the superior contender. After all, the Negro was always with the white Southerners, and personified their negative feelings every time he held office along with the Northern carpetbaggers. The Yankee was a transient, but the Negro was a fixture and had to work out some adjustment to this hostility if he wished to survive.

Undoubtedly Booker T. Washington was acclaimed as going as far as he could and not too far. His leadership was a comfort to both the white North and the white South since the one saw his persistence, industry, and moral character, and the other his modesty, good humor, and Christian helpfulness. One welcomed the tremendous boom he gave to Negro education, and the other drew a sigh of relief that his goals were so useful and limited. Both could shake hands over him.

Historical and sociological studies document the strong forces sweeping around him. At the start of his public life he was faced with certain choices. Once he felt the pull of opportunism there was no turning back. Experience, contact, travel finished shaping the shrewd diplomat. He learned the chords that brought response and eliminated all discord. That he might sometimes have had his tongue in his cheek about some aspects of the fine white world seems likely, but he was too disciplined to show it.

Thus in two ways can we explain the paucity of his autobiography. The internal evidence reveals a man who apparently has little self-knowledge. His drive for power has had such a satisfying outlet in race leadership that he lives for the cause as an idealist. He rejoices in setting an example and sacrificing for his group while discounting his pleasure in recognition.

On the other hand, the external evidence indicates that he deliberately selected a role to play with the white world. Naïve he may have been about understanding the deep, mysterious workings of human motivation, but not about the techniques of manipulating white public opinion. The later success of the "Tuskegee machine," so bluntly attacked in Du Bois' autobiography, points to a skilful and planned control. Only in this period, shortly before his death in 1915, does he feel his position so entrenched that he can at last afford to make some concessions to his Northern opponents—for example, concerning the dangers of segregation—without fear of reprisals from his white supporters.

But not one word of fearless speech creeps into his autobiography. It is written at a time when Tuskegee and his career are still in the making. It is to serve as the final stamp of approval. Each page seems to be tempered to his white audience. Conscious suppression of the unpleasant side of intergroup life, no matter how important for public sentiment, could only result in stilted and superficial writing. Ironically enough, his expediency undermines the very concept of happy and healthy race relations which it constructs.

In Spite of the Handicap

JAMES D. CORROTHERS

Up from Slavery served as an inspiration and a model to many Negro leaders in the next generation. Bishops, ministers, social workers, and teachers who devoted their lives to the betterment of their group met similar needs for coming to working terms with the white group, and accepted the solution offered by Booker T. Washington. Born from ten to twenty-five years later than Washington, and with more Northern than Southern experience, they escaped the direct onus of slavery. Today they are dead or belong to the older generation. Yet they still bear witness to the pioneer leader. Several of them, writing towards the end of their careers, and reminiscing about their early struggles and decisions, not only mention specifically the influence which Washington's thought exerted on their own life patterns, but prove the fact by conforming to his type of autobiography.

Three instances should suffice to gauge the strength of the tradition. Variations there are, and occasionally more honest self-analysis, more outspoken resentment of felt injustices, but the bonds of restraint, the criterion of "good taste" for a white audience, seem to play the decisive role in shaping the material. A mood of hope, even though not entirely in keeping with the circumstances of their lives, is carefully maintained. Always there is a picture of the deserving Negro who never falters from the humanitarian task he has set himself, and who rises above hardships to achievement in the spirit of brotherly love. Even the titles of these autobiographies have family connections: *In Spite of the Handicap, Bursting Bonds,* and *A Nickel and a Prayer.* They echo the humble origin, the rough path, and the victory through faith suggested by the title, *Up From Slavery.*

No shadow of the plantation fell on James Corrothers. He was born in the "chain lake region" of Michigan where Quaker abolitionists had established an underground railroad station and where there was a colony of free Negroes before the Civil War. He has more knowledge than Washington about his white ancestry. His father's father was of Scotch-Irish and Indian stock, with a second wife who was Negro, a black Zulu. His father came from this marriage, grew up to be a Union soldier, and married a woman with France and Madagascar in her background, and with "Caucasian features."

James Corrothers' original conditioning towards white people was favorable. When his mother died at his birth, he was taken and raised by his white grandfather. What could be more fascinating to the small boy than a grandfather who had traveled from Canada to South America, who was a hunter and a teller of tales? The affection was so genuine that, as a young boy, he tried to support the old man when his other children tired of the responsibility.

He grew up in South Haven, Michigan, where there was no particular color problem. To him it was an advantage to be the only colored boy in the public school. He learned to speak correct English, unmarred by Negro dialect, and received better instruction than Negro children in the South. Although poor and shabbily dressed, he quickly impressed the teachers and pupils by his determination to "make good."

He liked this white world he moved in. Later, as a public man, he regretted that lack of early contact with the masses of Negroes which would have given him "intuitive understanding." But at the time he had no apparent reservations. Some initial coolness he detected in his schoolmates. But he explains that it was just because he was "new" to them. When he went to work in Muskegon, Michigan, there were only about fifty Negroes in the town. He sensed "no particular prejudice," as long as a Negro was a good worker, and accepted the lack of social intercourse between the groups.

Yet, after his grandfather's disappearance, he seems to lose his foothold among white people and "bums" his way to his mother's people in Ohio. From then on, his expression of identity with the Negro group is uppermost. His move to Chicago starts the train of events culminating in a Negro ministry.

Hard work and devotion to learning prepare him for this leadership. At fourteen he had worked eleven hours a day in the lumber mills of Muskegon and held his own. He describes himself as "rough and ready, but virtuous." He had felt the stirrings of higher ambitions which liquor and fast living would have hampered. Now, while he works for seventeen hours daily in an Indiana hotel for board and $2.00 a week, he reads at night. Drawn to the poems of Gray, Burns, Tennyson, Longfellow, Whittier, and James Whitcomb Riley, he decides to become a poet himself. He joins a Young Men's Republican Club and is encouraged by the "bright men" in it, whereas he leaves a good paying job on a lake steamer because he dislikes the "vulgar men" who are fellow workers.

During his early years in Chicago he begins to see the disparity between his ambitions and the opportunities open to him as a Negro. He does not enjoy earning his living as a porter or in restaurants. So discouraged does he become with his chances for a career of writing that he even contemplates turning boxer. At least that would mean money. The climax of his resentment came when he made a month's study of the Chicago Negro for the *Chicago Tribune* only to receive no pay and to have it rewritten and distorted by a white reporter. Corrothers' protest, on top of his expressed wish to become a reporter, lost him his porter job on the newspaper. He had been told, "You already have a better job than the average coloured fellow of your age. Sensibly *stick* to it, by conducting it and yourself properly." His reaction was sharp. "A bitter realization crept over me—the boding anathema of my colour! And then—I expressed my feelings quite too bitterly."

But this unhappy episode is more than canceled out by the kindness of influential white friends. While working in a white barber shop he had been discovered by Henry Demarest Lloyd, "a reformer upon whose shoulders the mantle of Wendell Phillips might well have fallen." This new friend continues to help him with odd jobs, introduces him to others, and backs him in starting at Northwestern University at twenty-one years of age. Corrothers meets distinguished white people like Jane Addams, Governor Altgeld, and Charlotte Perkins Gilman. Miss Frances Willard gives him financial support in his college days. "Very lovingly, by deed, and not by word, she taught me that the sweeter way was the better way." Undoubtedly this conclusion is fostered by his friendship with the Negro poet, Paul Laurence Dunbar, and his meeting with Booker T. Washington.

Even his brief experience in the South, as a student and as a teacher, does not shake his renewed faith in the decent white man. He speaks of the support and friendliness of the whites in their home communities. Negroes sometimes meet prejudice when they travel, but "I have never had an unkind word spoken to me in the South by a white man who knew me personally."

From this point on, in his autobiography, any bitterness he feels is directed more against his own group than against the whites. It is almost as if there were a transference of emotion. The Negro becomes a convenient whipping post for his negative feelings. Taken as a whole the Negro group suffers in comparison with the white group just as much in *In Spite of the Handicap* as in *Up from Slavery*. Moreover, Corrothers lacks Washington's benevolent touch to soften the charges.

Corrothers' original point of attack is the Negro churchman. Back in Chicago, his efforts at free-lance journalism are hampered by race. The problem of a living is acute. Married to the daughter of a Methodist minister, he entertains the idea of entering the ministry himself. However, attendance at a Methodist convention checks him temporarily. "I could not see wherein these ministers were much superior to the Negro boathands among whom I had once worked, and I did not particularly relish the thought of close association with them." He speaks of their "unlovely personal traits" and their "mental unpreparedness" for their work.

But after a strenuous period of trying to support his family by odd jobs, unloading cargoes and picking fruit, his resolution wavers. Perhaps the way to improvement of the church is from within. The church "had enthralled my race to ancient things" instead of to "progressive and beneficial ideas." It lacks leadership. He asks himself, "Why not ally myself with the church, and be the ideal minister that I want others to be?" According to him, this self-searching is in the nature of a call. At the moment of decision, "A sunburst fell upon my being."

Although his start in the East was propitious, misfortune soon struck, and with it came his renewed antagonism to Negro churchmen. Accused of plotting against his bishop, he is ousted with a bad reputation, black-listed, and reduced to hunger and unemployment. He has no money to fight the necessary legal battles, and, by the time the courts clear him, the damage has been done. He now feels qualified to put his finger on the greatest single weakness of his group. "Ah, *that* is the curse of the American Negro!—jealousy, silly bickering, and inherent deviltry on the part of those who would *lead!* . . . They find a sinister delight in kicking every honest heart that knows a better way." It is strange to see him dwell on the punishment his persecutors ultimately receive at the hands of a just Providence. One becomes "a raving maniac," another "a fugitive from justice," although "I have never lifted my hand against one of them." The press which printed the falsehoods against him was smashed and the building burned to the ground while he was a thousand miles away.

This preoccupation with the flaws in Negro character follows him in his further church experience as a Baptist. Near his boyhood town he starts a Baptist church which fails because the community is opposed to an influx of Negroes. But less attention is paid to this attitude than to the error of Negro ways in New England. In general, he is disappointed in the "commonplace" people he finds there, especially the foreigners who are "jolly well up on strikes" and who have no knowledge of Whittier and Emerson. "But the New England Negro was the greatest disappointment to me!" The group does not benefit from its "unusual advantages." The reason is that "Many are merely transplanted Southern 'ne'er-do-wells' " He is glad to resign and leave the "one long nightmare of fuss-dodging" among colored Baptists. We see him finally making a change for conscience' sake to the Presbyterian faith. It is never clear from the author's account of his life which handicap he singles out for special mention in his title. It might be argued from the evidence that his association with undesirable Negroes assumes a worse aspect in his eyes than white discrimination.

Yet, in spite of all his troubles and grievances, he closes his personal history with positive affirmations. He asserts that he has delighted in labor, in service, and in learning. He has envied no man, and done his best with a life which held "so humble a beginning." On the whole, he regards it as a privilege to have been allowed to work in God's "wonderful, beautiful world." Friendly help has never failed. "What if the lights have dimmed along the shore and I have had to build my life all over again? I have been enabled to do it, and to move up again into God's free sunlight where the air is fresh and pure."

Again, the idealism cloaks a well-developed shrewdness. We find a strong urge towards "the best people," the moral life, and a respectable status. White people have the lion's share of those values he is seeking in life. By ancestry, early environment, and later friendships, he feels a legitimate claim on their esteem. At the same time it is obvious that he resents his forced identification with a less cultured group. His autobiography eases his sense of inferiority by distinguishing him from the vulgar and bickering elements of his race. He gains recognition as a worthy race leader without having to share the stigma of the race weaknesses he exposes.

We know little of the man aside from the role of cheerful martyr which he assumes. Even though removed from the fears inbred in slavery, he develops his autobiography in the spirit of the tenet that the white masters can do no wrong, and that the Negro masses still have far to go in the scale of evolution. With progress promoted by the right people, there is cause for optimism.

Bursting Bonds

WILLIAM PICKENS

Of greater stature as a leader and thinker than James Corrothers, William Pickens shares even while he qualified many of the same views. More outspoken in his realism about the race problem than Booker T. Washington, he nevertheless follows his spirit of conciliation.

Originally, his autobiography was published in 1911, when he was thirty years old, under the title, *The Heir of Slaves.* His concluding words are meant to convey encouragement to other heirs. "I have been impressed, not that every single thought and deed in the world is good, but that the resultant line of humanity's movement is in the direction of righteousness, and that human life and the world are on the whole good things." In 1923 he revised and enlarged his book with the name of *Bursting Bonds.* He informs his readers that, during the interval, he has learned to be more realistic about many things, but that "the world still seems good, not all good, but altogether interesting, and always improving." His optimism, no matter how shorn, clings to its bony structure.

The circumstances of his early life certainly did not offer grounds for cheer. He was born in South Carolina, the sixth of ten children to a mother who died of overwork when she was forty-five years old. His father was a tenant farmer and day laborer whose inability to make ends meet necessitated twenty moves for the family. There was a hard struggle to escape the cold, hunger, and debt of wage slavery which even involved secret flights at night. The young William was thus unable to start school before the age of eleven, and could remain through the years only by a severe work schedule and a supreme effort of will.

Work and schooling, guarded by character, fall into the pattern now familiar to us. So determined is he to learn that from thirteen years on he earns his own way. His summer jobs include work on a shift ferry, in a stove factory, and on the railroad. He was up against stronger and rougher men. One seasoned worker, on a job of pitching and stacking boards with him, tries to "get" him all summer. Instead of being discouraged, William Pickens regarded him as "one of my appointed teachers," because he inadvertently taught the boy resourcefulness and skill. For this reason he never bore him ill will. While earning money for college, he is subjected to the strain of blasting and mixing concrete. He attributes his survival to the fact that he had no bad habits. Like Corrothers, he is carried over the rough spots by his virtues.

All during these years he maintained high scholastic ranking. His mother had been ambitious for him and would release him from family responsibilities so that he could study. When she died in his fourteenth year he did not deviate. One teacher called him "Always Ready" when he memorized his history lessons and had perfect papers in mathematics. His scanning of Vergil was considered so remarkable for a Negro that a newspaper featured it. Finally, reaching Talladega College on faith, with only thirty dollars saved in his pocket, he was tested and placed in the Sophomore class. Beyond this Negro college came two years at Yale, with Phi Beta Kappa honors. A career of teaching opened up as a natural outlet for his endowments.

The intensity of his intellectual drive he explains partly by his Negro background. In the beginning race does not seem to constitute a problem for him. His father was of African heritage, though not markedly so, his mother half Cherokee. In one small town, his father and his white employer practically ran the town between them. There is "extraordinary good feeling" between the races. Disagreeable white bosses are taken for granted. But when he enters the competitive field of learning it irks him that white people expect so little from colored people. He finds that he wants to change this negative attitude to an attitude of awareness about Negro achievement: "My ambition to win was stimulated by a desire to further the acquaintance of other peoples with my race. I had noticed that when I did my classwork among the best, more curiosity was awakened than when a Jew or a Japanese ranked among the best. The surprise with which I was taken struck me as due to a lack of expectation in my fellows, and I would succeed in order to cause others to expect more of the American Negro."

In such ways he is drawn towards the ideal of service. Possessed of sensitivities and mental acumen, William Pickens was cut out for race leadership. However, there is a faint condescension in his approach. Like Booker T. Washington, he dedicated his abilities to the welfare of his slower brothers. Like Washington, he tends to generalize about racial traits while considering himself an exception. For instance, his father's gullibility in believing the false promises of an agent is a symptom of "the unquestioning faith and good cheer of our race." That the father might have learned to be just as canny as the son, granted the same education and experience, does not occur to the son. Unthinkingly, Pickens upholds one of the favorite Southern notions about Negroes: the childlike group which requires the guidance of kindly-disposed white masters together with wise Negro leaders. It is almost as if he were willing to peddle popular opinions of his group in return for the approval of the influential whites.

In keeping with a race leader who seeks alliance with the "best people" is the care he takes to level any criticism of the superior race at the "poor whites." Even here he adopts an air of tolerance and pity rather than of reproof. "It has always appealed more powerfully to my sympathies to behold poor, degraded white people than to behold the same class of my own race . . . it is a less sad spectacle to see a man simply *down* than to see a man *downed*." On this issue he can stand in safe agreement with the better class of whites who have more cause to blush at any failure in their own white racial stock. In this tactful manner he can also suggest indirectly his own worthy attainments.

It is true that Pickens, in contrast to Corrothers, broadens his concept of the race question. The years beyond his first attempt at autobiography bring him experiences harsher and broader than those in *The Heir of Slaves.* He says of his teaching days in the Deep South that "real living is the great educator," giving a close view rather than the ideal perspective from an airplane. In 1913 he travels in Europe with his wife, then assumes the Deanship of Morgan College, Baltimore, and finally, in 1920, becomes field secretary of the militant organization for Negro rights, the National Association for the Advancement of Colored People.

Culled from these years are specific criticisms of white policy: the absentee control of missionary colleges, the double standard of salaries and promotions for white and colored teachers, the brutality towards innocent Negroes, the injustices of segregated facilities, the danger of

Pullman travel for Negroes even when interstate and legal, and finally the risk for a Negro citizen in standing up for his rights when a white man—or especially a white woman—intervenes. As an illustration of this last point he relates a personal incident about the collection of a debt in Texas. A simple and direct matter in itself, it required polite manners and guarded speech over a long period of time because the man was white and had an opinionated wife.

Yet, knowing his status as a Negro intellectual, his opposition to the Marcus Garvey Back-to-Africa movement, his support of Negro officers' training in World War I, his association with noncompromising leaders in his N.A.A.C.P. work, all of which antedate the last edition of his autobiography, we can well wonder why this side of his life is treated so slightly. While external evidence about his later activities would thus push him in the direction of Du Bois' school of thought, the autobiography as it stands bears the indelible mark of Booker T. Washington. Evidently the formula of a good world, good whites, and good Negroes, if not too convincing to his mind, was at best useful and at worst the line of least resistance.

A Nickel and a Prayer

JANE EDNA HUNTER

OUR first glance makes us relegate *A Nickel and a Prayer* automatically to the Booker T. Washington school of autobiographies. Here we have the story of one of the first Negro career women. The title calls our attention to the modest beginning and the progress through faith. She, too, feels that she has burst the bonds of handicap. She, too, wishes to lighten the way for others. On her climb upward she gives repeated credit to the influence of Booker T. Washington. At the peak of her life work, in 1938, she receives an honorary degree from Tuskegee Institute for her direction of the Phillis Wheatley Association, "the embodiment and essence of the industrial philosophy maintained by Dr. Booker T. Washington."

But we must remember that this book was published in 1940. While it is remarkable that the Washington pattern has persisted so long, it would be more remarkable if the decades between 1900 and 1940 had not brought new points of view which would affect Mrs. Hunter's presentation. And our further inquiry does, indeed, confirm this supposition.

First of all, her painting is not flat. She is the only one out of this first group of four who attempts to delve beneath the surface of her own life, to examine her motivations, and to analyze the source of her conflicts. Although her terminology is moralistic rather than psychological, it bears witness to the more advanced scientific knowledge of the individual which we have a right to expect from the later publishing date. So many discoveries about human behavior have been popularized in this century that no literate person can overlook them entirely.

The frankness of her self-probing carries over to such "delicate" subjects as intermarriage. Again, in 1940, this no longer ranks as taboo. Edna May Hunter had "white blood" in her veins and felt free to mention the consequences. Booker T. Washington, James Corrothers, and William Pickens all had white ancestry but elected to skirt the matter discreetly.

As a result of this new scientific thought which encouraged more self-awareness and the loss of inhibitions, Mrs. Hunter was better qualified than her forerunners to be realistic. That she succeeded to a certain extent we shall see. Certainly she made headway in understanding the roots of her ideal of service. That she still remained a child of Tuskegee thought we shall also see. In autobiographical method she was modern, but in conclusions a member of the old school. A play-by-play account will confirm our first impression. It will show her course of reconciliation.

The problem of miscegenation begins for Jane Edna Harris in childhood and is so acute that it becomes the focal point of her introspection. Born in slavery, her father, Edward Harris, was the son of a plantation overseer and a full-blooded Negro woman. "In complexion and features he was Anglo-Saxon, and his English blood ruled his thoughts and actions." His small daughter, born in 1882 in South Carolina where he was a sharecropper, was named for her English grandmother, Jane McCrary. He early had ambition for her future, sold his farm to be near a school, and was willing to work as a ditchdigger and hod carrier. She, on her part, resembled him, and was "conscious of father's predominant traits in me." In family quarrels she always took his side. She had a strong loyalty to this "white" father.

On the other hand, she was not oblivious to worth on her mother's side. The first ex-slaves in the region to own land, her maternal grandparents had bought sixteen acres for $250. "Even as a child, I derived an enormous pride from the reflected glory of this distinction; and it remains a source of pleasure to me that the homestead still belongs to the family."

The child seems to have the proper setting for a happy childhood. The mother is a neat housekeeper. The two-room house is in a sloping field near her great grandparents' original home. She remembers with sentiment the old well, the apple orchard, the garden with okra and turnip plants, and the rows of cotton and corn in her father's fields. The morning-glory climbed to the eaves of the porch and the purple wistaria brightened the tall cedar. Down the red clay road waited adventures, from hunting frogs to fighting water moccasins. As a small girl she had outer security. Her folks had status in the community. Her grandmother was a "refined and cultured mulatto," a mother of nineteen children and a local midwife who still found time to work in her garden and pray.

But emotional stability is lacking. She observes the constant friction between father and mother. Although her father is industrious, he has a jealous disposition and a violent temper. He attempts to dominate his wife while she seeks to thwart his will. Inevitably, the child took sides and inevitably paid the emotional price. "I have never doubted that my life was shaped by this initial pattern of conflict with Mother and unswerving loyalty to Father . . . I came to feel a deep remorse for my aversion to her."

The pendulum swing between this hate and remorse governs her life. Her father dies when she is ten so that she no longer has a buffer between herself and her mother, or between herself and the harsh demands of poverty. She learns what it means to be miserable, lonely, and mistreated by her employers, and to receive no sympathy at home. Before the age of fourteen she has only three scanty years of schooling. Instead, she cooks, cleans, washes, and irons for a white family of six. Inside, she is rebellious and unadjusted; has no personal convictions about religion; plays cards and dances when such recreation is questionable.

When she is fourteen her situation seems to change for the better. She comes under religious guidance which bids fair to train her unruly ways and to soften her antagonism to her mother. Presbyterian missionaries provide the opportunity for her to attend Ferguson and Williams College in her home state. Gradually she learns to evaluate domestic work in a new light. "There is always joy in the humblest household task for the worker who is proud of her position, and who possesses a lively sense of appreciation of the contribution she is making to the total happiness of those around her. Given this, she ceases to be a rebellious drudge and becomes a cheerful co-operator in human service." These new values of unselfishness and usefulness are bound to predispose her toward a new adjustment with her mother.

But one final blow damages this process of reconciliation. As a young woman she is forbidden by her mother to choose the boy she loves, and is urged, instead, into a loveless marriage with Edward Hunter, a man forty years her senior. It is this event which precipitates her into apparent independence. After fifteen months she leaves him and starts a career which is to take her from nursing experience in Charleston to social reform in Cleveland, Ohio. Yet, by so doing, she fails to ease the familiar burden of conflict about her mother.

In 1910, when she is thirty years old, her mother's death brings about a spiritual crisis. "The grief of the next thirteen months robbed me of all interest in my profession. I had waited too long to bring about the reconciliation I so greatly desired, and now it was forever beyond me. At moments of despair I contemplated suicide."

In her choice of a lifework her feeling about her mother is presented as the strongest conditioning factor. Originally, the ideal of service taught her at college had provided an escape from hate. "To atone for this bitterness, I undertook the work to which I have devoted my life." Now, when she suffers the "agony of remorse and frustration" on her mother's death, she hunts desperately for a solution to her problem: "How could I best give to the world what I had failed to give her?" The answer is a home for Negro working girls; the following year the Phillis Wheatley Association is founded.

More important than her description of father-mother-daughter tensions is her explanation of their origin. Here she sets the blame squarely on racial mixture. "Wherever the blood of the white man flowed in the veins of the Negro, there was a conflict which conditioned his reaction to the people of his own race as well as to those of the white race." Thus husband could not possibly feel harmonious with his wife. In response, the wife "disliked and feared the characteristics of the white race" in both husband and "white" child. She saw in her unsympathetic daughter "the living expression of this difference which made happy family life impossible." If we could, at this point we might well ask her why "the blood of the white man" on her mother's side did not cancel out these differences. In any case, cultural if not biological factors propelled the father towards the white group and the mother towards the Negro group.

As she goes out into the wider world, Jane Hunter feels impelled to choose between these opposite pulls, exerted "by the dark and mysterious forces of the blood." Her first tendency was "to escape racial heritage as a Negro." She explains it as an unconscious motive at the time: "I would have denied it indignantly had anyone formulated it for me—but in the years to come it was to carry me far away from my native environment into new and strange ways of life." Earlier, in

Charleston, she had deplored the color snobbery in a Negro church, with "high yellows" to the right and "chocolate browns" to the left; at the same time she learned the direct connection in her nursing training between her own lighter complexion and certain favors and privileges. But the temptation to take the easier path is finally overcome: "Then the miracle! Having escaped, as I thought, the curse of being a Negro —poverty, contempt, subjection, the badge of sufferance which my people had worn for so many years—I was to be overwhelmed by the realization that I was, above and beyond all, my Mother's child—a Negro; that I was proud of the blood of my black ancestors; that my life henceforth was to be a solemn dedication to the people of my Mother's race!"

In this way, the personal problem and the social problem join forces to propel her into Negro leadership. After extending her aversion of her mother to her mother's group, she resolves her conflict, she believes, by accepting both. Instead of withdrawing, she embraces. Instead of futile words of regret she decides on deeds of goodwill. Her dedication is like a call. There is an enlightenment, but there is also an act of will. From this point on she becomes as conscious of the cause and as disciplined to the hard work it involves as any of her predecessors. Although she is more aware of a tortuous motivation in her preparatory period, once her mind is made up she is as eager as they to fight for the right.

The particular form of service Mrs. Hunter selects is ready-made for her. In 1905 she had come to Cleveland by chance. Immediately the bad housing situation for Negro working girls impresses her, "the dark, little rooms under the eaves; lumpy straw mattresses, dim gas lights which had to be turned off at ten o'clock." With no decent place to live, they imperil their moral reputations and their health. With limited job possibilities and no training, they lessen their chances for adjustment. Because of discrimination Negro girls are subjected to extra "dangers and pitfalls" in the big cities. They are more easily exploited by commercialized vice closely linked with corrupt politics. With righteous indignation, Mrs. Hunter investigates the night clubs where white men come to see Negro girls dance. "The whole atmosphere is one of unrestrained animality, the jungle faintly veneered, with civilized trappings." Behind it all she sees "the hideous god of greed," the landlords, the gangsters, and the racketeers who are profiting by an appeal to "the dark and violent desires of man's nature."

Mrs. Hunter begins the battle to eliminate "the worst that my race has to offer" by providing a better way of life. Faith and a singleness of purpose are her only weapons. Dr. Fosdick's book, *The Meaning of Prayer,* helps her through trying periods. She concentrates on the task before her. Early in her nursing career she had decided that "racial prejudice was an obstacle that could be overcome only by unusual devotion to duty and outstanding success; my prayer was not to lose a single case." Now this lesson is applied to the saving of souls. Starting without capital, she finally achieves not only a residential building but a community center with employment offices, gymnasium, recreation facilities, and cafeteria. Moreover, the years ahead hold for her additional duties of social worker, lawyer, civic and educational reformer.

Parallel with her determination of deed goes a determination of conviction. The experiences of the child and the young woman have at last crystallized into definite form. Like Booker T. Washington, she develops a system of thought on racial issues.

Boiled down to its essence, Mrs. Hunter's code for race relations becomes segregation. This covers everything from schools to marriage. The slogan of "separate but equal" she adopts without question. She insists that this is what the Negro wants and needs, as illustrated by the educational system: "In the grouping of pupils on bases of nationality and race, there exists an opportunity for the development of group and race consciousness." In order to give the proper direction, Negro teachers are indispensable in Negro schools. Through their common racial experiences they can understand their Negro pupils more fully than white teachers.

After all, Mrs. Hunter points out, is it not up to Negroes to take care of their own? When Richard Allen was not permitted to participate in the Lord's Supper he did not protest against the unchristian white attitude. Instead, "he walked out of that church building, rallied his brethren," and became the founder of the African Methodist Episcopal Church. When Booker T. Washington sensed the mood of the South about Negro education he adapted himself to it. "These two leaders did not waste their energies in futile attempts to abolish segregation, but addressed themselves to the task of educating Negroes to find a way to better citizenship." Similarly, she affirms that it is better for Negro working girls to have a separate home of their own rather than to seek admittance to the white Y. W. C. A. where they would not be welcome.

She is even prepared to suffer for her conviction when necessary. To her Negro critics Mrs. Hunter's answer is sarcasm or silence. Her first opposition in Cleveland came from Negro club women "who, blessed with prosperity, have risen from the servant class and now regarded themselves as the arbiters and guardians of colored society." In the case of those who continue to prefer suspicion to reason, "I have found it wise simply to preserve silence—following in this the example of Booker T. Washington."

Her conscience can sustain segregation in all its implications. Rather than an admission of inferiority, it is a means to group improvement which should not be weakened by miscegenation. Negroes should feel proud of the unique contribution they can make to the world as Negroes and should try to foster it biologically as well as socially. "By thorough and complete miscegenation we should lose our richest heritage."

By stressing the evils of intermarriage at the end of her autobiography, Mrs. Hunter completes the circle started in childhood. Always troubled by this problem, undoubtedly she feels a certain satisfaction in her final conclusion. It is as if the ghost of the white father-dark mother feud were laid forever by her choice of segregation with her mother's group.

Mrs. Hunter has taken us as far as she can in analysis. She starts probing into the layers of personality only suddenly to stop on the very threshold of awareness. For her problem is even more complex than she is in a position to recognize. Her account is filled with psychological data the significance of which she misses. Unwittingly, she offers the clues for a further interpretation.

The direct evidence of the autobiography leads us to postulate that Mrs. Hunter's unconscious identification has always been with her father, never with her mother. Race and sex factors wove a strange web around the growing girl. The natural attraction of daughter to father was increased by the color likeness to the stage of a fixation. Their white appearance became a bond in common which symbolized their exclusion of the wife and mother. Back of the girl's remorse towards her mother simmered a strong guilt feeling. Her anxiety prompted her to atonement. Yet her unhappy marriage fed her aversion.

When she seeks escape from her husband, her mother, and the Negro group her attraction for her father is uppermost. When she swings back to her mother's group the burden of her guilt is lightened. In the effort her final decision demanded we can read its falseness to her underlying nature. On the surface her life is integrated around a goal of voluntary service. But no march under the banner of idealism can stamp out the deep emotional longings and frustrations of the child and the girl. The more she strives to identify herself with the Negro group on a conscious level the more she feels an unconscious preference for the white group. Even while she trusts that her early resentment of Negroes has dissolved in loving kindness, it is expressing itself in a constant alignment with white attitudes. Even while she cultivates pride in them, she has a buried wish to believe in their inferiority.

The first link in the chain of evidence is her apology for the rule of the Southern white man. Like Booker T. Washington, she sees "the friendly interdependence of the earlier relationship of slave and master continuing to link tenant and landlord with ties that were personal and human." From the memories of her childhood she can sort out no gloomy pictures. "At least, the faces I knew and loved were untouched by the melancholy and despair that are written in the faces that have been brought to notice by Erskine Caldwell and Margaret Bourke-White." Observation of later years only confirms her optimistic view of Southern conditions. "From both races I learned of the cordial relationship of the Negroes and the whites."

Essential to this friendliness is the Negro acceptance of his humbler role. Only the colored servant who is loyal to his white master through long years wins contentment. His kind-hearted employer will respond by a "continual paternal interest" in his welfare, which will include the awarding of responsibility and training. The rightly disposed Negro will acknowledge his debt of gratitude, for the white man "laid the foundation stone for his rapid progress."

Negroes owe it to themselves and to their white employers to seek advancement first in those fields where they can be useful to the community. Here she is in accord again with Tuskegee objectives. From her vantage point in Cleveland, many years after Washington's death, she regrets that so many Negro men have come North. Had they remained in southern agriculture, they could have "continued to be one of America's greatest assets." As for Negro girls, she agrees that domestic training is basic and does everything in her power to implement this value. Out of the girls who come to her Cleveland shelter she feels that "poor endowment" and "inadequate training" bar a large percentage from certain occupations as surely as racial prejudice. While she does not wish to go so far as to condone inequality of opportunity for Negro working girls in the North, she thinks it is more important to eliminate "square pegs in round holes" and equip them for jobs where they will be welcomed. With the right spirit of cooperation they can also learn traits of skill and character from their white employers that will improve their lot.

Mrs. Hunter does not stop with precept. All along she has set an example of the advantages of proper connections. In fact, her predilection for the "best white people" forms the final support for our theory of father-daughter loyalty. That cooperation has paid dividends she often states. Back in her nursing days in the South she had the good fortune to work with cultured whites: "This was no snobbish feeling, but a realization that my success in these situations would give me a prestige valuable to my career. Then, too, I was able to acquire some of the gentler ways which my earlier underprivileged years had denied me."

It is doubtful whether Mrs. Hunter herself suspects the full implication of this passage. Especially revealing is the phrase, "a prestige valuable to my career." In it is contained all the strategy which promotes her later success in the Phillis Wheatley Association. Whenever organizational disputes of an interracial character arise, unerringly she casts her vote on the side of the angels.

One dramatic incident will suffice to illustrate her policy. At one point, white and colored civic leaders are deadlocked on the method of choosing a Board of Trustees for the Association. The "white friends" whom Mrs. Hunter has invited to join refuse to do so unless they can select the Negro members with whom they must associate. The colored candidates object to this procedure. As a countermove, they oppose a new constitution unless it allows for "Negro domination." In chorus with her white friends, Mrs. Hunter indignantly brands them as "insurgents" and "recalcitrants." She justifies her course of action in what she hopes are fair if positive terms: "I was faced with a choice between offending members of my own race who had given far more than they could actually afford, and yielding to influences which could give our organization a sound financial basis. I was called upon to make a decision which gave to us the support we needed. It seemed necessary to sacrifice personal feelings for the sake of the cause." The paradox of her reluctance to discard the "insurgents" does not confuse her. She is pleased with the subsequent "interracial harmony."

In its strange mixture of self-interest and idealism how symbolic of her whole life is that single explanation. How smoothly does reference to "the cause" gloss over her frank concern for white financial support. Not without profit has she sat at the feet of her hero, Booker T. Washington. Like him, she has no desire to batter at stone walls of prejudice. Like him, she selects the pleasant and sunny detours. The "right people" will approve of her and speed her on her way. If the "wrong people" oppose her, she can find consolation in the fact that she acts in their best welfare anyway. She is, first and last, a martyr to her mother.

She is a Negro as long as it is convenient to be one, as long as it gives her the prestige of group leadership. But when the question of Negro inferiority arises she is no longer a Negro in her own mind. Opportunism facilitates her natural inclination towards white people. She can afford to feel superior to racial contamination because of her private concept of herself: she is an exceptional Negro with "white" characteristics. Her reward lies in the hands of her father's group.

PEACE AT THE "WHITE" PRICE

In approaching these autobiographies we are at first inclined to hold their very existence as a miracle. It seems incredible that a first generation removed from the restrictions of slavery could so quickly learn to voice their experience. Sufficiently impressive would be a mere historical record of their early rise to leadership. That they also cultivate the tools of writing, find the time, and take the trouble to fashion their thoughts and deeds into words suggests a compulsion which is not ordinary. Only as we lay bare the roots of this compulsion do we remove all mystery about authorship.

If we start with the individual, we immediately recognize that we are in the presence of exceptional mentality. As our sample group of four illustrates, these men and women were hungry for knowledge and well equipped to absorb it. It is typical for them to be ahead of their classes in school, even while time and energy were consumed by self-support. All of them knew the extremes of poverty yet none of them faltered in the pursuit of education and training, nor failed to profit by their chances. This placed them in a position not only where the mechanics of writing would be no obstacle but also where they could attain sufficient success to justify writing about it.

But *could* is not *would.* Whether they reached their goal or not depended on further factors beyond their native endowment. They soon learned that cooperation with influential white people on their terms meant the difference between self-advancement and mediocrity. They soon sensed that only the right Negroes would be helped, that their leadership was, in the last analysis, a matter of white choice. Thus a process of accommodation to white attitudes developed. The starting point was not in the individual Negro but in the racial feelings of the white group which acted as a strong selective force. The standard was the subservient Negro.

Undoubtedly there were many potential Negro leaders during this post-Civil-War period who would not accept victory at this price. Some of them we shall meet later in this study. Others many others, were the unsung rebels who planted the seeds for new ideas about race-relations while deprived of the fruits themselves. They were illiterate, so they wrote their autobiographies in the hearts of other men.

For those Negroes, North and South, who decided to conform, the price was perhaps greater than they realized. Their personalities suffered from the internal conflicts to which they exposed themselves. Seldom do we meet greater ambivalence of emotion than in this group. Love and hate jockey for position. Conscious resolutions and unconscious motivations play their conflicting part in shaping behavior patterns.

Circumstances do not allow their victims any normal outlet for their negative feelings. As human beings they are aware of their capacities. As Negroes they are reminded of the arbitrary limits set for them by the dominant group. Hostility is the natural reaction. But they have no legitimate object against which to direct this hostility. They do not dare to antagonize the white group which holds the key of their destiny. Loyalty to their own group is expected of race leaders. Yet identification with a low-status group has aroused feelings of inferiority. It is the line of least resistance to resent the Negro group rather than the white group as the cause of their suffering. Thus they develop an unconscious hatred of Negroes to compensate for their own sense of inferiority and to provide an excuse for establishing themselves on a higher rung of the ladder. It is an ironic fact that some of these early pioneer leaders, apparently prompted by social consciousness and a love of their dark brothers, underneath have less love and are more opportunistic in their guidance than those who do not profess this idealism. They preach the way of social accommodation, often convincing themselves that it is the only hope of salvation for the Negro masses, and that they are Christian martyrs for the cause rather than appeasers for their own ends.

To rely upon the aid of religion becomes essential. It is doubtful if they could have weathered their mental strain and stress without it. The type of religion handed down to them from plantation days offered them a ready-made formula of humility, sacrifice, and forgiveness and of future reward through faith. The consolation in this assurance acted as a salve for their buried fears and hates, and allowed them legitimate emotional outlets. At the same time, the moral code of hard work and virtuous living, fostered by the Christianity of the group in power, promoted self-discipline. These Negro leaders had a fixed moral framework within which to operate. Its very narrowness protected them from having to deal with complexities. Self-doubts and confusions could be ruthlessly stamped out or twisted into convenient shape. In this manner their religion gave both sanction and support to their conduct.

Their autobiographies reflect all these efforts at adjustment. They must symbolize the good life. They must describe the path taken by men of humility, consecrated to their God, their white benefactors, and their own people. They must inspire less gifted Negroes and impress more gifted whites. Carefully pruned to the point of artificiality, these life histories present a monotonous front, and suggest a plan more calculated to encourage white approval than colored emulation.

As products of their day, then, these four books exhibit more natural than surprising features. They form such a direct response to group pressures, they illustrate so clearly one kind of group-interaction that we might just as readily place them on our social science as on our literary bookshelves. Even as we scan the titles we can note the conformity of pattern and purpose which subordinates their normal individual differences to a common policy. Moreover, we can see other titles stretching beyond, of which these are typical. Beside Booker T. Washington's *Up from Slavery* rests *Finding a Way Out,* the autobiography of Robert Moton, Washington's successor at Tuskegee. Next to James Corrothers' account of his rise to the ministry in *In Spite of the Handicap* comes Rev. Adam Powell, Sr.'s *Against the Tide.* Common need bound the authors together in a struggle for status. The family resemblance of their books was no accident. It was seized upon as a useful technique of advancement. Yet these men and women, as they wrote down their stories, were blinded to the full realization that they were footnoting social history.

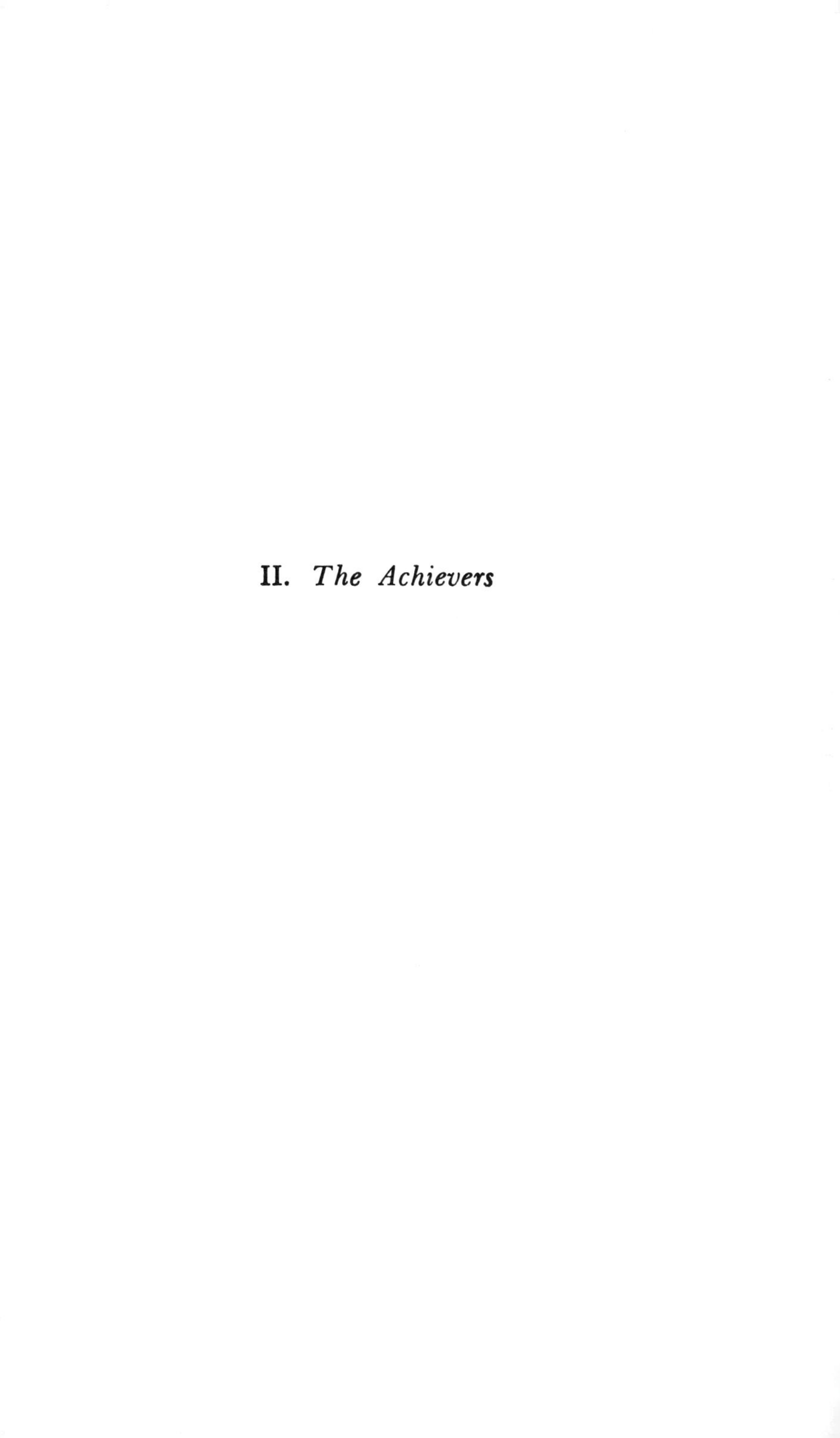

II. *The Achievers*

THE ACHIEVERS

THE relationship of individual and group is turned topsy-turvy in our next group of autobiographies. Instead of Booker T. Washington's emphasis that the good of the group should come first, and that the good of the individual is incidental, we have writers who boldly put self-interest first. Their attention is riveted upon their own special achievements. It is true that they are conscious of achieving as Negroes, and that they are eager to cast glory upon their race by so doing, but group benefit is nevertheless secondary.

The mood of these books expresses a direct contrast. Gone is the air of apology to white overlords, of submission to lower status. Here we find attitudes ranging from self-confidence to aggression. These writers have developed skills and have won recognition in a variety of fields from sports and exploration to music and public service. They feel a legitimate pride in their accomplishments which they see no reason to disguise.

Because they are not sidetracked by any pseudo idealism they are more apt to be realistic about discrimination, less apt to be grateful for white kindnesses. They are not concerned about currying white favor because they have tasted the pleasure of their own independence. Lifting themselves up by their own bootstraps, they feel that credit should go where it is due.

It is not that they ignore the race problem. It is just that they prefer a new approach. Their way is the way of individual protest. By their own lives they believe they can offer the best proof of Negro worth. By taking the offensive and challenging the white world to look at their records, they believe they shatter stereotypes of inferiority.

This spirit of protest does not necessarily express itself in bitterness.

Nor does religious motivation suddenly disappear. But by and large these authors show more tendency to analyze and make articulate their criticism of the course of white justice, wherever and whenever it is misused against them. The matter becomes personal. In their struggle to achieve, often in direct competition with white men, they do not brook interference patiently. They put the blame where it seems to belong and have recourse to their own wits. On the whole, they take a certain pride in forging ahead on their own initiative.

The process of placing their special skills in the foreground results in a fragmentary type of autobiography. Details are omitted or presented in so far as they bear on the author's particular center of interest. Thus we often are not told the complete story of a life but are given a full account of one phase, including every technical point. As we investigate sample autobiographies, we immediately notice this common tendency in the titles: *The Fastest Bicycle Rider in the World; Black Wings; A Negro Explorer at the North Pole;* and *Father of the Blues.* These Negroes do not profess to be writers. They are specialists and often use the written word only as a stumbling means of communication. Failures as literary masterpieces and as personality sketches sometimes result. Nevertheless even the crudest attempts succeed in capturing a certain enthusiasm and pride.

The Fastest Bicycle Rider in the World

MARSHALL W. "MAJOR" TAYLOR

IN 1900, when Booker T. Washington was publishing the story of his career, a twenty-one-year-old Negro was winning fame in quite a different manner. Known variously as "The Ebony Streak," "The Black Cyclone," and "The Worcester Whirlwind," Major Taylor had already broken world records in bicycle racing. For the next ten years up to his retirement we are given a description of spectacular but hard-won victories before crowds of thousands. Not only America but Canada, Australia, England, and the Continent form the background of his activities.

The subtitle of his autobiography, published long after his bicycle days are over, suggests his preoccupation with his specialty. He plans to give us "The Story of a Colored Boy's Indomitable Courage and Success Against Great Odds." The material is strictly limited to this objective. The issue quickly becomes drawn between individual skill, on the one hand, and group prejudice on the other.

He ascribes his start as a bicyclist to "a break of fate." We learn nothing about his ancestry, parents, seven brothers and sisters, or boyhood except the one fact that his father was a coachman to a wealthy family in Indianapolis. The small son became fast friends with the small son of his father's employer. They played as equals, and the Negro boy had access to all the gymnasium equipment in the luxurious home. He learned to excel the white boy and his friends in various sports and exercises. But one day he met an obstacle: "There was only one thing, though, that I could not beat them at." Because of his color, he was not allowed to join the Y. M. C. A. and go on the gymnasium floor with his white companions. Even though the boys protested to their parents, the policy of discrimination was upheld. The boy was "first introduced to that dreadful monster prejudice, which became my bitterest foe—and one which I have never as yet been able to defeat." In compensation, his white friends gave him a bicycle and he became a trick rider, teaching himself.

Soon his skill won public attention. A bicycle shop hired him to put on shows. At thirteen he began to win races. Although he was barred from the Indianapolis tracks because of color, he was fortunate enough to elicit white sponsors. A favorite device was to offer prizes attractive enough to bring the best bicycle riders in the state, and to keep the Negro boy's entry a secret until the last minute. By such means he gained his chance to demonstrate his ability. So impressed was Louis Munger, the owner of a bicycle firm, that he selected the boy as a protégé. The author informs us that when business associates asked Mr. Munger why he "bothered with that little darkey," he answered that he was an unusual boy, with excellent judgment and a cool head, and that he was going to make him the fastest bicycle rider in the world. When the criticism continued, Mr. Munger moved his factory to Worcester, Massachusetts, and took the young Negro with him. In Worcester he could at least join the Y. M. C. A. By this time the aspiring cyclist has gathered two conclusions from his experience: that a few white people are "too big" for prejudice but that most of them are so small-minded that only extraordinary skill can impress them.

This early observation explains the policy of rigorous training Major Taylor always followed. He took daily body-building exercises, and avoided alcohol and tobacco. While traveling he maintained habits of proper eating and rest. Patiently he acquired a store of technical information about bicycles and about racing as a profession. Tirelessly he practiced his routines. By 1896 he was ready to make his debut at Madison Square Garden as the only Negro professional.

From this point on, most of Major Taylor's autobiography is devoted to details of his many races, complete with names of competitors, dates, places, audience reactions, and press dispatches. The layman is taken back into an era before the automobile, when human speed and endurance were respected to the tune of big money. This American Negro won international fame for his racing form and his "jump" which helped him become a champion sprinter. To bring him to Australia he was paid £1500, reputedly the largest sum ever paid to a racing cyclist. He cut down his own one-mile world record of 1:22 2/5 to 1:19, by working with a steam motor pacing machine. In 1901 he competed in sixteen European cities and defeated the best riders of six countries. Already in 1899, in Montreal, according to one newspaper account, "He was cheered and cheered by an enthusiastic crowd of eighteen thousand people who loyally greeted the new world's champion, Major Taylor, U. S. A."

But the champion soon found that his right to the title was denied, ignored, or opposed by foul means. Although the press and the public recognized that he was a drawing card and were often on his side, demanding fair play, the prejudice of his white rivals found innumerable opportunities for expression. Sometimes, as was the case in St. Louis, these men would persuade hotels and restaurants not to accommodate him. Sometimes they would arrange that entry blanks to the race tracks bore the words, "For White Riders Only." Once, in Savannah, he received a threatening, anonymous letter from the "White Riders."

But the worse danger occurred on the race track itself. Perhaps the clearest evidence that race prejudice was used as a convenient mask for professional jealousy can be seen in the extreme measures his competitors took to handicap him. Bicycle racing had its normal share of the "dirty tactics" connected with all commercialized sports. Ironically enough, Major Taylor, who had always refused to participate on that basis, and who was so strait-laced that he would neither split purses nor ride on Sundays, now found himself abnormally victimized.

The devices ranged from deliberate fouls by individuals to the secret agreement of the whole group. The author relates one instance of the first type which occurred to him in New England and showed him that prejudice was not confined to the South: "Just after we had crossed the tape Becker wheeled up and hurled me to the ground. He then started to choke me, but the police interfered. It was fifteen minutes before I regained consciousness. The crowd threatened Becker who claimed that I had crowded him into a fence. However, the judges disqualified Becker, and ordered the race re-run, but I was too badly injured to start." Often he lagged behind in order to keep away from group tricks. Sometimes, in spite of precaution, he would be "pocketed," thrown, or tossed by the others. On other occasions they would pool their efforts towards the victory of one of their number. For instance, they would share the "pacing." One rider, following closely behind another, could gain an advantage that increased with the speed of both. "It is as though the man behind were being actually towed with a rope." Teamwork could thus be fatal to the one excluded from it. Several of his American enemies in Australia were fined or disqualified for a period because of their collusions against him, but that did not prevent their success in introducing American prejudice to foreign countries. Taylor's archenemy, for example, Floyd MacFarland, managed to indoctrinate the Australian champion.

After sixteen years of competition on such a life-and-death basis Major Taylor deserves honorable retirement. His pride in the laurels he has won is both heightened and tempered by a knowledge of the sharp realities he has had to face. He feels that the least he can do is to relate the unvarnished facts. In his foreword he expresses the hope that the statement of his case "proves to the world literally, that there are positively no mental, physical, moral or other attainments too lofty for a Negro to accomplish if granted a fair and equal opportunity."

Not all idealism has been killed. The author does not forget his wish to benefit the Negro race, "to inspire other Negro youth" to follow his example, and "to solicit simple justice, equal rights, and a square deal for the posterity of my downtrodden but brave people." He does not lose sight of his few loyal white friends. At the same time he invokes the spirit of Booker T. Washington towards his white enemies. "As the late Booker T. Washington, the great Negro educator, so beautifully expressed it, 'I shall allow no man to narrow my soul and drag me down, by making me hate him.' "

Yet the dominant note is struck in the next passage, at the close of the book. "I am a Negro in every sense of the word and I am not sorry that I am. Personally, however, I have no great admiration for white people as a whole." Here speaks a man who has carved his own way and is not afraid to name his enemies. Without intellectual pretensions, without group ties, he has compensated for his handicap by the development of individual courage and skill.

Black Wings

LIEUTENANT WILLIAM J. POWELL

Black Wings precipitates us into modern times. The image of the bicycle fades into almost ridiculous insignificance before the sweep of the airplane across the uncharted skies. Lieutenant Powell became an aviation enthusiast in the days of Lindbergh's fabulous flight across the Atlantic, and much of that pioneer spirit of wonder and exaltation marks his own approach.

In no way does *Black Wings* satisfy the criteria of adequate autobiography. The material is sketchy, the presentation awkward. The author starts his account abruptly with his first airplane ride in Paris, in 1927, and never looks backward. No memories of childhood help us round out our impression. It is as if a schoolboy had been assigned the task of describing his hobby and nothing but his hobby. The scratch of pen on copy paper is often audible.

However, the devotion to the hobby is obviously genuine. It manages to shine out of the labored pages and to give them an excuse for being. It opens up an area of human potentiality and endeavor which we should not overlook in our study of life histories. Against discrimination as stern in its way as that which Taylor faced, Powell succeeds in demonstrating his skill and spreading his enthusiasm to other Negroes.

The first plane ride started out as an end and finished as a means. The young Negro felt an excitement which stayed with him like a fever. He experienced an urge to master all the secrets of this marvelous manner of travel, an urge which carried him through the initial barriers of race. Refused point-blank at the aviation school in Chicago, he applied to the Army Air Corps School. There his rejection was tactful and by degrees. To the specification that all candidates must have had two years of college he replied that he was a graduate of the University of

Illinois; to the further explanation that only majors in engineering were acceptable he replied that he had majored in electrical engineering. When they finally admitted that he was not eligible because of his color he had no answer. But he persisted in his efforts with other schools until he was finally admitted to the College of Aeronautics at Los Angeles. Along with a hundred white, three Japanese, and a few Chinese, Hindu, Mexican, and Filipino students he settled down to work.

It was soon evident to him that a lone individual could not succeed in aviation. One man might both buy and pedal a bicycle unaided, but the financing and mechanics of airplane travel were on a large enough scale to require teamwork. Lieutenant Powell realized that his best bid for cooperation lay with the Negro group. Practical considerations forced him out of a "lone eagle" psychology into a move towards other Negro aviators and aviation fans.

He becomes entrepreneur extraordinary. His plans are ambitious and include a tour of the United States by pioneer Negro aviators. He hopes to find and train mechanics, navigators, parachute riggers, aeronautical engineers, radio men, parachute jumpers, and flyers. An executive committee is set up in Los Angeles to raise $10,000 capital and to promote "aero clubs" named in memory of Bessie Colman, the first licensed Negro pilot. Publicity stunts alternate with misfortunes. At one time Bill Powell has his friends functioning smoothly together, only to have them, shortly after, working at cross purposes, discouraged at the odds, or hampered by jealousies. One month he is triumphantly advertising his idea through performances of his play, "Ethiopia Spreads her Wings"; another month he and his best friend have wrecked a $3500 plane below the Mexican border and are lost in the desert, without instruments, maps, or food. Other planes have accidents and the debts mount up. Yet he has the satisfaction of laying the groundwork for the first successful transcontinental flight in 1932.

Just as the organizer supersedes the aviator, so does the propagandist finally supersede both. Bill Powell is not the type of person to take discrimination calmly. He is not a theorist or a philosopher. As a man of action he is impatient with conciliatory words and timid behavior. Conscious of his own worth as an individual, yet constantly reminded that he is a Negro, he takes an immediate line of attack. At the close of his book he issues a call to other Negroes to follow suit: "Black men and women—arouse your imaginations. Act before it is too late. Do not let the aviation industry become completely monopolized and built up by other races who will only give you and me the most menial jobs of porter, red cap, and washer; but get into aviation now while we have a chance to have black airplane designers, owners of black air transport lines, and have thousands of black boys and black girls profitably employed in a great paying industry." He urges that Negroes should "get in on the ground floor" as producers, not just as consumers. This would involve the united support of Negro businessmen. It would involve employment of Negroes as skilled workers at the airports and in the factories, as clerks in financing companies and distributing agencies, and as salesmen. He summons Negro leaders, ministers, editors, to arouse the populations of their towns, to sponsor student attendance at aeronautics schools, and to raise money, if necessary, by a voluntary tax of 5 or 10 per cent on Negro affairs.

Black initiative is the rallying cry of *Black Wings.* The author has no intention of depending on the prestige of white ancestry, or the power of white men and their white God. When his color interferes with his self-development, he proceeds to build it into an asset by his own resourcefulness.

A Negro Explorer at the North Pole

MATTHEW A. HENSON

Among these Negro candidates for fame none has a better claim than Matthew Henson. He worked with Commander Peary for over twenty years, accompanied him on all of his arctic expeditions except the first, and was the only American to stand beside him at the North Pole in 1909. He rose from messenger boy to chief aide on the strength of his qualifications alone. Commander Peary was quick to recognize and utilize them: "This position I have given him primarily because of his adaptability and fitness for the work and secondly on account of his loyalty. He is a better dog driver and can handle a sledge better than any man living, except some of the best Eskimo hunters themselves."

With such a record, it is small wonder that Matthew Henson confines his autobiographical material to this one aspect of his life. Exploration monopolized his hopes and fears during the best years of his manhood. Between the ages of twenty-five and forty-two he eats, sleeps, and breathes with but one goal in mind, and its attainment gives meaning to his life. So single-minded is he, and so isolated in his arctic wilds from ordinary human contacts that even problems of race do not enter into his consciousness directly.

The only significant aspect of his childhood seems to lie in an inclination for adventure. He mentions the fact that he was born in Maryland in 1866, that his parents were freeborn, and that he attended grammar school in Washington, D.C. But life really begins at thirteen when he ships to sea as cabin boy. The world spreads before him: China, Japan, North Africa, Spain, France, and Russia stir his imagination. But in 1888, when he meets Commander Peary, then a civil engineer in the U. S. Navy, he is more than ready to exchange his general enthusiasm for a specific interest.

In mastering the science of exploration, Henson does not skip any stage of apprenticeship. He turns into a veritable Jack-of-all-trades. A list of his duties on any one trip would include: navigation, overhauling and storing supplies, rearranging sledges, trading with the Eskimos, cooking, walrus hunting, taxidermy, carpentry, making sledges and building igloos in from 45° to 59° below zero. He also functioned as barber, tailor, and interpreter. In addition, Commander Peary counted on him to handle the Eskimos in the right way.

The ease of his negotiations with these natives sprang from a fundamental personality trait. He had an unusual capacity to understand and appreciate new and different ideas. There was nothing of the dogmatist about Henson. When other Americans felt superior to or baffled by the Eskimos, his mind was flexible enough to evaluate them in terms of their particular culture. Sometimes he lived more than twelve months at a time with them, wearing the same clothes, eating the same food, speaking the same language. He grew fond of them to the point of adopting the orphan boy, Kudlooktoo. On the whole, he judges them to be an affectionate people with no bad habits of their own but with a tendency to assimilate the vices introduced to them, such as the use of tobacco. Furthermore, the Eskimo dogs come in for their share of admiration. The author makes the flat statement that, without them, the North Pole could not have been discovered.

At the same time Henson is too shrewd to idealize these people. In times of crisis he notes that many are cowards and some are heroes. To his mind it becomes a question of individual differences. Yet it is a fact that four Eskimos stood beside Peary and himself at the North Pole. These same four had also accompanied them in the unsuccessful attempt in 1906. They had the needed combination of stamina and skill: "The cowardice of their fellow Eskimos at the 'Big Lead' on this journey did not in the least demoralize them, and when they were absolutely alone on the trail, with every chance to turn back and return to comfort, wife, and family, they remained steadfast and true, and ever Northward guided their sledges." This tribute is signed and sealed by his personal indebtedness to them. On the return trip from the Pole one of them saved Henson's life, for when he lost his footing and slipped into the icy water the Eskimo lifted him out with one quick jerk. Only a short time previously a professor in one of the return parties had fallen in the water and frozen before his Eskimo helpers could reach him.

Henson's adaptability is not confined to people. In the frozen North lurk the dangers of impersonal forces threatening the puny efforts of man. But this explorer is fascinated, not repelled by them. He feels exhilarated and challenged to meet them. His book shows a familiarity with arctic topography and weather conditions and a pride in adjustment. He takes us into a region of crevasses, floes, and "leads" or open water, of pressure ridges and hummocks. Terrific winds hurl one hundred and fifty pound rocks to the edge of precipices and topple them over like toy blocks. Sometimes the snow is soft like "loose, granulated sugar"; sometimes, when packed by the wind, almost as solid as ice and excellent for igloo building. Through thick ice the men pickaxe their way. Over thin ice they hurry and hold their breath: "We forced the dogs and they took it on the run, the ice undulating beneath them, the same as it does when little wanton boys play at 'tickley benders,' often with serious results, on the newly formed ice on ponds and brooks down in civilization." It was a common mishap to camp and go to sleep, wake up and find themselves isolated on an ice island, a floe surrounded by swirling water. Yet neither the fear of drowning nor the pain of snow blindness daunts Matthew Henson.

Even the extreme cold and the long marches hold no terrors for a man who has carefully built up his endurance. At Cape Sheridan, which the final expedition reaches by ship, the temperature already ranges between 45° and 59° below. Then there is the hard ninety-three mile sledge trip overland to Cape Columbia. Beyond that still stretches four hundred and thirteen miles of travel northward across the ice-covered ocean. Peary and Henson are gone from the ship, dependent on their supplies and their own resources, for sixty-eight days. So cold does it become that: "Our hoods froze to our growing beards, and when we halted we had to break away the ice that had been formed by the congealing of our breaths and from the moisture of perspiration." Snow cannot be used to drink because it would reduce the body temperature and cause death. Yet at 86° 38′ North, before the last dash to the Pole, Matthew Henson has the presence of mind to read the twenty-third Psalm and the fifth chapter of Matthew.

He is so at home in this world of danger that he can afford to note its beauties. Just as he saw both sides of Eskimo character, he is able to find redeeming features in the "inhospitable country." Although he claims that he has "no poetry in his soul," no words to describe its "irresistible fascination" and its "unique beauty," he succeeds in communicating some sharply etched impressions: "Imagine gorgeous bleakness, beautiful blankness. It never seems broad, bright day, even in the middle of June, and the sky has the different effects of the varying hours of morning and evening twilight from the first to the last peep of day. Early in February, at noon, a thin band of light appears far to the southward, heralding the approach of the sun, and daily the twilight lengthens, until early in March the sun, a flaming disc of fiery crimson, shows his distorted image above the horizon. This distorted shape is due to the mirage caused by the cold, just as heat-waves above the rails on a railroad-track distort the shape of objects beyond."

He observes the color effects as snow-colored peaks reflect "the glory of the coming sun," and the cloud effects after the sun has "balanced on the brink of the world" and started its daily circle. As vivid reds disappear before the bright sun, "the shadows in the mountains and clefts of the ice show forth their beauty, cold blues and grays; the bare patches of the land, rich browns." The dazzling whiteness of the snow and the bright blue of the sky, "bluer than the sky of the Mediterranean," complete his color symphony.

Such an ability to merge into and yet master his environment, to enjoy the good and endure the bad, to develop his skills while retaining his sense of values, may explain his success where others failed. It was sensitivity as well as sound physique which placed him alone, of the Americans, at the North Pole by the side of Peary. Henson was relieved when Peary didn't choose to send him back in the last returning party, but Peary must have sensed that there was a useful combination of elements in this Negro, whether he ever analyzed it fully or not.

Certainly Henson himself never stopped to admire the fine balance in his personality, as reflected in his autobiography. But he was conscious of considerable pride in his achievement, which we may find excusable. As the journey nears its climax, the author conveys some of the drama to us. "Day and night were the same. My thoughts were on the going and getting forward, and on nothing else. The wind was from the southeast, and seemed to push us on, and the sun was at our backs, a ball of livid fire, rolling his way above the horizon in never-ending day." The small group was bound together with a sense of destiny: "As we looked at each other we realized our position and we knew without speaking that the time had come for us to demonstrate that we were the men who, it had been ordained, should unlock the door which held the mystery of the Arctic." Increasing the high excitement of this moment was Henson's realization that his skill had helped make it possible. Because of his "proven ability in gauging distances," he enabled Peary to go ahead without solar observations until "within a hand's grasp" of the Pole.

Seldom could circumstances be more ideal for the exclusion of thoughts about race. In this struggle against natural forces each was dependent on each, and only manhood counted. Strange as it may seem, however, Matthew Henson does not forget that he is a Negro, and that he has won his spurs as one of a long line of Negroes: "Another world's accomplishment was done and finished, and as in the past, from the beginning of history, wherever the world's work was done by a white man, he had been accompanied by a colored man. From the building of the pyramids and the journey to the Cross, to the discovery of the new world and the discovery of the North Pole, the Negro had been the faithful and constant companion of the Caucasian." Henson has wrested success from his environment as an individual, but he chooses to share it with his racial group.

Had his attainments not been eloquent enough to speak for themselves, Matthew Henson would have lacked the temperament to fight for freedom from lower status. He had much of Booker T. Washington's tolerant attitude, which would not have allowed him to attack or accuse white society, especially when his own contacts were pleasant. Underneath, however, he is fully awake to the racial significance of his story. He knows that both Negroes and whites will agree with Peary that his triumph "is a distinct credit and feather in the cap of his race." Therefore his autobiography becomes a subtle form of protest. In all modesty he reminds the world that hasty conclusions about Negro inferiority are unwise, if not unjust.

Father of the Blues

W. C. HANDY

THE composer of the *St. Louis Blues* needs no introduction. In terms of American culture, W. C. Handy offers a distinctive gift. The story of his life really becomes the story of the blues, their origin, composition, and influence on modern American music. With the blues in the center, it does not matter much, according to his analysis, in which direction we go. On the one side we find their "first cousins," the spirituals. On the other side stretches ragtime, jazz, swing, and boogie-woogie. Beyond both we see the impact of Handy's folk themes in modern works, in Chiaffarelli's symphony, in Gershwin's *Rhapsody in Blue.*

W. C. Handy assures us that the blues, just as surely as the spirituals, are essentially Negroid: "The art of writing blues or spirituals can be assumed but cannot be delegated outside the blood." Both are derived from a type of suffering which only Negroes have experienced; both are typical responses, one on a secular, the other on a religious plane. Only as a Negro does W. C. Handy feel he is qualified to understand and capture the primitive rhythms and melodies of Negro folk music. Hence it follows that the very nature of his special achievement makes the author of *Father of the Blues* conscious of his Negro status.

As in Matthew Henson's case, Handy's reasons for pride seem legitimate enough to persuade his readers. In fact, his faith in his contribution is so strong that it lends a certain unity to the uneven presentation of his autobiography. Arna Bontemps, Negro scholar and writer, has edited the jumble of material which Handy furnished, but, wisely enough, he has not tried to organize the life out of it. As a result the original Handy flavor is preserved; the spirit of the struggling musician is allowed to flow through the book and do its own integrating.

In flashes here and there we catch sight of the driving force which helped him, as an artist, pull genius out of mediocrity, and, as a Negro, lift superiority out of inferiority.

He is no bitter protagonist for his race. He makes no direct battle for Negro rights against white wrongs. Just as Henson's preoccupation with exploring comes first, so is Handy's love for his music the guiding star of his life. Yet, equally with Henson, he does not fail to relate his success to the fact of being a Negro. He has felt what it means to be discredited and discounted because of race. In proportion to the maturing of his talents comes a natural inclination to give the lie to false assumption, to bring glory to himself as an individual Negro, and hence to his whole group. Therefore we must always remember that while W. C. Handy decides to present his case to us primarily as an artist, he is always building up credit for his race, albeit quietly. The emphasis of his autobiography thus reflects both spontaneity and careful planning. He follows his enthusiasm while deciding that the best technique of persuasion is anyway an indirect one, that the bare facts of his phenomenal musical career can speak most eloquently for Negro recognition. His attitude towards the title of his book illustrates his method of approach. Originally he chose the name, *Fight it Out,* but since it "did not express a musical career," he dropped it in favor of *Father of the Blues,* a title suggestive of status.

W. C. Handy would have us believe that his dual wish, to protest injustice and yet to maintain diplomatic relations with society as the most effective means to that end, can be traced back to his own grandfathers. His paternal grandfather had a defiant history. He had run away from his masters in Princess Anne, Maryland, by the underground railroad. When he had been caught and sold into Alabama, he had retaliated by starting an insurrection. Secretly, he acquired a liberal education and ultimately became a respected citizen. In contrast, Handy's maternal grandfather, when given his freedom, preferred to stay near his master as a trusted servant. Under torture he refused to disclose the hiding place of his master's money to the Yankees. The grandson is led to conclude: "It is probably my inheritance from these two characters that enabled me to submit to certain hard conditions long enough to fight my way out and yet be considered sufficiently 'submissive' by those who held the whip hand."

He fails to note that the grandfathers have one characteristic in common, no matter how dissimilar their application. They have tenacity, and without the same quality, whether as a result of biological or social inheritance, their grandson could never have clung to his particular purpose. He was not pitted against any white owners, like his paternal grandfather, but he was opposed in his ambition by a *status quo* which did not allow for potential creativeness in a mere Negro. He was not tortured by Yankees, but he was ridiculed and reprimanded for his musical urges by those who were supposed to be on his side. Only a stubborn faith in his own impulses kept him going.

His family was not in a position to understand him. They were not musically inclined, they were too hard working to regard the pursuit of music as anything but wasteful, and they were too respectable to do less than uphold the religious prejudices of their community against secular joys.

His parents owned several strategically located acres, known as Handy's Hill, in Florence, Alabama. The poverty in the family was of cash, not of food. Consequently the father, who was also a pastor with strong convictions, backed a program of work for his growing son for two reasons: necessity and principle. The small boy picked berries, worked in the fields, sold iron and rags, and learned to make lye soap. At twelve he was a water boy in a rock quarry; in his teens, an apprentice in plastering, shoemaking, carpentry, and printing.

But this was not his real life. He went through the motions of obeying his father while his imagination was enthralled by the sights and sounds of nature. From early childhood, "I knew every haunt of this woodland for whatever my fancy conjured, and I knew the music of every song bird and all the symphonies of their unpremeditated art." From some strange source the boy developed a need to reproduce these sounds. Except for his grandfather Brewer, who sometimes fiddled at dances, he found no musical bond with his relatives. "With all their differences, most of my forebears had one thing in common: if they had any musical talent, it remained buried." Yet, years later, Handy can look back on nature as his "kindergarten." He can compare the cry of the blue jay to the French horn, the tappings of the woodpecker to the reverberations of a snare drum, the raucous call of the distant crow to a jazz motif. He sensed the bass of the bull frog, the obbligatos of the million crickets, the syncopation of horses' hooves. As he grew older he added the saxophonic wailing of the cows and the clarinets of the moody whippoorwills. The mature musician cannot give too much credit to these early impressions. He feels that the genius learns from all aspects of nature more than from books. "He hears the music of the stream, the brook, the ocean, and makes notes out of them."

At first the boy's need for expression had to content itself with crude devices. Broom handles, fine-tooth combs, and tin pans were pressed into service. Sometimes he and his playmates invented more original instruments: "We Handy's Hill kids made rhythm by scraping a twenty penny nail across the teeth of the jawbone of a horse that had died in the woods nearby." But there is a limit to living off substitutes, and the growing boy began to feel an intense longing for a real musical instrument. Setting his mind on saving his money for a guitar was "like falling in love." It gave him a secret source of happiness: "All the world seemed bright and changed."

Not until the guitar was in his possession did he realize the full strength of his opposition. His parents were horrified when he proudly brought it home. The father prohibited its use and delivered a stern warning. The son was stunned: ". . . the words [seemed] dim and far away, like words spoken in a dream. A devil's plaything. I wanted to dispute the charge, but I knew that argument would mean nothing. My father's mind was fixed. Brought up to regard guitars and other stringed instruments as devices of Satan, he could scarcely believe that a son of his could have the audacity to bring one of them into his house." The conclusion was foregone. The young Handy was forced to exchange his purchase for Webster's dictionary.

At the same time this reaction was duplicated in school. His reply to the teacher's routine question about his pupils' future intentions was disastrous. "A bomb explosion could not have been more effective." His teacher denounced musicians as idlers, whiskey drinkers, and social pariahs, and prophesied that Handy would land in the gutter if he did not abandon his present course. That same evening his father put the prevailing sentiment into final and drastic words: " 'I'd rather follow you to the graveyard than to hear that you had become a musician.' "

Yet the boy continued to extract what he could from his environment. At least there was singing at school, even though without instruments or piano. The tonic sol-fa system was taught under the blessing of tradition, and this musical pupil learned to sing in all keys, measures, and movements. By ten years of age he could already catalogue almost any sound by this method, whether the whistle of a river boat or the bellow of a bull. One spring day, when the doors and windows of the school were open, he heard the song of a Negro plowman half a mile away. For years this snatch of song rang in his ears until it became part of a blues composition.

Such single-mindedness deserved reward. At last the wheel of fate revolved in his favor and a violin player came to town. He was no ordinary player. Traveling aimlessly to ease a broken heart, he landed in this small Alabama town from famous Beale Street, Memphis. Under the magic of his tunes music came into its own with orchestra, band, quartet, and minstrel show. The young Negro learned the fingering of instruments from mere observation. A fever was in his blood and parental interference could no longer sway him. Even the white bandmaster's insistence that Negro lips were too thick to play the cornet could not deter him. Almost in the spirit of dedication, he bought a second-hand cornet. From that moment on, there was never any doubt that he was wedded to music for life. Years later, when he returned in triumph to his home town at the head of his own band, the praises of his father and of the same white band leader must have sounded bitter-sweetly in his ears.

Although the need for self-support forced him in the beginning to other jobs, none of them held enough appeal to sidetrack him for long. His high grades in school qualified him for teaching, but when he learned that he could earn $1.85 a day as a moulder's helper instead of $25.00 a month as a teacher he quickly left Birmingham for Bessemer until work slackened and wages dropped. Back in Birmingham again it was enough just to hear a quartet singing in a saloon. Obviously money was no longer an issue, and he joined them in spite of their uncertain future. As they traveled westward, stealing rides or giving performances according to their luck, the new partner had no regrets. Even when hard times brought an eventual disbanding in St. Louis and a poverty such as the young man had never experienced before, the would-be musician still kept his hope untarnished. He was reduced to sleeping in vacant lots, on the cobblestones of the Mississippi's levee, or in the chairs of poolrooms in between police roundups of vagrants. He could have returned to the security of his home. But something more than pride held him. Unconsciously, he was following his boyhood habit and absorbing the sights and sounds of this environment, too, for future use. "I have always felt that the misery of those days bore fruit in song. I have always imagined that a good bit of that hardship went into the making of the *St. Louis Blues* when, much later, that whole song seemed to spring so easily out of nowhere, the work of a single evening at the piano."

From "hobo and member of a road gang" he suddenly attained status as a professional musician. Joining Mahara's Minstrels in Chicago, in 1896, he won instant success. "The dove descended on my head just as it descended on the heads of those who got happy at camp meeting." When he was raised to $7.00 a week, he "bought a spanking new C. G. Conn gold-plated trumpet and began practicing like an archangel from four to six hours a day." He organized a quartet, became a cornet soloist, arranged orchestrations, and discovered the strange pleasure of hearing his work played by a good orchestra. With prosperity under President McKinley came smart outfits and bouquets from the musical press. "Dressed to kill, I became a figure on the Avenue." The assignment of a second Mahara band to his leadership capped the process of recognition which had lifted him so far above the St. Louis cobblestones.

By the turn of the century, as Booker T. Washington is circulating his views of education, Major Taylor winning fame as a bicyclist, and Matthew Henson exploring with Peary, W. C. Handy is bringing popular music to thousands of Americans. Except for a brief and unsatisfactory interlude of teaching music in a Negro college where only classical music is countenanced, Handy spends many years with the Mahara bands. He travels from Cuba to California, from Canada to Mexico while ragtime has its heyday. He stays with them until minstrel shows are no longer popular, and until the next and most important stage of his musical career presents itself.

The time for specialization has arrived. His next locale is the Mississippi Delta, his next task the discovery of the blues. Although offered the directorship of a white municipal band in Michigan at a higher salary, Handy accepts the directorship of a colored band in Clarksdale, Mississippi. "For no good reason that I could express, I turned my face southward and down the road that led inevitably to the blues." In the coming years he learns by heart every foot of the Delta, every branch of the Yazoo Delta or "Yellow Dog" railroad, and every chance strain of folk melody that he overhears. At first these snatches of song "were kept in the back rooms of my mind while the parlor was reserved for dressed-up music," but gradually he begins to observe "with the eye of a budding composer."

The excitement of this creative period dwarfs all other events in his autobiography. Although he has told us more about his boyhood than our bicyclist, aviator, or explorer, it was necessary in his case as a portrayal of embryonic musical talent. Now that his account comes to the full flowering of his genius, he devotes most of his remaining space to detailed analysis of his one central interest. It is true that we learn of his wife and six children, of his later troubles with copyrights and publishing firms, of his move north to Harlem and financial success, of his failure in business and health in middle age. These are facts, dutifully recorded. We are even made aware of certain emotions connected with these events. While temporarily blind, he compares himself to Job and wishes for death. During the years of his national acclaim in the '30's, from the parades in Memphis to the ovation at the Golden Gate International Exposition in San Francisco, he experiences pride and elation frequently. But somehow all these happenings appear to be peripheral. It is as if we chanced upon them casually as the years carry us further away from the center of the author-musician's interest. Only there where he found his completest musical expression do we see the fine focus of thought and feeling. "If, as my teacher predicted, music brought me to the gutter, I confess it was there I got a glimpse of Heaven, for music can lift one to that state."

As W. C. Handy stands on the threshold of blues composition, the habits of a lifetime support him. Where other musicians have listened and not heard, he has listened, remembered, and even written down musical ideas. Thousands, he claims, have been exposed to the material which went into the making of the blues, without realizing it. His band men ignored the two-tone song of a blind woman on a Memphis street corner while he stored it away for future reference. Past memories feed into his present experiences traveling through the Deep South and sharpen his powers of observation. There was the plaintive song of the Negro plowman from his school days, and the simple melody about the legendary John Henry which he picked up from other Negro workers in the stone quarry. There was the improvisation of his "shovel brigade" in a furnace, making music by beating the shovels against the iron buggies, withdrawing or thrusting forward to alter the tone.

Now there is the lean, loose-jointed Negro who plunks his guitar beside him in a Mississippi railroad station: "His clothes were rags; his feet peeped out of his shoes. His face had on it some of the sadness of the ages. As he played, he pressed a knife on the strings of the guitar—the effect was unforgettable. His song, too, struck me instantly. 'Goin' where the Southern cross' the Dog.' The singer repeated the line three times, accompanying himself on the guitar with the weirdest music I had ever heard. The tune stayed in my mind." He discovers Southern Negroes who sing about everything from trains, steamboat whistles, and sledge hammers to fast women, mean bosses, and stubborn mules; who accompany themselves on anything from which they can extract sound and rhythm, from a harmonica to a washboard. Out of their suffering and their hard luck, these uneducated people "set the mood for what we now call the blues."

Yet, responsive as he is, W. C. Handy requires one last proof of the potentialities locked in this folk music before he commits himself wholeheartedly. After all, he is a "respectable bandleader" who had been trained to accept certain musical conventions as correct. It is not easy for him to concede "that a simple slow-drag and repeat could be rhythm itself" or that the public would like it. But one night a local string band in a small town, led by a "long-legged chocolate boy," showed him the beauty of primitive music as the coins fell at their feet. "They struck up one of those over-and-over strains that seem to have no very clear beginning and certainly no ending at all," but they had what the people wanted. As they outshone Handy's professional band in popularity, "a composer was born, an American composer."

Out of the wealth of his raw material W. C. Handy is now ready to shape his own blues. Rather than constructed out of "the snatches, phrases, cries and idioms" he has heard, his compositions are suggested by and built around them. For technical ideas he depends on Negro roustabouts, honky-tonk piano players, or footloose bards. Words and music are blended into his own unique whole. He uses the common medium of a twelve-bar, three-line form with its three-chord basic harmonic structure, but he also uses flat thirds and sevenths, even though the prevailing key is major, to suggest the typical slurs of the Negro voice between major and minor. Thus he introduces what are later adopted as "blue notes," and creates a personal medium. Or again, he notices the "breaks" or gaps in the folk blues which the singer fills up with spontaneous exclamation; by embellishing the piano and orchestra scores at these points he turns innovator. "The breaks become a fertile source of the orchestral improvisation which became the essence of jazz." His blues form a link with the past as well as the future. He does not shed all that ragtime has meant to him. But ragtime has put syncopation ahead of melody whereas he tries to team them together by stressing a real melody in the tradition of the spirituals.

With increasing public recognition, experimentation begins to mark his way of life. He stops at nothing to spread his new music. His is the first orchestra to add a saxophone. His musicians play new arrangements for politicians or for prostitutes. As they receive bids to play in less respectable places, they take it in their stride "on the grounds that music, like joy, should be unconfined." As they perform in the shuttered houses of the red-light district for the octoroons and their white patrons, they institute what is called "Boogiehouse music." The way leads directly to Beale Street, Memphis where they become familiar and popular figures. They add to the atmosphere of Pee Wee's saloon, with its painting from *Othello* and its gay patrons, "the heroic darktown figures of an age that is now becoming fabulous": cooks, waiters, gamblers in silk toppers and Prince Alberts, fancy gals, and chocolate dandies with red roses embroidered on cream waistcoats. Stimulated by this background, Handy creates his two musical hits, the *Memphis Blues* in 1912, and the *St. Louis Blues* in 1914.

But we must not lose sight of the fact that his blues were rooted in sorrow, underneath all associations with gaiety. Technically they did, indeed, provide a transition to the abandon of jazz. Unconscious mistakes in the fingering of clarinet or saxophone invited conscious imitation and further liberties with harmony and rhythm. Yet this artificial escape does not disguise the natural folk origin.

Perhaps W. C. Handy's greatest touch of genius is his ability to catch the emotional undertones of ordinary people. He reacts imaginatively to the poignancy of situations. One cold night he hears the mournful chant of a washerwoman as she takes in her husband's frozen garments, "Yo' clothes look lonesome hangin' on de line," and it serves as inspiration for one of his most popular works. When he starts to compose the *St. Louis Blues* he recalls his misery in that city as he stood before a lighted saloon, unshaven, shirtless under his frayed coat; as he slept in the streets, hungry and hopeless. But he recalls even more vividly "a woman whose pain seemed even greater." Heavy drinking had not helped her. As she stumbled along, she muttered, "Ma man's got a heart like a rock cast in de sea." Another woman explained to him, "Lawd, man, it's hard and gone so far from her she can't reach it!"

So deep an impression has this scene made that the composer now chooses to weave his plot around the moan of a lovesick woman for her lost man, and proceeds to write down his opening line, "I hate to see de evenin' sun go down." Not for one moment does he feel superior to this woman. Even as he objectifies her, he identifies himself with her as a fellow creature. In his simple statement, "her plight was too real to provoke much laughter," is embodied the basic appeal of the blues. Always, beyond technical variations and skill, W. C. Handy is seeking to express the real emotions of himself and others. Everything else is anticlimax.

Because of this peculiar susceptibility to the troubles of the common people, and because the Negroes he meets seem to have more than their due share, Handy is bound to feel the sufferings caused by race prejudice. When the blues get glorified, when they "put on top hat and tails" and are played by Paul Whiteman's orchestra in Carnegie Hall, he still remembers the shady side of the railroad tracks where they started. When white country clubs hire him and he plays before seven thousand in an Atlanta auditorium he still dislikes the violence he has witnessed in the South. A square is named for him in Memphis, yet this is the same city where he has seen a Negro skull tossed into a group of Negro workers to frighten and humiliate them, where he has known colored children who were not allowed to pass in review with white children during a Liberty Bell Parade. In his old age, when old troupers band together to give their specialties and go on the road, he is appalled by discrimination in the theatres of Washington, D. C., by the retention in the heart of the nation of "an ugly thing that should have died before now in a democratic climate." As a young man in the Deep South he had refused to work for a foreman who called him "nigger." As an old man in "democratic Manhattan" he is exposed to the pain of having his wife kept outside a hospital in an ambulance because of her color.

What better means of persuasion towards modifying such unkind attitudes can he use than his own genius? As an emotional appeal the blues can communicate suffering to its listeners. Perhaps he hoped that they might say, in effect, to their white audience, "Look, here is the Negro soul. How long will you choose to trample on it?" Perhaps he thought that by inducing sympathy they might lessen cruelty. As an appeal to reason comes the fact of the blues' existence, the fact of Negroid origin and composition. He implies that no individual and no race responsible for such creativeness deserves ignominious treatment. When a waiter in a Columbus, Ohio restaurant tries to embarrass Handy by bringing him his lunch in a paper bag, Handy informs him that he is the composer of the *St. Louis Blues* and changes his behavior.

A man with W. C. Handy's imagination would not be inclined to inflict suffering. His autobiography reveals realism but no bitter attacks on the whites. He never shies away from looking at the scars he and his people bear, but he approaches the future with an air of sweet reasonableness. The miracle of his own career generates hope: "It is a far cry from Handy's Hill to Harlem or from a rock quarry to Radio City, but we live in a new day and this is America." His thesis seems to be that, if this can happen in America, then surely much more of the good, the true, and the beautiful lies ahead. If men will but turn their heads and look, they will find the proof they need to persuade them to adopt new ways of thought about the Negro group. Handy's autobiography is meant to invoke sympathy for their sorrows and admiration for their gifts, not in the abstract, not by theoretical disputation, but through intimate acquaintance with one individual's journey towards his Golden Fleece.

A Colored Woman in a White World

MARY CHURCH TERRELL

A CONTEMPORARY of Booker T. Washington's, Mary Church was graduated from Oberlin College in 1884. While he was advocating vocational education for Negroes, she was proving the advantages of higher education. While he was temporizing with white attitudes, she was speaking her mind freely on a dozen controversial subjects. Of high intellectual caliber and unusual ability, she had all the prerequisites of leadership. But she never succumbed to the temptation of becoming a professional "race leader" and using her group as a stepping-stone to personal prestige. She replaced apologetic manners with assertions that were positive for her day and age. By the story of her accomplishments she wants to prove not that she is an exceptional Negro in splendid isolation from the inchoate masses but that she is one example of what many Negroes could do and become under the right conditions. A sense of pride in a work well done permeates her book, but it is not hoarded for her private pleasure. Unlike our first group and like our second group of authors, she shares it with her whole race.

Her pride is genuine, evidently stemming from calm appraisal rather than a compensation for a secret fear of inferiority. She tells us that during one period of her girlhood she was suddenly struck by the implications of a slave background but that she recovered her equilibrium when she studied history. It was reassuring to learn that "practically every race of the earth had at some time in the past been the subject of a stronger." As she grew older this fact tended to highlight for her the surprising progress of her race in the short time since slavery. It also helped her to evaluate her own career without undue depreciation.

Mrs. Terrell's talents are multiple, her contribution many-sided. In this one respect she differs from the other authors in this group. She has no area of specialization to describe, no one particular gift to present as proof of her distinction. This does not detract from the impressiveness of her story. We see her as brilliant student and teacher, as career woman as well as wife and mother, as clubwoman, civic leader, lecturer, and world traveler. Her achievement extends over a busy lifetime. Perhaps for this reason her autobiography lacks the fragmentary quality of the preceding ones. She publishes it in 1940 towards the close of her productive years, and she has a long and varied list of events to pass in review. It is natural that she wishes to include all her interests. Consequently we are treated to a full-scale story of her life.

The length rules out the possibility of much depth. With so much ground to cover, Mrs. Terrell cannot afford to linger too long on any one aspect of her life. In fact, we sometimes wonder if her writing does not suffer from the difficult task of all-inclusiveness which she has set herself. There is nothing clear-cut about her presentation. It shows signs of haste, is rambling, repetitive, and loosely organized. Instead of proceeding to her goal by a straight line, she falls into the associational method of "this reminds me." Clichés, from "in the twinkling of an eye" to "a thing of beauty is a joy forever" are not in keeping with the standards of a writer with her literary training and academic background. That Mrs. Terrell was over seventy when she wrote this book may serve as partial explanation of its digressive and careless features, but in the nature of the case a certain superficiality of treatment is inevitable.

There are two main threads of thought, however, which Mrs. Terrell never drops and which manage to tie together otherwise unconnected material. As her title hints, she is never heedless about the two basic conditions of her life, that she is colored and that she is a woman. These handicaps to her desired self-realization become further complicated because she is light-skinned and because she is a superior woman. She is faced with personal problems which might not otherwise have come within the ken of her experience. The more capable she recognizes herself to be, the more likely she is to chafe at the artificial restrictions of color and sex. Escape from her Negro group by intermarriage or by "passing" as white are open to her as actual, not theoretical alternatives. Emancipation from stereotypes of the woman's place in society poses a challenge to her. In both aspects of her dual role she must contend with injustice. Her decisions about how best to meet it in any given situation bestow not only continuity but value to her story.

The child Mary Church was comparatively sheltered from any of the problems she was to meet later. Although she was born at the end of the Civil War in Memphis, Tennessee, her family quickly obliterated any traces of slavery status. Her father was "so fair that no one would have supposed that he had a drop of African blood in his veins." He resembled his white father, Captain C. B. Church, whose sympathies had been on the side of the Union, even though he was a slaveholder. His mother had been taken away as a child from her own mother, but had become the close companion of her white mistress, joined the Episcopal church, and passed as a Creole for years in New Orleans. Going still farther back, Mrs. Terrell relates a tale of her great grandmother on her father's side, that mother who had to relinquish her child. She was not African or of African descent but a Malay princess, brought to the United States from the island of San Domingo as a fourteen-year-old captive. The islanders had been in a state of revolution and had overthrown the royal family. However, the young princess, with her straight, black hair and her deep red complexion, supposedly was never treated as a slave, spoke her own language and French, and became a valued seamstress in the best families.

It is true that Mrs. Terrell's mother had been a slave. Yet the child never heard her mother refer to this fact. Her master had taught her to read, write, and speak French. She had a cheerful disposition and was an excellent businesswoman. She trained herself to be a hairdresser, and after her divorce sold her shop in Memphis and ran a successful business in New York. Evidently this self-reliant and able woman inspired enough respect in the growing girl to prevent her from following the tendency we have noted earlier in Mrs. Hunter to associate all superiority with whiteness. Mrs. Terrell's appreciation of her mother is enhanced by her impression of her maternal grandmother, a very dark brown, almost black woman with straight, shapely nose and a small mouth. She remembers her as "Aunt Liza," quiet, refined, and reserved, helpful to and loved by everyone, black and white.

Thus, in her home circle, the small child has cause to feel as proud of her dark as her white ancestry. She feels no conflict about the matter. On the contrary, we can surmise that both combined to give her security and a sense of worth, even of aristocratic worth. As we read Mrs. Terrell's autobiography we often notice her pride in good breeding and a superior family background. She carries an upper-class air about her which seems ingrained, and probably explains her later predilection for European royalty. The log-cabin tradition is far removed from her experience. Poverty she never had to fight. Ignorance she was never exposed to. Illiteracy she never encountered among her family and friends.

Her family continues to furnish protection for her when she reaches school age. There is no abrupt transition from the sheltered home to the Southern community. At six years old she is sent North for a schooling which lasts through college. First at a "Model School" connected with Antioch College, Ohio, then at Oberlin High School and Oberlin College, she receives considerate treatment and able instruction in the classics. Her quick and eager mind is given the best training available in that day for women. Latin and Greek are favorite studies. Mrs. Terrell mentions the fact that one day Matthew Arnold was a campus visitor. He heard her read a passage of Greek and praised her performance without knowing that she was a Negro. This is indicative of the opportunity the young student senses in her environment to arouse by merit alone an admiration untouched by pity or condescension. Her whole educational experience gives her a self-confidence and an intellectual stability which facilitate her future work. Before the year of her graduation, Mrs. Terrell realizes that, according to available records, only two other colored women had received an A.B. degree from any college in the United States or anywhere else in the world. Yet her own case would lead her to interpret the scarcity in terms of limited opportunity rather than limited ability. She feels her powers as an individual. An intellectual fire has been kindled irrespective of race.

Perhaps for this reason the college graduate is now prepared to withstand any further protection from her family. By buying up real estate in Memphis during the yellow-fever epidemic her father has become quite wealthy, and does not want her to work. But she has a keen desire to use her talents and decides to teach in spite of his opposition. The process of broadening has started. She accepts positions at Wilberforce University and at a colored high school in Washington, D.C. She goes abroad for periods of study in Paris, Berlin, Florence, and Lausanne, assimilating languages rapidly, and appreciating the various peoples and cultures. France, especially, she enjoys now and on later visits.

She is loyal to the country in which she was "born and reared" and considers it her fatherland, but selects "dear, broadminded France" as her motherland, in accordance with Goethe's statement that everybody has a right to both.

Back in the United States, the young teacher discovers that she can also make room for marriage in her life. As an assistant in Latin to Robert Terrell she already has common interests with her future husband. Mr. Terrell possesses the background and the brilliance of mind to command her respect. When he was ten years old he had been brought from Virginia to Washington, D.C. for his schooling. He was among the first seven out of three hundred in the Harvard graduating class of 1884. His future career, as municipal judge for twenty years under Roosevelt, Taft, Wilson, and Harding, proves to the wife that her judgment of his worth has not been misplaced. Similarly, he seems to appreciate his wife's special talents rather than regretting her lack of skills in domestic matters. Mrs. Terrell takes her task of homemaking seriously up to a certain point; beyond that she offers her husband and two daughters other values from a personality enriched outside of household routine. She and her husband proceed on the simple principle applied to her by the son of Frederick Douglass: let those with trained hands use them, let those with trained minds use them.

Consequently Mrs. Terrell joins her husband in serving the larger community. For eleven years she is a member of the Washington school board. Although she receives no pay she feels her responsibility doubly as the only former teacher and the only colored woman in the group. In addition, she finds time to work with groups of colored women. Instrumental in merging two rival organizations, she is elected the first president of the National Association of Colored Women. Her activity is by no means confined to Washington. Selected as a Chautauqua lecturer she travels widely, spreading information to white audiences about the problems and progress of her race. A friend of Susan B. Anthony and Carrie Chapman Catt, she interests herself in the problems of her sex by alliance with the suffrage movement.

Wherever she goes she makes a distinguished contribution. Again she travels abroad, this time as a speaker at the International Congress of Women in Berlin. She confounds the audience by being the only English-speaking delegate able to make her address in German. Previously the Germans kept asking her, in all innocence, when "die Negerin" was arriving from America. They had evidently surmised "that she had rings in her nose as well as in her ears, that she would both look and act entirely differently from other women and that she would probably be 'coonjiving' or 'cake walking' about the streets." After the war, in 1919, together with Jane Addams, she serves as a delegate to the International Peace Congress in Zurich. She is the only colored woman in the group, but the white delegates ask her to represent them. Again she speaks in German and shows an intellectual grasp of still another subject. It is not strange that her college recognizes her successful career. At an early date they offer her the position of registrar. Mrs. Terrell regrets the necessity of refusing it: "I certainly deprived myself of the distinction and honor of being the first and only colored woman in the United States to whom such a position has ever been offered." In later years Oberlin singles her out as one of a hundred most famous alumni.

Her charm and her intelligence open up many circles which might otherwise have remained closed to her as a Negro. Because by education and temperament she fits in easily with these upper-class groups where even wealth is considered less necessary than intellectual attainments or good taste, she exposes herself to the danger of a certain snobbery. She knows important people in many countries. In England, H. G. Wells and the socialist Countess of Warwick entertain her. She is delighted to meet Prince Henry of Prussia, brother of Emperor Wilhelm, "to touch elbows and clasp hands with royalty," as well as to receive courtesies from relatives of John Jay and Cornelius Vanderbilt in America. "As I thought about the significance of these events, I felt I had grown an inch taller, believed that the recognition of our group coming from such a source would add a few years to my life." Her stress on group benefit does not hide the personal satisfaction all these contacts provide her.

Nevertheless, we can see that her penchant for important friends has a natural origin. She is not blind to the fact that she is an equally important person in her own right. Her training and experience have developed in her a poise which qualifies her for social intercourse with people of exacting standards. In addition, her interests, as a cultured person, coincide with theirs much more closely than with a great number of those identified with her by race who lack her opportunities. Mrs. Terrell has every logical reason to seek her own class level.

By virtue of her many pleasant associations with white people and the broadening effects of her scientific training on race issues, she is equipped to go more than halfway in the racial tolerance which mobility within her class group would require. She is strongly inclined to like rather than dislike white people. Beginning with the memory of her white grandfather who had been a benevolent slaveholder, continuing through the years of her northern schooling, and finishing with her European and American contacts with liberal-minded whites, she is led to two conclusions: that not all white people are "innately hostile" to her race, and that "broad-minded representatives of the dominant race" are largely responsible for giving her the chance to "make good." Often in her autobiography we come across evidences of her effort to see both sides, to attain perspective. For example, she always tried to impress upon colored school children "that George Washington was a victim of his environment and that he was a slaveholder because it was the custom of his section of the country and of his time and that he freed his slaves in his will."

But Mrs. Terrell's education has sharpened as well as broadened her mind. She cannot be easily fooled. Her temperamental alliance with aristocracy does not silence her tongue about the social abuses thriving in the shadows of their brilliance. Her tolerance of white people does not cancel out her sensitivities to their wrongs; if anything, it makes her more susceptible. With a complex and highly organized personality, Mrs. Terrell is bound to observe and react with growing realism to unfavorable elements in her environment. A Negro woman, she declares, can often dread more than physical attacks: "There are many cases of assault and battery committed upon the feelings and self-respect of colored people and I am no exception to a general rule."

Her own experience of race prejudice had a specific start in childhood. Ideal as her Northern school was in promoting equality, it did not function in a societal vacuum. With one blow the child's protective upbringing lay shattered. One day a group of older girls in the locker room teased her about her complexion. "It dawned on me with terrific force that these young white girls were making fun of me, were laughing at me, because I was colored."

This emotional conditioning affects the whole course of her life. Pain and indignation energize the mature woman's expression of her rational convictions. Thus she is able to identify herself with the pain of her dark-skinned great grandmother even while she does not speak harshly of her white-skinned slaveowning grandfather: "But the anguish of one slave mother from whom her baby was snatched away outweighs all the kindness and goodness which were occasionally shown a fortunate, favored slave." Such outspoken indictment of the system—from one far removed—we do not find in the life story of Booker T. Washington, an ex-slave who endured its miseries.

She also feels keenly about the lynching of Tom Moss, a childhood friend. He was a letter carrier who had saved his money and opened a store with two friends in the suburbs of Memphis. Because they gave good service colored patrons began coming over from the white-owned store. Mrs. Terrell informs us that these white men deliberately started a disturbance so that the police could arrest and a mob could lynch the three Negroes. Once again, when we turn to *Up from Slavery,* we find no lynching featured. Yet Mrs. Terrell carries the subject still further. She admits that her faith in religion is shaken by such events. She also comments on the brutalizing effects of this violence on those Southerners who participate.

Various forms of discrimination receive her attention in the course of her book. She sees a fallacy in the policy of "separate but equal" which Booker T. Washington countenanced and Jane Hunter defended. As applied to housing, for instance, it inevitably means "unequal" in practice. Her own difficulties in buying suitable property in Washington, D.C. in the face of restrictive covenants and segregated areas convince her that only old-fashioned and second-rate houses at first-rate prices are allotted to the Negro population. Even in government circles she meets no respite from slights due to her color. As a government worker in World War I, intent on performing her patriotic duty, she feels called upon to resign rather than submit to discrimination. When we recall her enthusiasm for the Prussian prince we must also mention that she was a charter member of the National Association for the Advancement of Colored People, an organization dedicated to win the democratic rights of Negro citizens.

Because she regards all forms of "Jim Crow" segregation as unfair, she has no qualms about ignoring them whenever possible. To her, whether the result of law or custom, they are the products of prejudice, should be changed by group effort as soon as possible, and meanwhile should be broken by those Negroes who can "pass" as white. Mrs. Terrell has taught her daughters to take advantage of their light color on trains, in restaurants, in theatres. She makes a sharp distinction between these temporary escapes from Negro status and a permanent desertion of the Negro group: "I have sometimes taken advantage of my ability to get certain necessities and comforts, and I have occasionally availed myself of opportunities to which I was entitled by outwitting—But never once in my life have I even been tempted to 'cross the color line' and deny my racial identity. I could not have maintained my self-respect if I had continuously masqueraded."

Along with the serious the author points out the ridiculous aspect of trying to classify people by color. She relates the incident of a southern conductor who boasted that no colored person, however fair, could escape his detection, but who forces the wrong woman out of a white coach into a Jim Crow car, almost gets murdered by the white husband, and brings a $20,000 loss to the railroad company. As a result of such incidents, one Supreme Court in a southern state decided "that a man who looks like white shall not be subject to conditions imposed upon Negroes." Looking at it from the other side, Mrs. Terrell feels that any prejudiced white southerner is subject to the fear that some day he may discover Negro ancestry. A friend of hers confirms this from personal knowledge: "Only last week a young woman who thought she was white committed suicide in a southern hotel because, in settling her estate, the lawyer made the startling discovery that her grandmother was a slave."

Since she is emphatic about both the immoral and irrational nature of color segregation, it may seem odd at first glance that this author never considered intermarriage seriously. She tells us that four white men made offers of marriage to her. The first was a blind musician in Europe who thought that, as an American, she must have money. The second was a German baron. She admired him, but wanted to live in the United States. Then came an American student who was eager to defy race prejudice and thought she was a coward to refuse him. Finally a prosperous American businessman suggests that they could marry and go to Mexico to escape the race problem.

But we have already noted that Mrs. Terrell had no intention of dodging the problems of her group on a long-term basis. As a believer in social equality she reasons that there is no logical argument against intermarriage. Poles apart from Mrs. Hunter's views on race purity, she feels that it is a matter of individual choice which should be determined by compatibility and not by accidental skin color. In light of this principle, she is quick to defend the action of her famous friend

Frederick Douglass in marrying a white woman. But she has reservations about such a course for herself.

In the first place, she is too conscious of the opposition of society to minimize the risks involved for Negroes. In her travels about the United States she has discovered a widespread fear of intermarriage among whites. In lectures and forums she was inevitably questioned about it. "From these experiences I became convinced that many white people believe that colored men lie awake nights trying to devise ways and means of marrying white women." Although she always did her "level best" to convince her audiences that white rather than colored people were dwelling on the idea, she finally concluded that the emotions involved were too deep-seated to be swept away by argument. Consequently she adopts a realistic position. Granting the theory, she is skeptical about much happiness deriving from the practice, "under existing conditions in this country."

But there is an even more important consideration determining her attitude. She believes that, in her own case, she could avoid the disapproval of society by "passing" into the white group. In the last analysis, therefore, it is a personal matter. She faces the stark fact that she could never have peace of mind married to a white man, even if no one ever suspected her own racial origin. Any white man, no matter how fine as an individual, belongs to a dominant group which has persecuted her group. "I have always felt very keenly the indignities heaped upon my race, ever since I realized how many and how big they are. And I knew I would be unhappy if I were the wife of a man belonging to the group which sanctioned or condoned these injustices and perpetrated these wrongs."

Thus we see logic and emotion often working at cross-purposes in Mrs. Terrell. On the one hand she regards herself as an individual, with special tastes and talents oriented towards like-minded individuals. Left to her own devices she would have adapted to groups with common interests within the class she found congenial. But even her high qualifications do not immunize her from the inroads of race prejudice. With all her knowledge she cannot entirely control her resentment and bitterness. Her suffering leads her to a voluntary preference for race instead of class alignment. Consciousness of color becomes the primary factor of her experience.

Her career as a writer illustrates the manner in which a natural interest is twisted by the fact of race into a problem. For many years she hoped to become a successful writer. Although she found it difficult to spare time from her exacting civic and domestic duties, she loved to write and received encouragement from well-known authors like Mary Roberts Rinehart. Yet her sympathies and her information usually confined her to subjects connected with Negroes. She believed that she could perform a real service by developing such material: "I have thought for years that the Race Problem could be solved more swiftly and more surely through the instrumentality of the short story or novel than in any other way." "Bitter disappointment," however, came in the wake of her failure to obtain commercial encouragement.

In her autobiography, Mrs. Terrell analyzes the reasons in terms of discrimination. First, she is a Negro writer; second, her subject matter is about Negroes; third, her point of view, from the inside of the group, often runs counter to the popular notions current outside the group. "The only kind of article which found favor with the editors was one that emphasized the colored-American's vices and defects, or held him up to ridicule and scorn." The same criterion applied to stories, which were supposed to represent him as "a crap-shooter, a murderer, a bum or a buffoon." There is no market, she feels, for a description of a Negro's struggles to accomplish something worth while. "Nobody wants to know a colored woman's opinion about her own status or that of her group. When she dares express it, no matter how mild or tactful it may be, it is called 'propaganda,' or is labeled 'controversial.' " Mrs. Terrell's only recourse is to publish her articles in England.

Yet this victim of discrimination still prefers to live in America. In spite of the equal treatment she is accorded in Europe and the frustrations her own culture heaps upon her, she adheres to her native land. Without illusions as she nears the end of her career, she knows the price she has had to pay. "I cannot help wondering sometimes what I might have become and might have done if I had lived in a country which had not circumscribed and handicapped me on account of race, but had allowed me to reach any height I was able to attain." But there is something to compensate for her suffering, something to balance her sense of frustration. Like the other authors in this group, she is sustained by a knowledge of her own worth as an individual American and by a recognition of the heights she has actually reached as a colored American.

When she measures herself against the superior whites she does not find herself wanting, and therefore sees no cause to feel inferior. If white society never permits her to forget that she is a colored woman in a white world, she will not let them forget her achievements within these artificial limits. Her autobiography records no final, no inner defeat. She externalizes her enemies and takes pride in holding them at bay. Rather than submitting, asking for pity, or retreating, she interprets her situation as a challenge. According to the way she meets this challenge, she wants to suggest similar potentialities in other colored Americans.

Summary

RESPONSIBILITY OF RACIAL WORTH

As we end our first two groups of autobiographies we are bound to seek explanations for the sharp contrasts we find. Why do some Negroes accept the inferences of race inferiority, and others reject it? Why are some emancipated from slavery only in deed, while others succeed in sloughing off even the slave mentality? What gives the first group a negative psychology, characterized by internal conflicts, submission to white attitudes, and a hostility directed towards the weaknesses of Negroes rather than the unkindnesses of the whites? By what means does the second group attain a positive mood of self-confidence or even aggression, an independence which allows for open criticism of white policies?

Obviously no mere acquaintance with their self-written stories can supply all the answers to the many cross-currents of conditioning which sweep them hither and yon. Thousands of buried memories and unstated facts of their lives would have to be correlated with a detailed knowledge of their social settings before we could hope to gain a full understanding, and even this process would not entirely eliminate the mystery of human choice, the unexpectedness of individual behavior. Perhaps the one lesson which modern studies of environment emphasize most is the fact that no two individuals are exposed to identical sets of circumstances, whether within the wider framework of the same culture or the narrower framework of the same church, school, neighborhood, or family.

On the other hand, we should not let any futile longing for perfectionism block our adventure in understanding. In these autobiographies we find facts and opinions which add to our store of knowledge about the Negro in America. Straws in the wind, they indicate trends in group thought, feeling, and behavior which merit the serious attention of any student of American culture. As we look at the authors in perspective, we are impressed by the way individual differences do not prevent them from falling into two distinct patterns, according to their response to the race problems. This leaves us free to formulate certain generalizations about their group reactions.

Explanations for the greater independence of the writers from Major Taylor to Mrs. Terrell may be found primarily in psychological-economic factors. None of them ever faced the extremes of involuntary poverty. W. C. Handy was the least protected and Mrs. Terrell the most protected from any forms of economic hardship. Handy certainly was "down and out" at an early period of his manhood, but he makes it very plain that it was a voluntary matter. He could have returned to the safety of his family or the livelihood of teaching, but he preferred to be a wandering bard and take the bad with the good. Perhaps he could regard his temporary plight with more aplomb just because he had no harsh memory of deprivation from childhood. The hard work he was required to undertake as a boy was not occasioned by a scarcity of food in the family larder as in Booker T. Washington's case. Major Taylor, Lieutenant Powell, and Matthew Henson never refer to any personal poverty in their backgrounds. The young Mary Church did not need to drop her schooling at an early age like Jane Harris and go out to earn her living.

As a result, their personalities bear the marks of greater security in the formative childhood period. The freedom from want encouraged a freedom from fear that was to influence the way they met future difficulties. When they came of age their energies were not consumed by inner doubts and conflicts but were concentrated on achieving their special goals. They were able to assume that they had a rightful place in society, a state of mind foreign to the "struggle against odds" experience of Booker T. Washington's group. They felt that their talents transcended caste barriers of race and entitled them to social mobility. Self-respect enhanced their realism about the white man; no longer were his political, economic, and religious institutions so sacred as to exist beyond reproach.

Their self-assurance was further increased by the fact that their achievements did not have to stand or fall by white approval. They could be measured by objective standards, independent of any emotional bias. Time, space, and weather calculations do not change with race prejudice. Beating a bicycle-racing record, flying from point to point in an airplane, or reaching a certain latitude and longitude at a certain degree of temperature at the North Pole are tangible facts. To acquire a college degree and proficiency in languages constitutes an ability which is demonstrable and cannot be gainsaid arbitrarily by white foes.

Their special skills were almost like commodities which they could sell or withhold at will. When white bicycle fans loved good racing more than their prejudices, they had to pay for the privilege of seeing a Negro expert who did not always choose to race. Commander Peary was as dependent on Henson as Henson was on Peary. Various international organizations recognized that their work could be advanced by the talents of Mrs. Terrell. These Negroes are comparatively free of white control. Lieutenant Powell offered us the extreme example of a plea for financial self-sufficiency among Negroes, a plea almost amounting to chauvinism. None of this group fits into the categories of trained service for white welfare that Mr. Washington or Mrs. Hunter recommended. We find no bricklayer, carpenter, farmer, or servant among them. They engaged in pursuits which were definitely expendable from the point of view of American economy. Feats of skill and daring, accomplishments in music and public speaking were luxuries which their possessors offered to the larger American culture in their own fashion. When at the receiving end as consumer, white America had to acknowledge them, however grudgingly. The luxury tax was the admittance of Negro worth.

The conciliatory attitude of the Washington-Hunter group is far removed from this atmosphere. Back of the soft-spoken word we sense a compulsion, back of the compromise with white prejudices a necessity. In some cases these Negro leaders are directly dependent on white financial support, as the history of Tuskegee and the Phillis Wheatley Association revealed. In all cases they are dependent on white moral support. Childhood poverty and insecurity evidently provided a rich soil for the suggestions of Negro inferiority. Only by white approval could they rationalize away their feeling of individual inferiority and gain status on a level above their group. Acceptance of caste separation from whites was automatic.

Geographical factors do not seem to play much part in explaining the differences between these groups. Washington, Pickens, and Mrs. Hunter had southern childhoods, but so did Henson and Handy, coming from Virginia and Alabama, and Mrs. Terrell who lived in Tennessee until she was six. Taylor grew up in Indiana and moved to Massachusetts, Powell speaks mostly of Illinois and California, but Corrothers also has little connection with the south since he spent his boyhood in Michigan and worked in the midwestern and New England states. In terms of man-hours spent in the south, it is doubtful whether the first group could marshall a greater number than the second. Handy, as well as Washington, selected the Deep South as the locale for his most creative work. Mrs. Hunter has lived most of her long life in Cleveland while Mrs. Terrell's permanent home ever since her marriage has been Washington, D.C.

Similarly, chronological data is not conclusive. As we have observed, some of Booker T. Washington's caution seems traceable to his times. The oldest of these groups, the only ex-slave, and an observer of the aftermath of Reconstruction, he felt compelled to appease the temper of the South. These reasons would not apply with the same force to those who followed in his train, yet they are more akin to him than to many of their own contemporaries. Mrs. Hunter, writing in 1940, still reflects the limited educational objectives of Washington, while Mrs. Terrell, also writing in 1940, is an exponent of higher education. Born almost a generation earlier than Mrs. Hunter and therefore closer to Booker T. Washington chronologically, Mrs. Terrell knew this Negro leader personally, and is even ready to admit that his educational emphasis has fulfilled a need for many Negroes. But his moderate views on social equality were always foreign to her nature. The spirit of indignation burned within her during her frequent travels in the southern states familiar to Washington. Matthew Henson in 1912 shows more self-confidence and more faith in the potentialities of Negroes than James Corrothers in 1916.

If we take Negro autobiography, then, between 1900 and 1930, we find two parallel trends, instead of one trend following another. Including the books of Mrs. Terrell, Mrs. Hunter, and W. C. Handy, which are published later than 1930 but which center on events and opinions formed prior to 1930, our samples fall into two opposing schools of thought. According to particular experiences and opportunities the writers adhere to the popular and persuasive tenets of Washington or become the champions of individual rights and racial progress. In each separate case it is necessary to study the factors which send them one way or the other. No general prediction is possible.

This is a logical outcome of a period of flux. When the fixed status of slavery was abolished trail blazing towards new status became necessary. In a period of rapid advancement and quick change, Negroes in the forefront took one path leading around or another path leading through the dense thicket of white attitudes.

One characteristic, and only one, these two groups of autobiographies share in common. Whether the authors express accommodation or protest, they are intensely aware of white prejudice. Whether they are tolerant or bitter towards white people, they are conscious that whites are whites and Negroes are Negroes. This consciousness, even at their highest moments of endeavor, never leaves them. Underneath shame or pride, racial identity conditions their response to life.

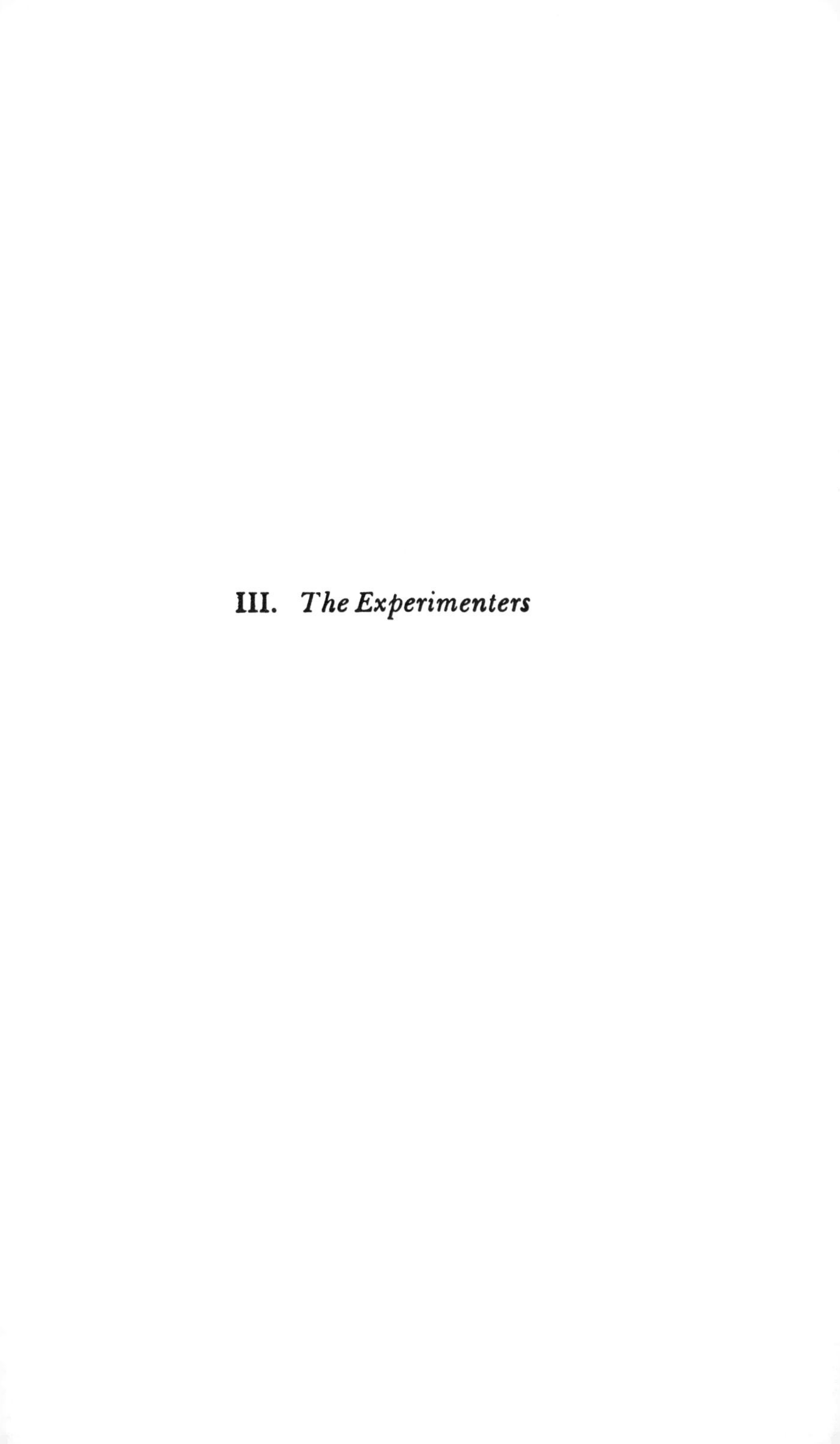

III. *The Experimenters*

THE EXPERIMENTERS

DURING the 1930's and the 1940's Negro-American autobiography expands. The number and variety of books increase, the literary style improves and the subject matter becomes more complex. The two tendencies we have noticed so far no longer hold true. It is necessary to turn to new family groupings.

Out of the wealth of fresh material which these recent years yield, we find seven autobiographies which are alike by virtue of their differences. Their highest good is individual self-expression. In agreement about the value of the process, they show no uniformity of result. The writers desire, above all, to discover and to be themselves, whether world traveller or regional folklorist, bohemian or Catholic, vagabond or classical poet.

In an important negative way the books resemble each other. No longer is the race problem featured. It is delegated to a minor role or it is excluded. Even the titles indicate this change of policy: *My Great Wide Beautiful World, A Long Way From Home, Born to Be, Dark Symphony, The House Under Arcturus, Dust Tracks on a Road,* and *American Daughter.* Gone is the *Up from Slavery* connotation, the emphasis upon handicap, struggle, and bursting bonds. Equally lacking is a preoccupation with color. Except for the word "dark" in one title, there is not the slightest hint of Negro authorship. In contradistinction, our previous group utilized "Negro," "black," and "colored" in unmistakable contexts.

The value contained in being true to one's self outweighs any considerations of race. It could be claimed that these men and women are undergoing a reaction to the "race uplifting" ideals of their predecessors. Weary of being a part of a problem, they seem to seek escape into more fruitful fields. In most cases, they have no special talents to develop, no special achievement to describe. They want to enjoy life as completely as possible. They want to free their minds and enlarge their experience. Self-expression becomes a law unto itself.

They have no monopoly on self-expression as such. W. C. Handy, Mrs. Terrell, and the others in their group also claimed their right to it. With them, too, the individual came first. Primarily they desired an unhampered chance to refine their natural gifts. But their reactions to race discriminations tempered their individualism. They developed such strong loyalties to their group that they could not think of their accomplishments apart from it. Our new group, however, has no corresponding sense of responsibility. It does not pride itself on doing great deeds in the name of the Negro race. It has no feeling of fulfilling any destiny beyond its own. It worships at no other shrine than the individual.

Consonant with less ambitious goals, the mood of these autobiographies is not shaped by pride. It springs from a search for happiness. As old moral ties are discarded new values form around the strange and exotic or the aesthetic. New facets of experience are sought. It is as if a burden rolled off the shoulders of these writers and left them footloose on the open road of discovery. Each to his own taste, they proceed.

My Great Wide Beautiful World

JUANITA HARRISON

IN Juanita Harrison we have evidence that not all cosmopolitans come from the privileged classes. World traveler extraordinary, she manages to work her way around the world for the love of it. A childhood dream materializes for this Negro girl, who was Mississippi born, with only a few months' schooling prior to the age of ten. Hard-working servant though she was, the travel pictures she found in magazines were enough to fire her imagination and feed her desire to see the world. The device she hits upon is to accept a job as a servant, and save enough money to move on to the next point.

One of these employers became sufficiently alert to the uniqueness of this odyssey to facilitate her servant's memoirs. Practically illiterate, Juanita Harrison probably needed a sponsor to encourage her and help her with the mechanical difficulties of editing and publishing material. Furthermore, her white friend in an introductory word provides us with what little background we have for understanding this original person. We learn that at thirty-six years of age she started her travels, that they extended from June, 1927 to April, 1935, and that she lived in twenty-two different countries. We are also told that she always looked younger than her years because she was a small, olive-complexioned woman who wore her hair in braids and often dressed in native clothes. For the most part, however, we are allowed to gather our impressions from the actual diary entries of the author who is not concerned about all the whys and wherefores of her past life but who only wants to convey her immediate joys to her readers. Out of the crude punctuation and spelling and the quaint phraseology crystallizes a real personality.

Strictly speaking, then, this book is more of a travelogue than an autobiography. At the same time, because it is devoted to the richest years of her experience it divulges more about the author's temperament and tastes than many a dull life-summary. Fascinated by strange places and new faces, she has an outgoing nature which enables her to enter thoroughly into each fresh adventure. It is characteristic that she wraps herself in the ever-present moment with such zest that the past and future dim into insignificance. Thus she says about Paris, "I think I love it best of all but I can't help but love the last place best," and again about Leningrad, "I thought the world were small until I arrived here Leningrad is a world in its self. I wouldn't give it for all the 25 or 30 countries and city that I have seen." In every spot she settles, she takes on the protective coloring of her environment. The fact that she feels like an insider brings her acceptance on those terms.

Yet her participation never involves fear of situations or of people. Intrepid of spirit, she makes a joke out of storms on shipboard or out of a penniless state. Although she comes and goes wherever her fancy dictates, she never meets serious trouble. Undoubtedly her naturalness and good humor serve as a safe-conduct with everybody. She can beat down the resistance of the skeptical and inspire the loyalty of the rough-and-ready. Always she has men admirers, but always she manages to lose them at her convenience. Acquaintances of five minutes may become fast friends for a day or a month, but there is something transient about this bird of passage which is incompatible with any of the risks or responsibilities of permanent connections. Something inviolable in her nature gives her an air of aloofness in the midst of her mingling with the crowd. Possibly it functions as a check and balance so that her naturalness is never exploited by others as naïvete. Friendliness and reserve complement each other to form a well-balanced personality. Indicative is her comment that she likes people, but she likes her private room, too.

The child and the woman jog along companionably together. Along with her spontaneity goes a common sense which eases her over practical situations. Whenever her money runs out, she answers advertisements in the local paper. When she works, she really works, and is so quick and efficient that her employers usually beg her to stay longer. But she manages her affairs so that she does not always have to earn. She lives cheaply and with the minimum amount of baggage and clothes. When customs officials confiscate her one bag under the impression that she is a spy she finds that it is a blessing in disguise. She can drop one country off and be ready to pick up the next one when she reaches it. When she enters her new way of life as a native instead of as a tourist, she is more able to unearth bargains in food, clothes, and housing. This process of adaptation is speeded up by her foresight in learning enough French and Spanish for ordinary conversation.

Shielded by her shrewdness, Juanita Harrison piles one golden adventure upon another. Perhaps her greatest asset as cosmopolitan is her catholicity of taste. No dish is too exotic for her. She takes a natural interest in eating, so that a foreign concoction only whets her appetite. Restaurants of all kinds lure her. So do bullfights, the more spectacular the better. But she also likes good theatre and makes a special trip to Oberammergau to see the Passion Play. With a serious streak under her fun, she has a feeling for any true religion. While far away in China, she has occasion to express it: "Some Ladys at church ask me if I were a seven day member I said I was a member of every Church that believed in God and that I was nothing but a glob trotter that had faith only in Prayer." No dogmatist speaks here. There is a wisdom of common humanity in her that embraces all customs and all creeds.

So receptive to other cultures is she that we lose sight of her own racial and national identity. We can recall the same trait in Matthew Henson as he worked with the Eskimos, and we could even surmise that in both cases membership in a minority group had taught them the dangers of dogmatism and quickened their readiness to appreciate differences in other groups. Nevertheless, Henson made a virtue out of his Negro origin, whereas Juanita Harrison thinks and acts and talks only as herself. At no place in her memoirs does the problem of race assert itself directly. What bitterness there is, stored up from her earlier years, can be surmised only indirectly by the love she bears for freedom in every shape and form.

In Russia, for example, she thinks that she has stumbled on a new way of life: "the Saying of Mr. Lenin Learn, then learn some more then learn learn That's Their motto and are in big red letters on many buildings. its good to see it while its in the making. Here are no cast, and class, no who's who. Here you are more free to do what you want to than any other country thats if its clean and honest." But the author does not speak in the spirit of social reform. She responds to equality of treatment as naturally as she gives it, and there the matter rests. Eager to explore life modes which will not confine her particular temperament, she leaves others to their own solutions. On this basis, we find her, at the close of her travel notes, settling down to enjoy the tropic beauty, warmth, and harmony of Honolulu instead of returning to a harsher America. The complications of this choice she leaves to her readers.

The House Under Arcturus

WILLIAM STANLEY BRAITHWAITE

IN this fragment of an autobiography, William Braithwaite stands in direct contrast to our previous writer. By accident, they share racial identity. By intention, they minimize race. Otherwise, differences of age, sex, upbringing, physical environment, education, temperament, and interests separate them.

Instead of a wide, beautiful world seen through the eager eyes of a woman with outgoing impulses, we have a house, just one house, arousing a rush of feeling and fancy in a morbid boy. The thoughts of the young William Braithwaite turned in on themselves. What he observed was important only in so far as it could be translated in terms of his inner experience. During the first twenty-one years of his life with which *The House Under Arcturus* largely deals, Braithwaite did very little traveling. But, even if he had, it is doubtful whether exposure to many scenes would have made any deeper impression than the contact with his familiar, smaller environment. The unfolding panorama of life did not count as much as his absorbed response to any one little part of it. He did not reach out towards new people. The ones he did know furnished an abundance of speculation for his groping mind. Sense impressions and ideas lay all about him, in the face of his mother or on the page of a book.

Born in Boston in 1878 Braithwaite was raised in a time and place where certain restrictions for children were assumed. It was a cold world, with stress on parental authority and correctness of behavior. Soon, when he was seven and his father died, poverty further depressed the situation. His mother was obliged to take in lodgers and he was faced with a future of work and curtailed schooling.

But an undercurrent of feeling ran through these early years that was out of proportion to the mere turn of events. His reactions were always imaginative, rather than robust. On late winter days he observed the multicolored sunsets from an upper passageway of his home: "My childish emotions traced sources of the mysteries which fascinated my mind as I contemplated with excited awe the pattern of sunlight and shadow woven upon street and wall, roofs and moving objects in the city world of my childhood." Each room in the house had its own special meaning. The front parlor exerted "a dominant influence upon both my mind and temperament throughout all the long years since I was a child." As he returned from school each day, its window framed the face of his mother while she sat reading or sewing. His bedroom he associated with thoughts of death. It was here that his grandmother woke him one January dawn to tell him of his father's death and that the "grey, ghostly shadows" dissolved into "the icy melancholy of the fluting wind outside the frosted windows" to convey the meaning of death to him.

A preoccupation with death developed prematurely in the child. Although there were several occasions when he had to face the fact of death, he was unable to relegate it in time to the minor importance it assumes in the normal child's mind. The mood lingered and led to "a profound and speculative curiosity concerning the paradoxes of life and death which dominated my boyhood and youth." He was never satisfied with accepting surface explanations. He wanted to dig behind and into phenomena. The world of images served as a medium of deeper experience. When the small boy learned of his father's death, it is typical that he found no outlet in tears. Instead, he lay awake in bed, trying to sort out his immediate sense impressions into some sort of emotional pattern: "The universe of feeling was stilled, and all consciousness flowed into my mind, where I dimly tried to weave the dawn-shadows and the merciless chill of the snowy world outside into the mystery of the dead man who was my father lying in the hushed room downstairs."

Accompanying his introspective tendencies was a longing for affection. But we have seen that this value was not included in the code of his upbringing. Although he had a "fanatic devotion" to his beautiful mother, she displayed tyrannical rather than affectionate attitudes towards her eldest son, undoubtedly with the conviction that she was acting for his good and welfare. She failed to give him the warmth of relationship which might have fulfilled his need for emotional security.

His father equally blocked the small boy's search for identification with others. Not only was he reserved in his own nature, but, in addition, he kept his son in comparative isolation from playmates. Behind this policy was a fixed snobbery. He never believed that any other children were good enough to associate with his own. "We were, therefore, never allowed to play with any of our neighbor's children, and since our immediate neighbors were English, Scotch, and Irish, racial and color influences did not inspire his mandate." Always he spoke of the greatness of a few men, and the need to discipline one's life by these examples, to refuse to be content with anything but the best, to avoid mediocre relationships. With a background of medical study in England, he himself claimed friendship with the New England preacher, Phillips Brooks, with the artist, Groudman, and with President Eliot of Harvard. Surely his son could do no less than restrain his impulses towards common clay.

It is clear to the reader, if not to the author, that the aura of special distinction and reserve surrounding his parents impressed even while it chilled the boy. William Braithwaite devotes considerable attention in his short autobiographical sketch to details of family history which augment this boyhood picture of superior parents. His father's grandfather was a colored shoe merchant in Barbados and at the same time the best Latin scholar in the colony. His father's father migrated to Georgetown, British Guiana, championed political reforms for the natives, and ran a newspaper, the *Creole*. Here he met and married a girl of French and English background. Her grandfather had been a French nobleman and her mother had eloped with an Englishman from Martinique to Georgetown. She, in turn, with the French name of Henrietta, chose this enterprising darker-skinned journalist without arousing any color prejudice in the community. Her brother, William, achieved such distinction in the service of the British Empire that he was knighted. Her son, William, our author's father, found it natural with this ancestry to study in England and to pass on to his son a name which had won recognition.

But William Braithwaite does not omit tribute to his mother's side of the family. Although it was rooted in slavery, he manifests the same respect for its worth as did Mrs. Terrell in her case. At the end of the Civil War his maternal grandmother, Lydia DeWolfe, had come to Boston with three very light daughters. The eldest, Emma, was his mother, born in 1860, growing up with no knowledge of her white father. It was no easy task for this ex-slave grandmother of his to raise her three daughters singlehanded, especially since they looked so white that the colored community claimed she must have stolen them! But the grandson remembers her wise and gracious spirit, her personal integrity, her Episcopal religion, and regards these as the signs of a lady just as surely as the birth and breeding which gave automatic status to his paternal grandmother.

Fortified by a sense of belonging within a tradition, within a framework of high ideals and character, the boy was enabled to disguise his inner sensitivities behind a certain aggressiveness. As we study the author's self-revelations, it becomes evident to us that he unconsciously sought for the social recognition of admiration in place of the love he was denied. He tells us that his ego grew both aggressive and ambitious, "superbly arrogant in the belief of its own faith and superiority." Small for his age and classified as a "sissy" in school because of the way his mother dressed him, he learned to fight offensively as well as defensively. He developed good coordination in sports, was part of a gang of boys in grammar school, and held his own on a newspaper route. Equally adequate in school work, with an excellent memory, he was especially drawn to English and history.

Although the end of grammar school necessitated a new adjustment, he made the transition successfully. Hired as a door boy at a "ladies' cloak house" in Boston, he soon won promotion to errand boy by solving a problem of delivery which had baffled even his employers. Other jobs followed. Meanwhile, determined to get an education, he decided to teach himself. He frequented libraries, ran a bookstore, and at twenty when he met William Dean Howells was a well-read young man. He had covered a wide range of books from the *Kreutzer Sonata* to the *Golden Bough,* and established acquaintance with a variety of authors from Ruskin to Freud. He had delved into both the natural and the social sciences and taught himself languages. Starting with pluck and quick thinking in childhood, he had continued to utilize his resources to escape the anonymity of poverty and the mediocrity of the average citizen.

A happy synthesis of two sides of his nature now lay open to him. As a poet he could find expression for his natural inclinations and simultaneously gain a measure of public esteem. Mr. Braithwaite does not indicate by any direct statement that his choice of career reflects an attempt at reconcilement of personal conflicts, but he supplies adequate data for our own conclusions. We can trace the pattern of inner repressions and outer aggressions which his parents first encouraged, which grew habitual, and which conditioned the type of poet he was to become.

His first conscious alliance with poetry corresponded with a direct experience in adolescent years. While apprenticed as a compositor at a publishing house he had occasion to grow familiar with pages of poetry. He states without qualification that this opportunity changed the whole course of his life. English poets like Keats and Wordsworth especially stirred his imagination while impressing on him "the cultural training necessary for an artist." Undoubtedly such a conclusion helped motivate the long period of self-study he undertook. His apprenticeship was no longer as compositor but as poet.

What a satisfaction it must have been to find a legitimate outlet for his bottled-up feelings. His nervous system had always "reacted agonizingly to the world of images," to sense impressions of all kinds, and always he had attempted discipline. As an example we have his reaction to religion. His aesthetic response to the ritual of the High Episcopal church frightened him. The appeal of the incense and pageantry, of the elements of pagan beauty in the service was so strong that he felt it might draw him to a merely sensual instead of a sensuous life. Consequently he discontinued attendance, in spite of the fact that his mother then judged him an atheist, and concentrated instead on the inner meaning of religion as embodied in the personality and life of Jesus.

Sometimes he sought surcease for his mystical longings in nature. He could stand at a window for hours watching the rain fall, "waiting to capture some unguarded secret of nature." His daydreams became enmeshed with the ebb and flow of the sea. Full of "spiritual and mystical symbols," the sea finally seemed "an element in my blood." He identified himself with the "cosmic force" of the tides, with vastness and eternal motion. Just as the child tried to plumb the mysteries of death, so did the growing boy wonder about natural phenomena.

But it took poetry to unlock the floodgates. Here at last he found the answer to his quest. "Here was the spirit of a man flaming with a strange new mystery of life and nature." One man could transmit his feelings to other men. "I received communications, impressions, and revelations which transported me into realms, and awakened sensibilities, that remade my world in terms of poignant imaginative desires."

There was no more need to fear his sensuous responses. There was only the need for crystallizing them in memorable words and phrases.

On the threshold of realization he is forced to grapple with the problem of race for the first time. Up to this point in his autobiography there is only occasional mention of racial factors, in connection with his slave grandmother, or with job discrimination, "the inferior employment reserved for my kind." He sometimes goes out of his way to show that race plays no part in some experiences. For instance, in the case of his schoolboy fights he stresses the fact that they sprang from personal disagreements, rather than racial antagonisms. In his native Boston, and later in the summer resort of Newport he moves largely in a white society and is accustomed to being regarded as an individual. He is able to claim that, up to the age of twenty, "I had not been conscious of color, for though I had recognized the limitations and restrictions of both the social and economic relationships of the white and colored worlds, the former had not yet impinged upon the active pathway of my ambitions." But a winter in New York, trying to make his way as a writer, changes the picture. Barred from newspaper work and bookstores because of color, the young poet is thwarted in making his living by methods consonant with his objective of writing.

A crisis in his thinking takes place on his twenty-first birthday. During his meditations in a darkened room on Fifty-Seventh Street he recognizes the difficulties and injustices of his situation in even more fundamental ways than work exclusion. He senses the possibility that prejudice can turn him into a race poet, using racial themes, producing for racial welfare. He feels that cultural discrimination follows closely on the heels of economic discrimination, and that the natural reaction on the part of its victims is to build up their own distinctive cultural values.

Yet this solution he rejects with all the vigor of his convictions. On impersonal grounds he disapproves of a separate body of Negro literature. It would lead to a double standard of criticism in American letters. However high its quality, if confined to racial materials it would be appraised differently and thus threaten "artistic sincerity." On personal grounds he does not believe in writing as a Negro. No special importance adheres to his life by virtue of his racial classification. No unique experience is connected with his color, clamoring for poetic expression. Although more realistic now about the obstacles of prejudice he must face, he falls back on the validity of his original belief as a guide for the future, "that Beauty and Art were the leveller of all distinctions, and that the source of this transfiguring power was in the common unity of all men, sharing and participating in the same interests and the same privileges." He anticipates that neither white nor colored people had the power to prevent him from creating in this spirit, no matter how much influence they might have on the eventual reception of his poems.

In reaching his decision, the young man does not regard himself as a deserter of the Negro group. He cannot desert something with which he has never felt any organic identity. Personal ties he recognizes, but blind mass loyalty he considers a delusion. He feels some of his father's "superb abilities" potential in his own nature, but does not see any reason why credit for origin or for results should rest with the Negro race rather than with humanity. He does not scorn or embrace any group as such, nor does he wish to be scorned or embraced on any terms except individual failure or success. In his attitude of independence from claims of race we can read once again the signs of parental influence, the summons to significant living judged by an absolute standard of comparison with all men, not by a relative and apologetic approach accorded to a member of an underprivileged group. His conditioned aggression has the final word.

The careful reader should bear in mind the unmentioned but crucial importance of the title of his autobiography. William Braithwaite has confined himself to the house of his own dreams and aspirations, but the house is under Arcturus. The symbolism of a giant fixed star suggests the dominant ambition of the poet. He can save himself from the neuroticism he dreads by keeping his gaze steadily on his permanent goal. Consequently he brushes aside the cobwebs of his own racial classification which obscure his vision and singles out those poets whom he feels are great enough to help him in his efforts. The fact that Keats, Wordsworth, Burns, and his other British models have whiter skins than he does not deter him. If he is charged with white favoritism, his reply will be that he is concerned with the thoughts, not the appearance of his beloved poets. Predisposed towards the conventional literary themes and forms of an Anglo-Saxon culture, he cannot afford to be disturbed by extraneous questions of race, whether colored or white. Classical examples which have passed the scrutiny of time seem more fruitful to him than any experimentation in terms of his particular status in a modern America. Carl Sandburg would be as alien to him as the Negro dialect poet, Paul Laurence Dunbar.

In retrospect, writing in 1941 at the age of sixty-three, the author takes only small account of the disapproval which his views occasioned during the long years since his twenty-first birthday. He mentions that the present autobiographical material is "the first recorded explanation of a course which had invited some criticism from my own people who had accused me of retreat from, and discrimination against, racial materials and interests." Nevertheless, he does not care to have us view his autobiography primarily as a rationale of his position in relation to race. Since he has permitted more than forty years of silence on this issue to pass by, he evidently means to suggest a stronger motive for his brief self-portrait. Why does he concentrate on his first twenty-one years? We are left to conclude that it is these years which formulate his life values so decisively that no further deviation is possible, and no further story is necessary. No more convincing proof can he muster for the singleness of purpose which moves him. His subjectivism develops into a devotion to self-expression which is the only ultimate loyalty he chooses to admit. We carry away the picture of a young man who is already achieving moderate success with his poems, and who is going to spend his adulthood carefully distilling his emotions into more refined essences.

Dust Tracks on a Road

ZORA NEALE HURSTON

OUT of her abundant stores of vitality Zora Hurston fashions an autobiography which shoots off bright sparks of personality. She has all the robustness which William Braithwaite lacks. A woman of courage and action, she would scorn any academic retreat from the touch and feel of ordinary life. Not only is there nothing of the recluse in her nature, but there is, to state it positively, a preference for the jostling of the crowd. She feels a challenge to elbow her way along her traffic-jammed road with a roving eye for adventure. Tracks she leaves behind her in the dust, witnesses of her presence which only she among all those people can make. Mixing with others only enhances her individuality.

Like Mr. Braithwaite, Miss Hurston is a writer by profession. As the author of several novels, she is as well qualified as the poet to communicate her life story in telling phrases. In contrast to the autobiographies of our first groups, *The House Under Arcturus* and *Dust Tracks on a Road* are the products of minds trained in literary expression. Greater skill with words combines with sharper psychological insight to achieve a three-dimensional effect which we sensed dimly in Mrs. Hunter's *A Nickel and a Prayer* and more closely in Mrs. Terrell's *A Colored Woman in a White World.*

At the same time, both Mr. Braithwaite and Miss Hurston treat their special gift of writing as incidental to their individual search for happiness. If they were composing in the same spirit as our last group, the story of their lives would become the story of their writing. Their talents would be employed for racial purposes. Just as Handy accumulated evidence of the Negroid origin of the blues, so would they collect every detail to glorify the creative process in Negro authorship. Instead, the use of words becomes for them only a means of fulfilling their own private needs.

At this point, however, they part company. Their definition of happiness would, of course, be quite dissimilar. On this score, Zora Hurston would have more in common with Juanita Harrison. With her wealth of curiosity and sympathy, she also stands ready to embrace a wide world and find it beautiful.

Born in 1886, in Florida, at the opposite end of the Eastern seaboard from Braithwaite, Zora Hurston was subjected to an environment which was the complete antithesis of Boston. Instead of living in a city largely populated by whites, she was part and parcel of a small all-Negro town, the first incorporated Negro community in the United States. Her father helped to write the local laws and served as Mayor for three terms. She was accustomed to seeing Negroes in positions of authority. Their self-respect was further enhanced by ownership of property and a comfortable standard of living. Her own family had several acres, a garden, chickens, and plenty of nourishing food. The eight children were expected to play at home, but they had plenty of space in this more or less rural setting to develop their personalities without too much friction.

During her formative years the child absorbed the spirit of this frontier-like existence where deeds counted more than high-flown sentiments. Her father came from a landless sharecropping background in Alabama. But he did not let this deter him. A light mulatto, he married dark-brown Lucy Ann Potts, even though he was from "over the creek," and labeled as "dat yaller bastard" by his mother-in-law who was a landowning snob and disowned her daughter. The enterprising young man was drawn to the opportunities of the embryo Florida community and functioned with equal ease as carpenter and preacher. Such instances of resourcefulness were not lost on the child. She sensed that personal strength and courage were the highest virtues in a country full of bears, alligators, wildcats, and rattlesnakes: "As in all frontiers, there was the feeling for direct action." No wonder that she grew up as a tomboy, disliking dolls, holding her own in fights with the boys. No wonder that her taste in reading included adventure tales like *Swiss Family Robinson* and *Gulliver's Travels,* the Greek, Roman, and Norse myths, and the David stories in the Bible where she found a full measure of "action and killings."

She always retained this feeling that a man was a man according to his own initiative. In her later years we never discover any signs of snobbery. In fact, she does not conceal her scorn of relying on "blue blood" connections for prestige. Whether this "blue blood" is "white" or "brown" does not matter. "Mixed-blood" she is, but she boasts "that I am the only Negro in the United States whose grandfather on the Mother's side was *not* an Indian chief. Neither did I descend from George Washington, Thomas Jefferson, or any Governor of a Southern State. I see no need to manufacture me a legend to beat the facts." Zora Hurston took pride in being one of the people and standing on her own two feet.

Her mother played an important part in arousing her ambition. She exhorted her children to reach out towards the sun. "We might not land on the sun, but at least we would get off the ground." She especially urged this favorite daughter of hers to meet the world bravely even in spite of race handicaps. Her father was more skeptical at this point. He did not think it was safe for a Negro girl to have too much hope, "but she didn't want to 'squinch my spirit' too much for fear that I would turn out to be a mealy-mouthed rag doll."

With her self-feeling nurtured in this way, the small girl became the exact center of her small universe. Even the moon was designed for her special benefit. "The moon was so happy when I came out to play, that it ran shining and shouting after me like a pretty puppy dog. The other children didn't count." When her playmates convinced her at last that she was not the moon's "exclusive friend," she consoled herself with the thought that she was at least still on the preferred list. It took her considerable time to learn fully that "the world didn't tilt under my footfalls, nor careen over one-sided just to make me glad."

A feeling of power bubbled up within her. It was as if she were poised on tip-toe, ready for anything. "I wanted to be away from drabness and to stretch my limbs in some mighty struggle." A child's normal desire to know what lies beyond the horizon was transformed into a consuming curiosity. She tried to carry her friends along with her. "We sat up in the trees and disputed about what the end of the world would be like when we got there—whether it was sort of tucked under like the hem of a dress, or just a sharp drop off into nothingness." It was characteristic of her temperament that she was not satisfied with mere speculation but wanted to implement it by action. She began to lay plans immediately for a trip of exploration.

She was equally outgoing towards her human environment. People stimulated her. She loved to sit on the store porch and listen to the gossip, the tall tales, and the folk tales. Both the teller and the tale held a fascination for her. She liked to observe and compare these grown-ups who were so totally unaware of the parts they strutted on the stage for the benefit of one little spectator. When preachers gathered at her home she luxuriated both in the warm interplay of personalities and the colorful stories they exchanged.

Yet underneath all the eagerness with which she sought to master her little world lay a deep vein of wonder. Any tendency to accept life on easy terms was soon balanced by a growing seriousness in her nature. Never content with the smugness of her elders or the stupidity of her companions, she often turned inwards to her own resources. Sometimes her imagination worked overtime. The birds and the lake talked to her. She concocted stories of her imaginative adventures that were real enough to win the approval of her mother and convince herself. Even though she rejected any conventional play with dolls, for months she transformed a corncob, a bar of soap, a doorknob, and several empty spools into real people with real emotions. In the Florida springtime she could only be happy alone in the woods. "Then I hid out in the tall wild oats that waved like a glinty veil. I nibbled sweet oat stalks and listened to the wind soughing and sighing through the crowns of the lofty pines." The mystery of existence occasionally overwhelmed her so that she felt as if she "stood on a soundless island in a tideless sea."

The core of her apartness lay in a series of visions which started when she was only seven years old, and recurred at irregular intervals with the same details. The author gives us a description of these twelve scenes which would flash across her mind "like clear-cut stereopticon slides," and which she accepted as prophecies of things to come even while she shrank from them. She dreaded the experience largely because it made her feel different from other children. It gave her a feeling of "terrible aloneness" and subjected her to moods when she longed to be like everyone else. As she played, fought, and studied with other children, she would suddenly feel herself isolated. "Often I was in some lonesome wilderness, suffering strange things and agonies while other children in the same yard played without a care. I asked myself why me? Why? Why? A cosmic loneliness was my shadow. Nothing and nobody around me really touched me."

When she was nine years old, an outer event confirmed this inner

trend. Her mother's death precipitated realism. She had thrived under her mother's sympathy and now realized that it was time to put aside the joys of her childhood. Instead of clinging to the Midas gold sunlight, the shining meadow, and the halcyon days that had been, she wrestled with the problem of whether her mother had been unhappy, and whether her father was sincerely grieved at her loss. She began to analyze the husband-wife relationship and decided that, while her father appeared to be the dominant one, he had never been able to curb the spirit of her mother. Accustomed to being a hero in church or around the town, he was outdone at home. "I know now that that is a griping thing to a man—not to be able to whip his woman mentally." In seeing through her father's self-importance, she identified herself all the more intensely with her dead mother.

Her sense of estrangement from her father and home was increased by two factors. His favorite child, in turn, was Zora's elder sister, Sarah. It was she who received a parlor organ, a gold ring, and earrings and who was spared the punishments meted out to the other children. In addition, the father married again and inflicted a hated stepmother on the sensitive child. Driven to the extreme of physical combat with this new mother, Zora Hurston lost some of her early feeling of security. The moon no longer followed at her beck and call.

From the time she was ten years old she was shifted from home to home, poor and unwanted. She learned that poverty smells like death, that old dreams drop off the heart like autumn leaves, and that "people can be slave-ships in shoes." She did not even have access to the consolation of books for awhile. At fourteen she began supporting herself by domestic work. But it was a hard assignment. She found no pleasure in dusting or dishwashing. Preferring to play with the children or read the books lying around, she would soon lose her jobs. "Sometimes I didn't suit the people. Sometimes, the people didn't suit me." Or again, she would take a dislike to a certain house: "It frowned at me just as soon as I crossed the doorsill. It was a big house with plenty of things in it but the rooms just sat across the hall from each other and made gloomy faces back and forth." Finding herself either bored or upset by her work, she decided that she was "not the type." When she observed other young people on their way to and from school, she would become so depressed that she had to "mash down" on her feelings and "numb them for a spell."

But Zora Hurston's early conditioning was bound to reassert itself.

She had too much vitality and healthy egoism to stick in the sloughs of despair. Too curious about what waited around the next bend in the road, she began to push towards more solid ground. She began to seek a way of life which would still her restlessness.

The possibilities of intellectual growth first opened up to her. The author even provides us with a specific instance as a starting point. Retrieving a battered and discarded copy of Milton's poems from a rubbish pile, she delighted in the rhythms and images of *Paradise Lost.* Later she was inspired by *Kubla Khan* which made her realize how visual-minded she was: "Listening to Coleridge's poem for the first time, I saw all that the writer had meant for me to see with him, and infinite cosmic things besides." She widened her appreciation from good literature to good music. For a year and a half, she traveled as ladies' maid with a group of white actors. Soon a great favorite, she was more than willing to assimilate their tastes for classical music, light opera like Gilbert and Sullivan, and grand opera.

The next step to more formal education came naturally. The bonds with home had long since been severed. Only the problem of support remained, but, now that a definite purpose guided her, she seemed to meet no real difficulties. Starting with night school in Baltimore she succeeded in entering Morgan College as a high school junior. The job she undertook in return for her tuition did not distract her from her studies. So strong was her enthusiasm that she immediately memorized overnight Gray's *Elegy in a Country Churchyard.* According to her own explanation, "I acted as if the books would run away." With the wholeheartedness of her childhood, Zora Hurston entered into her new kingdom of learning.

Always advancing towards her horizon, the young student achieved her dream of Howard University. Her first assembly exalted her; her English professor filled her with a desire to be a teacher herself some day, and lean over her desk to "discourse on the eighteenth-century poets, and explain the roots of the modern novel." She discovered that she could write and received the encouragement of having her stories published in the Negro magazine, *Opportunity.* After mixing with the most able of the Negro students at Howard, she finally had the stimulus of competition with white students at Barnard College, only to find that she was more than adequate. Financially secure as Fannie Hurst's secretary, socially approved as "Barnard's sacred black cow," she took anthropology under Dr. Franz Boas, and immediately dropped her ambition of being an English teacher in deference to this new field.

Here at last Zora Hurston stumbled on to a permanent interest which promised to satisfy all the needs of her nature. She was fitted for anthropology because it was concerned with studying man, here and now. She was prepared for research by her childhood sense of drama, imagination, curiosity. To her, "research is formalized curiosity. It is poking and prying with a purpose." Anthropological research gave her, in addition, a chance to travel and a chance to write. Much as she loved to travel, she could not have been content, like Juanita Harrison, with that alone. Much as she loved shaping her thoughts into words, she could not withdraw into the isolated concentration of Braithwaite's world in order to write. Her quest for knowledge needed to be renewed continually by people, strange places, and adventures, as well as by ideas and the theories of scholarship.

As a folklore expert, she makes a name for herself. This particular content of her research links up with her past experience. Her desire to collect folklore material from Negro groups reflects the eagerness of the child, sitting on the store steps and listening to the picturesque speech. As she appreciates the primitive Negro types in the phosphate mines, on the railroads, in the forests of Polk County, Florida, as she captures the rhythm and melody of Negro dance and music in Nassau and the Bahamas, as she studies Negro culture in Jamaica and Haiti, she is extending further and further the original zest for living she felt in her all-Negro community. Her anthropological training equips her with a technique of approach and understanding which fulfils her deep-rooted spontaneities.

Now that her search for knowledge has reached this happy solution, her individualism loses the negative emotions so prevalent in childhood: the fear, the loneliness, the resentment. Making congenial friends on the intellectual level she craves, receiving recognition as a scholar and a creative writer, exploring out-of-the-way spots, she is too busy and too content to brood over visions. Her individualism asserts itself in such positive terms that it has a dynamic effect upon those around her. It is inevitable that her wit and her bubbling good humor, attractively clothing her independence, win her a popular place in literary and artistic circles.

At this point of attainment, the author is in a position to crystallize a set of values. In relation to three major aspects of her experience, love, religion, and race, Zora Hurston in her maturity manifests characteristic behavior and convictions. In each case she takes an unorthodox approach. Refusing to be bound by what she ought to do and think, she makes up her own rules. She seems to feel that she has carved out a philosophy of life, by dint of her own efforts, pragmatically suited to her unique personality.

Evidently her gaiety and personal magnetism bring her many opportunities to shape her views on love. She is certainly not afraid of it. She stands ready to fall under its influence at any moment, but she also insists on sincerity. She abhors the sentimentality of prolonging a relationship when it is dying. "Under the spell of moonlight, music, flowers, or the cut and smell of good tweeds, I sometimes feel the divine urge for an hour, a day or maybe a week. Then it is gone and my interest returns to corn pone and mustard greens, or rubbing a paragraph with a soft cloth." Yet, the next time, "when I fall *in,* I can feel the bump." Whole-hearted, whether she is in or out of love, guided only by her own feelings in the matter, she escapes from a temporary marriage, and finds her most permanent and satisfying relationship outside of marriage. The question of immorality would never enter into her scheme of things. She regards her private life as her own concern, her conduct as a product of a higher morality than society's, the a-morality of the free individual.

Sometimes, however, two free individuals can give each other a lot of trouble. She discovers that the one man who means most to her has his own ideas about their lives together. Born of West Indian parents, a brilliant graduate student at Columbia, he wants her to give up her career, marry him, and live outside of New York City. But she has things "clawing inside" her to be written. It isn't merely a question of a contract with her publisher, it is the principle at stake. She sees no irreconcilable conflict between career and marriage, whereas he is a "master kind." Zora Hurston cannot drown out the voice of her independence. "I really wanted to do anything he wanted me to do, but that one thing I could not do." Consequently, their relationship becomes one of these "on and off" affairs in which neither can be quite happy with or without the other. She cannot forget that she did not just fall in love with him, that she "made a parachute jump." She knows that his mental alertness will always attract her. "When a man keeps beating me to the draw mentally, he begins to get glamorous." At the same time she is temperamentally unable to countenance complete possessiveness.

Perhaps some inner reservations towards men linger from her feeling about her father. The small girl who had no patience with his pretences when they affect her beloved mother would be inclined to retain her critical attitudes and extend them to other men as she grew up. And so she generalizes about their conceit, their arrogance, and their need for flattery. She needs them and yet she does not intend to let them hurt her. It may be that a long-time loyalty to her mother has fostered her personal integrity, her role as an emancipated woman.

Similarly, her skepticism about orthodox religion stems from her father's shortcomings. Although he was a Baptist preacher, he dodged his small daughter's questions. Why didn't God want children to play on Sundays? How could anybody love a supreme being that he couldn't see or touch? How could a person sin with each breath he drew when he was already saved from sinning? It may well be that the lively debates his answers might have started opened up a prospect he hesitated to face.

In any case, Zora Hurston finally attains to a tolerance towards all forms of religion. All she asks in return is a tolerance of her lack of it. Any religion—and here she would even include Voodoo—is valid if it satisfies the individual. Creeds, prayer, and all kinds of worship are for those who need them. Her anthropological studies prove to her the amazing variety in man's interpretation.

For her part, she finds no comfort in traditional religion. She believes that she has "a mind and will-power" to work out her own destiny. Reliance upon religious help appears to her as a sign of weakness. Most people fear the uncertainties and responsibilities of life, so they "seek an alliance with omnipotence." Although "a creature of their own minds," this power makes them feel secure. But Zora Hurston does not want any false, wishful security. Once more, she chooses to dig into her own resources and unearth realities which hold meaning for her. "Somebody else may have my rapturous glance at the archangels. The springing of the yellow line of morning out of the misty deep of dawn is glory enough for me."

We are reminded of the little girl who hid among the oat stalks and listened to the strange song of the winds. But now her wonder seems to have reached certainty. No longer does she stand isolated on a soundless island in a tideless sea. She has a sense of belonging to the world beyond the boundaries of her immediate life, before "the sun rolled into shape" and "the earth was hurled out." The thought that matter changes but is never destroyed protects her also from any fear of death. Her particular consciousness will cease but the "stuff of my being" will continue in another form. Organized religion only stifles her spirit. "The wide belt of the universe has no need for finger-rings. I am one with the infinite and need no other assurance." Because of the danger of misinterpretation, Zora Hurston will not classify her experience under religion, and yet it is obvious that she is concocting a recipe to her personal taste.

But it is not until the author touches upon the subject of race that we know the full measure of her individualism. She does not ignore the question, like Juanita Harrison, nor give it incidental consideration like William Braithwaite. She has a great deal to say, and plunges characteristically right into the depths of the matter. Just as easily, however, she pulls herself out and shakes herself dry of conflicts. Her hands are too full with the problem of being herself to be occupied very long with the problem of being a Negro.

It is significant that in her autobiography Zora Hurston does not evaluate the part she played in the Negro Renaissance of the 1920's. This movement, centered in Harlem and spearheaded by Negro intellectuals, gave active encouragement to talented Negroes. With her quick mind Zora Hurston would naturally be drawn to this group. But it is from other autobiographies that we learn of her association with creative writers like Wallace Thurman, Rudolph Fisher, and Langston Hughes. When she speaks of this movement it is only briefly, in connection with Dr. Charles Johnson's publication of her first stories in the Negro magazine, *Opportunity*. Even here she qualifies the concept by referring to it as the "so-called Negro Renaissance." This omission leaves little doubt that this particular writer is wary about being caught in any pattern of thought which would make her conform. Obviously she does not intend to be an example of "the New Negro," and an exponent of race pride. When she writes a book, she wants to feel free to write as she pleases, and not according to some arbitrary standard which will show the Negro in a favorable light. She figures that Negroes don't deserve preferential treatment over whites. When she mixes with people, she wishes to enjoy them as individuals, and not as members of a racial group.

The genesis of this attitude lies in her lack of bitterness towards white people. Here again, we should bear in mind certain facts of her life which the author has related to us without attempting to show us their influence on her thought. First of all, she was protected in early childhood from race prejudice by the circumstance of living in a self-sufficient Negro community. Later, when she worked in white homes, she blamed her failure to adjust not on her white employers but on her own lack of interest. For eighteen months she was the darling of an all-white theatrical troupe. Her most inspiring teacher, Franz Boas, was white. Her most helpful friends were white: Fannie Hurst, who employed her as her secretary and who treated her as a friend, and her "godmother," Mrs. Mason, who supplied her $200 a month for two years in order to write. At Barnard College her white fellow-students seem to claim her as one of their own. Discrimination looms up only as a legendary monster.

With this background, why should Zora Hurston bear a grudge against the white group as a whole? She is inclined, instead, to forgive and forget their historical misdeeds. Why blame the sad days of slavery on the present generation of whites, she asks. Her ancestors who suffered are dead, as well as the white men who profited by their suffering. In fact, the whole issue is dead. So, she concludes, "I see no need in button-holing that grandson like the Ancient Mariner did the wedding guest and calling for the High Sheriff to put him under arrest."

So concerned is she with living in the present that she refuses to be sentimental about the past. "While I have a handkerchief over my eyes crying over the landing of the first slaves in 1619, I might miss something swell that is going on in 1942." Her contemporary troubles are of a different nature from those of nineteenth-century slaves, so there is no point in forcing an artificial connection. "For me to pretend that I am Old Black Joe and waste my time on his problems, would be just as ridiculous as for the government of Winston Churchill to bill the Duke of Normandy the first of every month."

Confining herself to the present, then, Zora Hurston sees no particular reason for getting excited about the sins of white people as such. According to her observation, all people, regardless of skin color, have the same weaknesses. She notes "the universal nature of greed and glory." She decides that "lack of power and opportunity passes off too often for virtue," and that "self-interest rides over all sorts of lines." She means to make the implications of these conclusions quite clear to her own racial group. With them in mind, at the close of her book she speaks of the attitude of those who walk humbly in the dust to those in power. Think kindly, she advises, for "there has been no proof in the world so far that you would be less arrogant if you held the level of power in your hands."

If forced to select a candidate for special criticism, she would concentrate on the Negro rather than the white group. As she studies the reactions of educated Negroes to their place in American society, she discovers certain absurdities in their behavior. The emphasis upon race achievement and race pride appears to her as a subject deserving satire. For Negroes to claim that their race has the most beautiful women and the bravest men on earth, and has made the greatest progress in fifty years of any comparable minority in history, seems presumptuous and exaggerated. She feels that it is not only far-fetched, but an admission of weakness to search frantically for evidence of superiority, whether of Negro genius in invention or Negro courage in battle, whether of Simon helping Jesus with the cross or of Crispus Attucks striking a blow for freedom in the Revolutionary War. She scoffs at the unhealthy state of mind this causes. The Negro is led to feel that his reward is not according to his desert. Out of his self-pity springs a boastfulness: "Were it not for the envy and greed of the whte man, the Negro would hold his rightful place—the noblest and the greatest man on earth."

If Negroes are so proud of being Negroes, she asks, then why is there so much color snobbery within the group? Why do mulattoes, with white ancestry, have more prestige? Why do the light-skinned children always receive in the school plays the coveted parts of angels, fairies, and queens? In actual practice, the most ardent "Race Champions" seem to be the first to protest against the use of anything definitely Negroid like the blues and the spirituals, or to make jokes at the expense of black women or "dumb niggers." She can recall that even in her high school days she sensed this inconsistency. "Were Negroes the great heroes I heard about from the platform, or were they the ridiculous monkeys of everyday talk?" Even before she notes the class stratification among Negroes, accentuated by color distinctions, she has wondered if there is any honor in being black. Thus Zora Hurston is far more conscious of intragroup than intergroup friction. Her message might be interpreted as meaning that it is important to put one's own house in order before crusading. Race relations begin at home.

In light of the contradiction between the theory and practice of Negroes, the author escapes from confusion by rejecting entirely the concept of "Race Solidarity." She regards it as a myth, in spite of all the fanfare about it. Since Negroes among themselves freely admit its absence, she wishes that they would not keep up the pretence. The true state of affairs holds out certain advantages. It prevents the danger of "an unmelting black knot in the body politic." The fact of differences between Negroes, whether taken as members of a class or as individuals, makes it more difficult for society to condemn them as a race, and easier for Negroes to find appropriate ways of life. "Personal benefits run counter to race lines too often for it to hold. If it did, we could never fit into the national pattern."

Any conscience she may have been given on the score of race loyalty is ultimately purged by her philosophy of individualism. She reaches the stage where all clichés about race ring hollowly in her ears. Her whole experience leads her to judge people only as individuals. "Light came to me when I realized that I did not have to consider any racial group as a whole. God made them duck by duck and that was the only way I could see them. I learned that ships were no measure of what was inside people." What they were depended on varying circumstances, conditions, and stimuli, not on inherent biological factors.

With all the strength of her convictions, therefore, Zora Hurston strong-arms the race problem. Along with her criticism of accepted views of love and religion goes her resistance to current attitudes about race. She shakes off any further consideration with a certain flourish: "I was and am thoroughly sick of the subject." Her frankness leaves no loophole for misunderstanding.

In her disavowal of any responsibility to her racial group Zora Hurston in her autobiography presents a contrast both to writers like Jane Edna Hunter and to writers like Mary Church Terrell. Belonging to a younger generation, making her creative efforts in a predepression and depression period, she has been exposed to more scientific evidence disproving racial differences, and to greater skepticism about the role of social uplift. Race leadership, whether based on shame or pride, is foreign to her nature. To be antagonistic, apologetic, or boastful about "my people" suggests impossible alternatives to her for the simple reason that Negroes form no separate entity in her mind. She sees "no curse in being black, nor extra flavor by being white." Product of a new realism, she anticipates no simple solution for race relations in the complex network of American society. Her only answer to confusion is that each man must struggle through the maze as best he can, supported by his own grasp of truth.

Thus her life experience has only tended to cultivate the deeply implanted injunctions of her mother. When the writer concludes her autobiography on the note that achievement is "up to the individual," that Negroes "will go where the internal drive carries us like everybody else," she is fulfilling the determination of her mother not to "squinch" her spirit. The encouragement she received to jump for a place in the sun has acted like an intoxicant. In the intensity of her living, she has enjoyed both the lean and fat years.

Convinced only of the path she herself must follow, she displays a tolerance towards the behavior of others which is a by-product of her consistent philosophy of relativism. She makes liberal allowance for points of view which have been hammered out in other forges. Because her personal feelings about love, religion, race, and individual happiness mean so much to her, she would not rob others of the joy of their own discoveries. To campaign for her pet theories would be futile in any case. "Nothing that God ever made is the same thing to more than one person. That is natural. There is no single face in nature because every eye that looks upon it sees it from its own angle. So every man's spice-box seasons his own food." This principle of relativity holds true all along the line, from matters of personal taste to opinions about social issues. In this way, Zora Hurston can produce a philosophical justification for her "hands-off" policy towards the race problem. She explains that she, too, longs for universal justice, but that it is impossible to do much about it when everybody is bound to disagree on ways and means of reaching it. "It is such a complicated thing, for justice, like beauty, is in the eye of the beholder."

Free of many routine moral obligations, Zora Hurston busies herself with unwrapping the happiness contained in each moment. She engenders an atmosphere of surprises both for herself and others who know her. Shrinking from the dullness of dogmatism, she blossoms out with an originality of thought and conduct. Although the author can hardly inform us that this originality is the secret of her charm, we can quickly detect it on each page of her autobiography. Even her literary style shows an out-of-the-ordinary quality, a concrete and earthy imagery, an uneven rhythm which reflect imagination, warmth, and impulsiveness. It is a safe guess that few people were bored in her presence. Angered sometimes, amused often, at least they must have responded positively to the unexpected course of her behavior. Sustained by her unflagging spirit, Zora Hurston is enabled to present a strong case for the doctrine of individuality in her own person.

Born to Be

TAYLOR GORDAN

IN some ways, Taylor Gordan's *Born to Be* could serve as a male counterpart to *Dust Tracks on a Road.* Published at the beginning of the depression it, too, reflects the lush days of the Negro Renaissance. Also a celebrity, this Negro singer was probably as frequent a guest as Miss Hurston at literary and artistic functions in New York. His book has much of the gaiety and enthusiasm for life as hers. It is filled with the same hedonism, the same scorn for stuffy conventions, the same forthrightness of expression.

Taylor Gordan does not profess to be a trained writer. In this respect, his work resembles Juanita Harrison's more than Zora Hurston's. Once again we have a case of editing—this time by Muriel Draper. Again we must depend on valuable information about the author in prefatory material. Muriel Draper's foreword and Carl Van Vechten's introduction prepare us for the kind of man we are going to meet in the autobiography. Yet, as Mr. Van Vechten mentions, he writes "with accurate observation and a poetic use of metaphor." Consequently, in spite of his deviations in grammar, punctuation, and spelling which Miss Draper admits, and his crudities of style and organization, he often approximates the colorful writing of Zora Hurston. This is possible because he is visual-minded; he thinks of his ambition as a "two-humped camel," of his face as a "passport stamped in full," of his boyhood playmates as having "many cant's tied to them" by parental laws. In general, we can sense a bond between all three writers which has to do with the fact that all of them are unashamed of the earth which bore them. Unlike Braithwaite, they use the idiom and raciness of everyday language to convey their frank enjoyment of everyday life.

Naturally, however, Taylor Gordan operated within a framework all his own, and arrived at fame and happiness from a unique background. He was Montana born, in 1893. His father was a "smooth black," the son of a Zulu who had come to America from Africa by way of Scotland. Both father and son learned to be expert chefs. Taylor Gordan's mother was born a slave in Kentucky and was nine years old at the time of the Civil War. With six children to raise, and a widow before her youngest was born, she had to work very hard as a cook and laundress. But she preferred to remain in the "free open country" she and her husband had immediately taken a fancy to when he became a chef for a gold-mining company. As a result this youngest child, Taylor Gordan, never knew his father, who was killed in a railroad accident, and scarcely knew his mother who was unduly burdened with practical tasks. But he grew to know his Montana so thoroughly that his personality always bore many of the marks of the typical Westerner.

White Sulphur Springs, nestling in a beautiful location between mountains, was both a hot-spring resort and a mining town. With such variegated sources of interest the young boy always regarded school as superfluous. He early decided that its sole purpose was "to keep kids out of trouble," so he proceeded to prove it by playing hookey in order to fish, hunt, explore caves, or "work on some contraption" of his own making. He avoided the timid souls and sought the companionship of boys who were willing to poke into every aspect of the town life.

Although he had more than his fair quota of children's diseases, often with serious complications, there was never any danger that illness would turn him into a sissy. As soon as possible, he would bounce back into activity of a strictly masculine nature. On summer evenings his gang would play a strenuous game of "Stray Goose" in which they could do anything to their human quarry except perform an operation or kill him. Sometimes the results were so drastic that the dividing line seemed theoretical. But this made the game all the more fascinating as a challenge. Learning to give and take constituted a sacred part of the boyhood code. Underneath ran a ready sympathy which prompted the gang to become friends with a murderer in the local jail.

The toughening-up process carried over from play to work. From his seventh year on Taylor Gordan earned money running errands for prostitutes. He served as page boy at the establishment operated by Big Maude, and learned the ways of the world with despatch. Sometimes his errands took him into the saloons of the wide-open town. At one period he worked in a bowling alley where he and his pal accepted bribes to bunch the pins. Then "Louie, the Chinaman," taught him how to sell opium and take care of the pipes for his ten hop-bunks. After such an apprenticeship, the would-be man in quick order considered himself a man. "I got high-heeled boots, a six-horse-roll on my pants, leather cuffs, Stetson hat, with a package of Bull Durham tobacco in my breast pocket" and attended dances where the music waxed loud and the fun waxed high. In the daytime he stuck to a man's job, learning to brand and dehorn cattle, to use a derrick and a bull-rake on a large farm for $2 a day. In addition, he picked up a knowledge of auto mechanics until he could drive and take care of a car. The rough-and-ready boyhood has now passed over into a self-reliant adolescence.

At this point, Taylor Gordan felt that he had exhausted the possibilities of the environment which had seemed so limitless in his early years. He was familiar with all the nearby ranches, mountain trails, hunting and fishing territory as well as the town proper, and all its inhabitants. "I knew everybody by their whole names, nicknames and businesses, as well as by their habits." It lay in the books that his strong sense of adventure should drive him to the city. He reasoned that other people were leaving, so why shouldn't he? It was as simple as that. He started his break with home by running away to Helena, Montana, then a city of twelve thousand, and by enjoying the races and the fair. He was still in his middle teens but he was long accustomed to handling his own affairs and squeezing out the maximum benefit.

His complete emancipation, however, came in 1910, when he went to St. Paul, Minnesota, as a chauffeur, in spite of his mother's protests. His only concession consisted in leaving his forty-five, his "Blue Steel Betty," behind him. It is typical of his masculinity that in the beginning he regretted this compromise. Schooled in direct action, he felt lost one day, in an unpleasant situation, when his right hand automatically fell to his left hip. "She wasn't there! I can't describe the lonely feeling that came over me. I have never felt like it since. It seemed as though everyone whom I knew had died at once." Yet he soon came to recognize that survival in a large city rested upon more complicated techniques than the exchange of blows or bullets.

For the first time he encountered situations in which direct action was a dangerous weapon against injustice. As he was taught the

A B C's of race prejudice by his friends and employers, as he experienced discrimination because he was a Negro, he learned to absorb the shock and adjust to new behavior patterns. This involved almost a complete turn-about-face. In his home community, his color had always been an asset. Belonging to the only Negro family, he had been so recognizable as to be trusted and treated like a privileged character about town. One ranch owner had shown such an interest in him that people had even mistaken him for an adopted son. But now in St. Paul his position was altered. "It baffled me to think that the mask that aided me so much at home was all against me in the cities I dreamed of." Yet his decision was to swallow the bitter pill that his dark face was no longer a passport, and to continue his adventures with his eyes wide open and his brain alert.

On the whole, Taylor Gordan's adaptation to city ways came rapidly. He liked the noise and excitement, the speed and the display of wealth and power. He found that there were advantages to urban living which balanced the disadvantages of race prejudice. In fact, he concluded that some of these disadvantages could be circumvented by following a strict line of self-interest. For example, accepting the American standard of success in terms of money, he ruled out the possibility of marriage. He wanted no extra pack on his back on his climb upward. Women were all right in their place but that was not in any home he would have to provide. Consequently, "church girls were out, for me." Besides, monogamy was not compatible with his temperament. Variety was as necessary to his well-being as breathing, and city life offered it to him in many fields.

During the following years, Taylor Gordan continues to be a perfect example of an extrovert. He welcomes change, fits into new situations, moves towards people. Always curious about his environment, he is too occupied with sampling it to have spare time for introspection. His autobiography becomes a running commentary on his experiences, and contains no descriptions of dark moods and no attempt at self-analysis.

Jumping from one job to another, he tries his hand at everything he can, and travels widely. The routine work of chauffeur, doorman, elevator boy, and pullman porter is varied when he makes whiskey, peddles women's lingerie in Harlem, turns bricklayer or dock worker, and escorts an insane man back to the West Indies. His only long-time employer is John Ringling of circus fame. First hired by Ringling in Montana days, he comes to New York to be his chauffeur, and alternates between New York and the winter quarters in Florida. The young Negro is fascinated by his contact with the circus, with important people, and with the trappings of wealth. He receives good pay, and plenty of leisure time.

It is while he is with Ringling that his chance for a career opens up. One day in 1915, working in Ringling's private railroad car in St. Louis, Missouri, he starts to sing along with a Caruso record. A passer-by hears him and recommends him to a musician in New York who specializes in the training of talent.

Gradually singing becomes the moving force of his life. At first he does not take his talent too seriously. Coming from a musical family in which he was supposed to be the exception, he had heard so much singing at home that "it really bored me." In addition, he receives no quick encouragement from New York experts or from Mr. Ringling who asks him why he wants to sing when he can cook sautéd kidneys so well. But the idea persists and even prods him into practicing on his own. He attends concerts, meets other Negro musicians, and seizes the opportunity of singing at parties and at army camps during the war. With the help of Will Cook and J. Rosamund Johnson he reaches wider audiences until he finally has the practical experience of three years with the B. F. Keith vaudeville circuit. Ten years after he first discovers his voice, he has won international attention. In 1927, he is a sensation in Paris and London.

Although his career gives his life the only stability and continuity it seems to have, Taylor Gordan does not feature it in his autobiography. Not only is there no inclination to publicize it for racial purposes, but there is also no undue preoccupation with his personal triumphs. His fame is a fortunate steppingstone towards his main interest in having a good time. The twin goals of money and success he had dreamed of as a young man now serve as the necessary means to his happiness. On shipboard, in night clubs and bars, in private drawing rooms, he enjoys meeting all sorts of people. The author treats us to many more details about the amusing incidents which occur at parties than about his concerts. The French customs or the conversation of English society make a greater impression on him than what the critics say about his voice. He immerses himself in the swirl of this new life to which his artistry entitles him.

After the long stretch of years, once again his color singles him out for favorable attention. As a Negro singer he is treated somewhat like a prodigy. He senses that his white hosts are often curious about him, but never hostile, always generous. Everywhere, during the 1920's, there is open house. He is wined and dined by the great, the gifted, and the wealthy, by Alfred Knopf, Carl Van Vechten, Heywood Broun, and Theodore Dreiser in New York. He becomes acquainted with writers and with aristocrats, with Somerset Maugham, John Galsworthy, Radclyffe Hall, and with the Astor family in London. Whether the setting is high society, intellectual, or bohemian, the atmosphere is always cosmopolitan. Typical is the party he and J. Rosamund Johnson attended at Heywood Broun's town house, "to meet some Big English Lord and Lady." Guests from Staten Island to Harlem thronged the doors. "There never was such a gathering at the League of Nations as there was at Broun's that night—unless they had some Gypsies in the League."

Taylor Gordan repays the social mobility accorded him in influential white circles by a revival of his boyhood adaptability with white people. He explains away the hate he has sometimes felt for them, in the transition period of city life, in terms of his own limited knowledge. Closer acquaintanceship with the right kind of white people persuades him of the existence of a mutual community of interest. This bold Westerner even holds a soft spot in his heart for the aristocracy of the old world. "You can say what you like about Kings and Queens, there is something about them that makes your blood tingle." He admires their nonchalance and their proud poise. King George, for example, "knew he himself was the ripe nuts and coffee without telling you how much the dinner cost." As he studies the royal British pair, King George and Queen Mary, in the closing days of their reign and of an era, he draws a conclusion which is characteristic of his basic outlook. To live and let live constitutes a bargain he is willing to strike with society. The strong and the clever deserve recognition. The frontier spirit of individualism which takes the law into its own hands can comprehend the drive behind the "divine right of Kings." Any misuse of their power he can overlook because of other values: "I thought of all the cruelty of all the old Kings, but if their way of living led up to giving people as much of a thrill as I got out of that day, they were justified in committing any kind of crime to get the effect."

According to the evidence of the autobiography, the author is not willing to stretch his tolerance to such length in relation to Negroes. In fact, he parallels Miss Hurston once again by leveling his strongest criticism at his own group. His starting point and his conclusions are of course, his own.

To begin with, he has no background experience of Negroes. Not until young manhood does he come into contact with people of his own color on any mass basis. Therefore his original impressions, gained in the Black Belt of Chicago, in Harlem, in the Deep South, are sharply defined. He anticipates these experiences with eagerness and correlates his opinions carefully. In Florida, he tells us, "I spent my time studying my people—their ways and actions." He confesses that he is disappointed in his expectations.

One fault he stresses is their failure to work together for their own interests. By all the rules of logic, Negroes should subordinate petty personal differences to group action in order to improve their lot. That they don't is as puzzling to him as perpetual motion: "I have never been able to find out why they pull apart so much." They throw away enough money to have the same facilities as the whites. With proper planning and cooperation, Negroes could develop their own businesses, and could start a treasury of a dollar a month from each member of the group.

But his main objection deals with a psychological flaw. He feels that too many Negroes suffer from inferiority and fear in relation to whites and transmit this emotional state to others. They will not recognize any talent in their own group without the stamp of white approval. He resents the effect in his own case: "They made me believe that nothing but things pertaining to Whites were advantageous. . . . It took me a long time to learn that that was the worst form of imprisonment."

By the time he writes his autobiography, however, he has reached the wisdom of thirty-six years and the satisfaction of personal success. Such freedom of mind and action has developed that any personal damage inflicted on him by current Negro attitudes about race seems theoretical. He closes his book on a nonproblematical note. He grants that Negroes cannot eat, sleep, or rent a house or get a job "where their fancy may lead them," but he refuses to accept these restrictions as grounds for pessimism. Instead, he suggests another side of the picture: "Everything else under the sun they do, all over the country."

He himself has been lucky. He has met "marvellous people," "the world's talked-of people," and they have helped him "to get lots of enjoyment out of life."

The light touch, the bantering air, the happy-go-lucky attitude suit him better than brooding or indignation about his lot as a Negro. Under the circumstances, "no wonder the Race Question has never been the big ghost in my life!" In any case, Taylor Gordan is not the man to take time off to consort with ghosts. He prefers the evidence of his trusty five senses.

Dark Symphony

ELIZABETH LAURA ADAMS

WITH one touch of her finger Elizabeth Adams topples down the house of cards so gaily built by writers like Zora Hurston, Juanita Harrison, and Taylor Gordan. Agreeing with them only in their individualism, she makes their quest for happiness seem frivolous. Their scorn of conventional morals and religion, their choice of a free-and-easy way of life would seem incredible to this serious-minded woman who finds her answers at last in the Catholic church.

No melancholy marked the earliest years. Unconsciously absorbing the loveliness of California landscape and climate, the small child was awakened to happiness. "I saw only the beauty of rose colored dawns. No clouds were visible to darken my path." The only child, she lacked neither material comforts nor parental solicitude. Her father provided steady and ample support for his little family, her mother graced the home with gentle manners and the quiet, good taste of an artistic temperament. She was also blessed with a loyal friend, a freckled face girl with taffy-yellow hair and a "winning front-tooth-missing-smile," who smoothed the way for her into the "happy, care-free kingdom of the first day of school."

Yet even this idyllic preschool period contained the seeds of future disturbance. Certain old-fashioned notions operated in the family circle. The dark, dignified head of the family spoke with the voice of authority. With a reputation as the best qualified colored head-waiter between the Pacific and the Atlantic, he believed in carrying over the ideal of dignified and courteous service from his job to his home, with the difference that in the first instance he gave, and in the second received its benefits. Convinced that his wife's place was the home, he surrounded her with every luxury he could afford. His love grew "like that of a curator of a museum" for the possessions in his guardianship. In return for his care, he expected a well-ordered home life.

His wife did not disappoint him. Her pliable nature bent to his sterner ways so that everyday routine showed no signs of friction. With her artistic resources, she had her own world into which she could withdraw at will, taking her little daughter with her. Left for the most part in her mother's hands during the first years, Elizabeth Adams was protected from many little realities by the fairy-tale coating her mother manufactured.

The little girl enjoyed this magic world. She couldn't imagine Easter without a real Easter Bunny. "Mother said his fur was as downy as the powder puff on her dressing table, and that he had pink-tipped floppy ears." Santa Claus had a shop of rainbow-colored ice which could never melt because he spent his life making children happy. Even the stork legend became glorified. It served the dual purpose of explaining happily the arrival of babies and the existence of color differences: "God had painted us different colors—then the stork selected us to blend harmoniously with the bodily color-scheme of our respective families." Only with reluctance was this story modified later. When the ten-year-old confronted her mother with schoolgirl tales of skepticism, she replied that "There *is* a stork and there *isn't* a stork," that it is necessary for little children to believe in this until they are old enough to understand "The Sacred Story of Life," the holiness of matrimony, the adoration with which expectant mothers should be regarded. As a result of this training, Elizabeth Adams was expected to use her imagination as a means of seeing only the beautiful side of life, and of behaving accordingly.

But sometimes her imagination backfired. Once she became habituated to fanciful flights there was no guarantee against morbidity. When her baby brother died and her mother had no ready explanation for death, the child concocted a figure: "Perhaps like the pirates in my story books. Powerful, Tall, Taller than our house, maybe; taller than a telegraph pole, a mountain. His laughter a loud, loud roar. Perhaps, like a pirate, he carried a sharp, gleaming knife between his teeth." Her nimble brain followed the train of associations to the logical end, that pirates were thieves and therefore Death was a thief. But the conclusion was too terrifying to face without screaming.

In her sensitive response to the thought of death, we are reminded of the young William Braithwaite. Like him she was exposed to the fact of death several times, with the loss of her little brother, her great grandmother, her grandmother and grandfather. Like him, she lay awake in her room at the mercy of her fears. The darkness became intensified. "Momentarily I waited for the sound. Organ tones kept roaring in my ears. Roared. Rumbled. Growled. Wailed. Whimpered plaintively." So overwrought did she become at one stage that her maternal grandfather decided to make her more robust. He took her out in the woods for rollicking good times, gave her food treats between meals, and showed her the gun he kept to shoot Death. Yet his attempts met ironic defeat when he himself died.

Other bitter realities besides death began to intrude upon the consciousness of the growing child and expel the soft-scented dreams. Her home situation took on a less pleasant aspect. Once she reached school age she entered her father's orbit more directly. He expected her to conform to the family pattern he had laid down. Conscientiously avoiding the danger of spoiling an only child, both parents required her to obey their slightest command. "If they had placed me in a circus I would have won out in competition with a well-trained seal without the slightest effort." Their aim of making her into a model girl was skillfully buttressed by placing her on an honor system. The results seemed above reproach. By the time she was ten, Elizabeth Adams was disciplined to be self-sacrificing and industrious and to help make things nice for her father.

But rebellious thoughts flowed beneath the surface. She knew that there were two sides to perfection. "Parents singled me out as the 'ideal child' and children yearned to throw brickbats at me." She recognized the inroads of duty on her spirit. As her father painstakingly taught her the correct way in which to serve a glass of water, she went through the motions while storing up her mental reservations. The cumulative effect was to turn her against the idea of marriage. "Who would want to get married, anyway, I asked myself, if it meant waiting on someone else the rest of one's life!" Assigned to dull household tasks, she sometimes took out her spite on her father's slippers, banging them against a chair or beating them with her fists, muttering imprecations against the crazy, silly, hateful husband she would not marry and wait on. She took precautions, however, to hide her resentment. When her mother asked her what she was saying, she was quick to reply that she was only talking to herself. After all, she had no desire to incur a whipping. And so the process of repression continued.

School life also held some shocks for her. Anticipating its pleasures, eager to adjust, she skimmed along smoothly until second grade. From then on she bumped into the unkindness of race prejudice which called for a completely new orientation on her part. For the first time she heard the word "nigger," on the lips of a new girl who refused to play with her, and saw the queer expression on the faces of her white schoolmates who had always taken her for granted. Not understanding what has happened, she was nevertheless only partially consoled by her loyal friend when she patted her hand and said "Never mind, Elizabeth. I love you." Laying the problem in her mother's lap didn't prove of much practical value. In keeping with her conciliatory approach, her mother admitted that "the word" was uncomplimentary, but affirmed that the child who used it did not know better. As a solution she urged her daughter to love the child anyway, and put her in her prayers. By this time the new girl had drawn several playmates away and the faithful friend had devised a vigorous plan of action. "Thus it was that while my mother saw to it that I implored the Omnipotent to bless Lillian, Mary Carty instructed me as to the proper procedure of turning up one's nose at an enemy."

This conflict between protest and direct action in school and tolerance of her enemies even to the point of repression at home continued for some time. Elizabeth Adams did not dare to report the fierce word battles of the school room in the artificial peace of her dining room. It was even worse when her overt behavior was discovered. One day a bully blew talcum powder into her face and jeered that it would turn her white. When she tried to retaliate by fighting, her parents were horrified: "There is nothing more disgraceful than a common brawl. We expect you to behave as a little lady should behave." Another day she felt insulted by the remark that "all colored people were supposed to be poor, wear rags and live in shacks." So she took the disbelievers on a tour of inspection of her home only to be informed scornfully that the nice furniture and dishes must be stolen. When her parents learned of this episode, they had no sympathy to spare for her chagrin. Instead, they accused her of vanity. They reminded her that character was more important than material possessions like beautiful rugs, engraved silverware, or hand-painted china. They stressed once again the need for her to discipline her emotions.

At the same time there was a sincere effort to satisfy the little girl's confusion about race. "The awakening of race consciousness wrought a series of bewildering revelations in my life" which called out for explanation. Her mother, especially, did not remain oblivious to this need, and often tried to heal her hurts with the same sweet reasonableness that had helped the preschool child. When her favorite teacher failed to include her among the flower girls at her wedding she was comforted by a parable of fences. According to her mother, "the world was a great, big patch of ground divided by fences" separating white, yellow, red, and black people. These barriers served the useful purpose of preserving racial customs and preventing arguments. Although practical affairs like school and work brought races together, social affairs were sacred to the members of one's own race. Her teacher's friends had a right not to like any black skins at the wedding just as the little pupil had a right not to like spinach. It was all a matter of taste.

This lesson in race relations was brought to an auspicious close by a consolation prize. Given half a yard of mosquito netting for a wedding veil, little Elizabeth Adams held a mock ceremony in the backyard. "Happy? of course I was happy! Does a wee bird cease chirping because its frail wings will not lift it beyond a high fence?" The atmosphere of make-believe still lingered.

Tirelessly, consistently, in situation after situation, her mother taught her not to look at the unpleasant side of race relations, not to magnify her troubles as a Negro girl, not to indulge in self-pity or bitterness. When a schoolmate asked if her mother took in washings and referred to her slavery background, she was to remember that other races had also been enslaved, that "if poor, despised slaves were honest, industrious and trusty their descendants for generations to come will be endowed with good heritage." When she observed that other children cried if they were called greaser, chink, jap or dago, she was to remember that she was "not the only hurt person in the world." When a colored schoolmate spread the rumor that there were some white teachers who refused to teach colored children, she was to remember that nothing in her own experience confirmed it. The supreme commandment was "not to take part in racial arguments anywhere at any time." It was beneath the dignity of the wise and the great to waste time trying to prove race equality.

Elizabeth Adams was caught between the upper and nether millstones of her mother's precepts about race and her father's authority. She sensed that if she couldn't become a little lady voluntarily she would be forced into the mold anyway. She felt the anger lurking behind the sweet reasonableness and knew that she would have to stack wood as a punishment for taking part in controversies. The rebel in her subsided.

It is true that in junior high school she went through a difficult adolescent stage when she became "aloof, indifferent, evasive." Reviewing this period, the author remarks that "the youth of my race resort to various means to conceal injured feelings and sometimes complete character transformation takes place." But the significant fact remains that in her case this change was only temporary. In light of such strong parental pressure on her sensitive temperament, it seems almost inevitable to us that she should finally accept their point of view wholeheartedly. Apparently, however, the author is unaware of this psychological process. In addition, although she furnishes us with ample data for our deductions, she draws no conclusions about any emotional damage these years of repression may have caused her. She is only conscious of reaching her parents' state of wisdom, of realizing her good fortune in having had the proper guidance to save her from bitterness and "consuming hatred." Her personality becomes stabilized around the principle of peace at any price.

The process is hastened by a long illness. With a heart weakened by "flu," she is led by circumstance into a quiet way of life. It is natural for her to fall back on the resources of her imagination. The shadows of the camphor boughs on the front walk turn into dancing puppets, thin grey smoke from a chimney changes to wisps of silvery fog, a lame cat takes on the proportions of a wounded jungle lion. She hears an anthem in the hum of the winds and a dirge in the murmur of the sea. The end result of this whole experience is the discovery of creative writing. Soon her poetry provides a socially acceptable outlet for her emotions. Her mother approves of the beautiful words she fits together to convey beautiful thoughts.

Another outlet her protected life affords her is music. At an early age she receives a violin and is told that the bows will make the strings sing, that the music will help her see stars in a starless sky and sunlight on a cloudy day. Her experience confirms this promise. Not only does she show talent herself, but she is unusually responsive to classical works. She is fortunate in the type of white teacher she has. The director of her first small orchestra "saw the soul of a child and not the color of skin." A junior high school instructor gives her the biographies of famous composers and points out that, although they vary in speech and nationality, they share the common language of music. "Shut your eyes and ears to the distractions and disturbances of the world and patiently listen," she is advised. Less and less can parental discipline, ill-health, or race discrimination bother her as she escapes into this new realm of gold. She cannot keep abreast of the activities and chatter about the latest fashions which come so easily to other school girls, but she knows all about young Schubert, Chopin, and Liszt. When she hears Verdi's *Aida* and Wagner's *Parsifal* she sees the Pyramids and the Temple of the Grail. She likes to play the Miserere from *Il Trovatore* in order to listen to the solemn toll of the bell, the deep chant of the priests. Beethoven, Mozart, Bach, and Hayden each contribute to her emotional enrichment.

In the years to come she is going to need all the inspiration which poetry and music can hold out to her. Disappointments and responsibilities lie ahead. When she is fifteen her father dies. Unwise investments eliminate her hopes for a college education. Her mother's failing health places the burden of financial support on her shoulders. Her own heart trouble at one time becomes so severe that she loses the desire to live. In addition, she has to meet the strains of the depression which, in her case, means such curtailment of job opportunities that she is forced into distasteful domestic service. She has no time for dates or recreation. Without the normal activities of youth she grows old for her years. She is not freed from the shadow of her family even when her mother marries again, for it is an unhappy marriage which brings emotional involvements for the daughter as well.

As all these experiences chasten and sober her temperament, Elizabeth Adams relies increasingly on still another resource. She finds that even the beauty of music and poetry fades in importance before the comfort of religion. It is her search for satisfying religious experience that forms the major purpose of her life and receives the final emphasis in her autobiography.

This is no sudden interest. The problems of race and family were always accompanied in childhood by the problem of God. From the very start Elizabeth Adams revealed a keen and analytical mind which naturally influenced her towards religious inquiry. Her conclusions were often so unorthodox that she learned to keep them to herself. While still very small, she wondered "how God would like it if someone called him 'nigger' " and then remembered that no one was supposed to wonder about the Creator. Later she reacted to the noisiness of Methodist conversion when the Holy Ghost descended. In fact, she could not understand the Holy Ghost at all. "I thought it very impolite of the Holy Ghost to impose Itself upon people, to make them do unsightly things." Moreover, God couldn't be so unkind as to want to see children cry repentance. And since God was all-wise surely He knew her sins anyway and expected her parents to punish her. So of what use was the Holy Ghost? "Secretly I decided that perhaps if I did not think about the Holy Ghost, the Holy Ghost would not think about me. We could avoid one another." However, this reasoning brought her only cold comfort. She developed "a spiritual sense of inferiority" because she felt that "everybody in the world" knew more about the subject than she.

As a young girl she noticed acts of discrimination by churchmen. For example, during one communion service the white clergyman ostentatiously wiped the chalice when it passed from colored to white communicants, and later asked the colored members to discontinue their attendance. This cast reflection on the nature of God. How could He lay down rules and not allow for methods of observance? Perhaps He belonged to the white race and listened only to their prayers. Yet she could not go so far in her skepticism as some of her colored friends who lost all ideals and became frankly materialistic. She shrank from their practical advice: "White people want the whole world and God, too. Let them keep God—but get your share of the worldly goods before they beat you to it." Instead, she resorted to her habit of withdrawal and sought for better spiritual guidance.

She could not rest in doubt. For along with her active mind went sensitive feelings which also needed to be salved. As her personal troubles multiplied, her longing for peace and beauty within some sort of divine protection must have grown strong. She might sometimes question the nature of God, but not His existence, since a belief in the unseen and in the possibility of miraculous powers had accompanied her since childhood. An act of faith, on her own terms, followed naturally.

The final solution is Catholicism. While still adolescent she was attracted to it. At the time, she was living in Santa Barbara which formed a picturesque setting with its crescent-shaped strand sprayed by the sea, its paths winding up to mountain peaks, its fruit trees blossoming in the sun. She entered into the mood of the Good Friday service in the mission, with the quiet prayers, the rosaries, and the Ave Maria.

"As a mirror reflects images, so the memory of the old Santa Barbara Mission and its ancient form of worship were always to be reflected in the mirror of my soul."

In spite of this inner "conversion" she was prevented by a strange irony from joining the Catholic church at once. The whole impact of her parents' influence upon her has sent her in this direction. Taught to avoid the brawls of this world and love her enemies, to subordinate material possessions to character, and to discipline her behavior for the welfare of others, she was even eager to take the ultimate step of withdrawal and enter a convent. Certainly there was nothing in her proposed plan which was incompatible with her parents' injunctions to act like a "little lady." Yet her father voiced determined opposition and forbid the initial step of membership.

The author does not take cognizance of this irony. Apparently she holds no bitterness against her father, and does not recognize his inconsistency at this point in light of the values he has always upheld. She seems to accept his decision as a simple matter of religious conservatism rather than suspecting that the familiar habit of father-dominance may be operating once more. It may well be that his daughter's independence of choice is more unwelcome to him than the nature of her choice. It may also be that her resolve to fulfill her purpose some day is strengthened unconsciously by stored-up rebellion against parental authority. It is true that she is ready to submit to an even higher authority, but perhaps she cherishes a feeling of free will in this case. This new religion represents a way of life which corresponds to her inculcated tastes, her environmental conditioning, and at the same time is peculiarly her own.

What Miss Adams does stress in her autobiography is the joy of self-realization when she becomes a Catholic at last. After her father's death, her mother grants her permission at the time of high school graduation. Forced by practical responsibilities to postpone indefinitely her plan to enter a convent, she nevertheless feels a part of a great spiritual reality already. By participating in the ritual and worship of Catholicism she learns that she can accomplish her daily chores with more grace and fortitude. New hope wells up for the future. In a spirit of humility for all these gifts, she closes her personal memoirs on a note of prayer: "Ave Maria . . . let earth's last sunrise break on me, Still reaching arms and heart to thee."

At the same time, her devotion does not blind her to one drawback in the Catholic church. She finds that race prejudice is not confined to other churches. She notices that some priests ignore Negroes waiting at a confessional, or instruct them to come to the altar last for Communion. In the face of such discrimination she can understand why more Negroes aren't Catholic. She herself never feels moved to pray for suffering for the simple reason that her dark skin guarantees a sufficient amount. On the contrary, she always prays at the altar: "And if, dear Lord, anyone should pass me by . . . help me to have faith in Your Presence in the Blessed Sacrament just the same." Eventually she trusts that the many noble priests and white laity will eradicate this evil of race prejudice in favor of "Catholic Catholicism—nothing less."

Meanwhile her reaction to this new sorrow is one of adjustment rather than of disillusionment. She has long ago cultivated the art of endurance. Injustices within the church only yield fresh proof of the folly of expecting too much. "I have learned what it means to be Colored. The Negro who tries to be spiritual learns more about being detached from earthly things than many people who are in Religious Orders." With the proper frame of mind, a liability could be turned into an asset. Out of the negative springs the positive. "Out of the conflicts of my life I could compose a symphony, a symphony to be played in the unseen music-chamber of my soul."

The title of Miss Adams' autobiography is now self-explanatory. The music of her life, like the music of this world, is "sorrowful, yet triumphant." *Dark Symphony* acknowledges the synthesis. The author chooses to subordinate immediate troubles to a "glory yet unseen." No circumstances can deprive her of the inner harmonies to which she alone is attuned.

For her, the road to happiness is essentially the road to individual salvation. Miss Adams is under too great pressure from personal problems to feel obligated to attempt the solution of larger social questions. The fact that she is a Negro is only one of several difficulties she experiences. It never occurs to her that she should feel responsibility for Negroes as a group any more than she would expect the group to help her. Although she mentions a good many instances of discrimination because of race, they are important to her largely as they affect her private struggle to achieve inner beauty and goodness. They become relatively unimportant to her the moment she discovers the spiritual resources to transcend them.

This autobiographer presents us with an extreme case of withdrawal before the encroachments of parental and societal discipline. It is difficult to say what might have happened to her without the compensations so readily attainable by her imaginative powers. That she achieves a measure of personality integration through her music, her poetry, and her religion cannot be gainsaid. That her approach is utterly different from the other individualists in this group of autobiographies also cannot be denied. The rough-and-tumble boyhood of Taylor Gordan shared nothing in common with Elizabeth Adams' careful upbringing. His enthusiastic reception of all aspects of experience would frighten her just as her introspective musings would seem unintelligible to him. Zora Hurston would have more patience with her values, for she too knew what it was as a child to live in a vivid realm of imagination. But she would have little patience with stabilizing experience on that plane and would probably categorize it as "escapism." Zora Hurston was sensitive to the touch of strange dreams but she also was sturdy enough to strike back at her stepmother. She was not afraid either to love or hate. Both she and Taylor Gordan were "of this world" in a manner completely foreign to Elizabeth Adams.

Our author is the product of a middle-class mentality. Above all other criteria her parents placed respectability. With adequate income and only one child to raise, living in a predominantly white area, they had every opportunity to gain status by means of the correct material possessions and manner of living. Perhaps unconsciously they molded their daughter's tastes and manners to win the greatest amount of social approval among both white and colored townspeople. They must have felt that they were doing her a great service. As a "nice" little girl she would have many doors open for her which otherwise would remain barred to a dark face. They could not be expected to foresee that the final door might be a convent.

In contrast, Zora Hurston, Taylor Gordan, and Juanita Harrison never had the problem of a strict parental code to wrestle with. Frankly and unashamedly lower class in background, they had no set standard of behavior imposed on them as the private way to social acceptance. Only William Braithwaite can approximate Elizabeth Adams in this respect. The New England boy whose father will only let him play with nice children can reach hands across the continent to the little girl on the Pacific coast whose father censors her every move. In both cases, the death of the father and the realities of poverty relax the discipline of proper upbringing but do not erase the habits of thought and taste in the children. Braithwaite repays his family training when he soberly enters the temple of classical poetry to the exclusion of contemporary distractions. Elizabeth Adams is true to the spirit, if not to the letter, of parental ideals when she kneels at the altar of the Catholic church and finds peace of mind.

A Long Way from Home

CLAUDE McKAY

WITH Claude McKay the pendulum swings back into this world. There seems to be little which he has not observed, participated in, or speculated about. As eager to travel as Juanita Harrison, he operates on an intellectual level to which she does not even aspire, which means that his progress is punctuated with analysis. A long way from his Jamaican home, this brilliant young Negro tastes life and finds it both good and bad in America, Africa, England, France, Germany, and Russia. Often his autobiography becomes a series of impressions and digressions about people, cities, women, art, politics, and race.

Once again we are carried back into the swirl of the Negro Renaissance. Celebrities meet, big ideas are afoot, creative efforts are applauded. Negro Harlem and dark Africa beckon to Negro intellectuals, but so does white Park Avenue, so do the European centers of the white man's culture. In these years of mental stimulus among the torchbearers for new values, social barriers of race lose much of their sting. People are on the lookout for personality and talent. Dark skins only enhance their presence. White and colored elite take pleasure in their common language. In such an atmosphere of expectation foreign-born Claude McKay, coming from the West Indies to the United States as a young man, finds himself singularly at ease.

He had much to commend him to the attention of select circles. He was a poet to begin with, and had not been long in this country before he published his well-received book of poems in 1922, *Harlem Shadows*. Before the 1920's were over, he had received recognition both as a poet and a novelist. In addition he had a wide background of reading, an urbanity of manner, and a liberalism of views which spelled his success, whether in New York or Paris.

The theme song of his life story is his independence. Starting back in his native Jamaica, he evinced an early proclivity for this trait. Of peasant origin, growing up in a reputedly remote and backward colony, he learned to do his own thinking. Religion became a favorite target. In their high mountain village he and his young friends must have shocked the conservative peasantry with their "free-thought band." They seemed to be "heathen from their own primitive thinking, without benefit of books." In Claude McKay's case, this tendency was supported by a lack of religious instruction at home, by an older brother who sandwiched free-thinking in between his denominational school-teaching and lay-preaching, and by a later program of omniverous reading. Contact with scientific thought confirmed his initial skepticism about orthodox religion: "And suddenly like a comet the discovery of the romance of science in Huxley's *Man's Place in Nature* and Haeckel's *The Riddle of the Universe.*"

His intellectual curiosity was not merely iconoclastic. It was avid for information which would enlarge his horizon. In books he unearthed new enthusiasms. Starting with the thrill of the Waverly novels and Dickens in thin blue covers, he rapidly pushed on to *Paradise Lost,* to Shelley, Keats and Byron, to Dante, Villon, Goethe, Schopenhauer, and Baudelaire, to a range of poetry from Elizabethan love lyrics to *Leaves of Grass.*

This love of literature is to remain with him and forms one of the major threads in his autobiography. He becomes a literary critic of sorts, evaluating with celerity modern writers like Shaw, D. H. Lawrence, James Joyce, Ernest Hemingway, Edna St. Vincent Millay, and Sinclair Lewis, some of whom he meets. Shaw he considers "the wisest and most penetrating intellectual alive," an impression which his visit with him does not dispel. Hemingway he classifies as typically American: "I find in Hemingway's works an artistic illumination of a certain quality of American civilization that is not to be found in any other distinguished American writer . . . the hard-boiled contempt for and disgust with sissyness expressed among all classes of Americans . . . a conventionalized rough attitude which is altogether un-European." He is attracted to D. H. Lawrence because he reflects the confusion of the times and a "psychic and romantic groping for a way out." With especial pride he points to Antar, the son of a Negro woman and an Arabian chieftain, who is "as great in Arabian literature as Homer in Greek," and whose love poetry has influenced European literature even though never taught in schools. Whether exploring the main stream or the tributaries of world literature, Claude McKay is intent upon making his own way, forming independent judgments about authors and their enrichment of human experience.

His flair for unconventionality throws him towards support of radical literary movements. Faced with the problem of a living in New York, he fluctuates between Frank Harris' magazine, *Pearson's,* and Max Eastman's *The Liberator.* "Because of my eclectic approach to literature and my unorthodox idea of life, I developed a preference for the less conservative literary organs." As associate editor of *The Liberator,* he comes into contact with many of its left-wing contributors, with Art Young, Adolph Dehn, Louis Untermeyer, William Gropper, Mary Heaton Vorse, and Michael Gold. This is the period when proletarian literature is having its heyday in American letters and Claude McKay is not immune to its excitement.

Yet he asserts his individuality in this field as well. Not wishing to shelve artistic integrity, he insists that the criterion for judging good literature stands quite apart from the question of its social purpose and importance. One of the first literary critics to appreciate the innovations of the modern poet, E. E. Cummings, he defends their "intrinsic beauty" as weighed against their lack of "social significance." He proceeds on the assumption that he can compartmentalize his "aesthetic emotions" and his genuine "social sentiments" so that there will be no occasion for a head-on collision. In the last analysis, he contends that no art or literature can endure which does not wrap its content in appropriate form and animate it with deep personal feeling.

From this point of view Claude McKay chooses to speak of a proletarian period of literature, rather than of proletarian literature. Each work should be assessed on its own merits instead of claiming the blanket endorsement of a current fad: "I preferred to think that there were bad and mediocre, and good and great, literature and art, and that the class labels were incidental—that whenever literature and art are good and great they leap over narrow group barriers and periods to make a universal appeal." External handicaps will always plague the creative artist. Southern states may boycott the works of Negroes, Hitler may burn books by Jews, the Pope may index anti-Catholic literature and the Communists may blast criticisms of international communism, but "if the works are authentic they will eventually survive the noise and racket of the times." Thus he contends against

Michael Gold that it isn't enough for workers to write, that they must learn to write "good stuff" compared to others.

Coming closer home, he strives to apply the same general principle to Negro literature and to himself as a Negro writer. Just as workers should write out of their basic experience as workers, so should Negroes express themselves as Negroes. At the same time, they must avoid propagandizing for their group and must not expect special concessions in criticism because of their race. The individual must stand or fall according to his special vision and strength.

A case in point is his reaction to the Negro writer William Braithwaite, whose desire to ignore Negro themes we have already noted in his autobiography, *The House Under Arcturus.* Claude McKay expresses the utmost scorn for Mr. Braithwaite's professional advice to him to "send to the magazines only such poems as did not betray my racial identity." He deplores the fact that in this Negro poet's work "there was not the slightest indication of what sort of American he might be." As a result he produces "purely passionless lyrics."

In contrast, Claude McKay feels that his own racial angle has advantages. He does not intend to disguise it. In every poem and every novel "a discerning person would become immediately aware that I came from a tropical country and that I was not, either by the grace of God or the desire of man, born white." On this score he claims the goodly company of many great writers who reflect their particular circumstances. Turning to the poetry of Blake, Burns, Walt Whitman, Heine, and Verlaine he discerns "their race, their class, their roots in the soil, growing into plants, spreading and forming the backgrounds against which they were silhouetted." Only by being true to one's origins can one write with deep conviction and authenticity.

Yet this Negro writer wants to make it very clear that the loyalty is to self rather than to group. He will describe what he really observes and feels and not what the Negro group wishes. There is little point in idealizing Negro life in fiction for the sake of improving race relations. Instead, he cherishes the thought that he creates his Negro characters "without sandpaper and varnish."

To him, literary realism is a form of sincerity. He is confident that he has more first-hand knowledge of the masses of Negroes than the Negro intelligentsia who are offended by this realism: "I knew the unskilled Negro worker of the city by working with him as a porter and longshoreman and as waiter on the railroad. I lived in the same quarters and we drank and caroused together in bars and at rent parties. So when I came to write about the low-down Negro, I did not have to compose him from an outside view." He doesn't have the academic approach of a speaker at a public meeting nor the bohemian approach of a café-conversationalist, and therefore it is impossible for him to give a "pseudo-romantic account" of these people. When he steers clear of prudery and portrays a hero in *Home to Harlem* who "lives and loves lustily," and when he is subsequently accused by one Negro journalist of "betraying" his race, his answer is that it can never be betrayed "by any real work of art."

With this point of view the author both embraces and rejects the Negro Renaissance movement. Attracted by its brilliance and glamor, stirred by the idea behind it, he breaks with any and all of its moral implications. The very thought of utilizing his art for "noble" purposes, for "uplifting" Negro status, runs counter to his particular brand of morals. He suspects that, underneath the idealism, the real business of selling talent for social prestige goes briskly on. Better to be realistic than pseudo-idealistic.

Very distasteful to his sense of proportion is the pressure to conform which he imagines emanates from this movement. Whatever else his inclinations, Claude McKay is definitely not a joiner. To mix is essential to his well-being, but to join is another matter, threatening his jealously guarded idea of self and his sense of a higher morality. Consequently, he prepares himself to meet opposition. When his work arouses resentment among some elements of the Negro Renaissance he is hesitant about returning from abroad to Harlem. He reasons that "the cream of Harlem was in Paris" anyway, so why bother with the second-raters? He wears his isolation in foreign fields like a badge of merit.

The same problems which dog his footsteps as an author invade his life. Behind the academic issue of the Negro Renaissance is the practical matter of his wider racial adjustment. How can he live both as an individual and as a Negro? Is each Negro only a special human being or does he share common racial traits? Is he doomed to color consciousness through discrimination? Should Negroes distinguish between whites or are they entitled to direct bitterness towards the whole group? Claude McKay never poses these questions as such, but in the course of his book he wrestles first with one, then another, apparently at the expense of consistency.

Initially he seems to feel that the Negro race has some special virtues which he prizes. He refers to its "primitive vitality," its "simple, unswaggering strength," its "hidden soul," its capacity for joyous, carefree living. "Many a white wretch, baffled and lost in his civilized jungles, is envious of the toiling, easy-living Negro." Sometimes he fears that his "damned white education" has robbed him of this heritage and yet he claims a strong sense of identity with the unspoiled Negro masses. In Marseilles, for example, he is relieved to be surrounded once more by "a great gang of black and brown humanity—all herded together in a warm group—it was good to feel the strength and distinction of a group and the assurances of belonging to it." He goes so far as to assert that this is a value he wishes to preserve at all costs. One day in Toulon, France, a white sailor predicts one fraternity of men in which white, black, and yellow will be forgotten. Claude McKay's answer is as positive as it is spontaneous: "My sense of the distinctive in the difference of color was outraged, and I said, 'We can still remain a fraternity of men and guard our complexions.' "

At the same time he admits to a constant restlessness from color consciousness. Only in Africa does he lose it entirely. For the first time, "I experienced a feeling that must be akin to the physical well-being of a dumb animal among kindred animals, who lives instinctively and by sensations only, without thinking." But back in New York it is a different matter. Discrimination in restaurants and theatres reminds him of his color and incites him to anger.

He cannot easily surmount this obstacle of white behavior. Sometimes white people seem to him like descendants of "medieval torturers," sometimes they resemble a "world-embracing Anglo-Saxon circus" in which the black clowns are slapped. Often he speaks scornfully of Anglo-Saxon prudery and puritanism and is glad that he is not a part of it. "I am a pagan; I am not a Christian. I am not white steel and stone."

As a self-respecting Negro he sees one effective weapon against white prejudice. Negroes must develop group pride and must learn to work together for the common good. They must not depend on the help of whites who, no matter how well-meaning, can never enter into the experience of a suppressed and persecuted minority. "Whatever the white folks do and say, the Negro race will finally have to face the need to save itself."

The success of such an effort will involve a necessary distinction between segregation and aggregation. Many Negroes are frightened away from supporting Negro institutions and causes by the accusation that they would then be as guilty as whites of the sin of segregation. Yet, Claude McKay points out, the entire world is in groups—family, tribal, language, class, religious, labor, women—each with its special interests and special institutions. Why should Negroes be an exception to this rule? As it is, the American Negro group is "the most advanced" in the world, yet possesses "very little group spirit" and no "group soul." It cannot solve its problems by "passing" or by miscegenation, on the one hand, or by a separate Negro state on the other. Therefore the logical solution is to organize according to numerical strength and to counteract white discrimination by the power of aggregated enterprises. It must be remembered that the man who now recommends this procedure is the same man who condemned the emphasis of the Negro Renaissance on race pride and group effort.

How all-pervading is this color-consciousness which makes him turn against whites and towards Negroes? How does it affect his personal relationships? The evidence is contradictory. At one point in his autobiography Claude McKay seems to think that only "super-souls" are capable of interracial friendships. However, he states elsewhere that he has probably had more white than colored friends. On principle he deplores any false emphasis on color one way or the other. "Neither the color of my friends, nor the color of their money, nor the color of their class has ever been of much significance to me. It was more the color of their minds, the warmth and depth of their sensibility and affection, that influenced me." Evidently this is no idle theory. His white friends range from the pickpocket, Michael, to the philanthropist who finances some of his European travels. In taking this position, Claude McKay completes a cycle of reaction and asserts his individualism once again. It is as if he willed to follow this philosophy in spite of all emotional setbacks and practical expedients.

The key to his apparent shifts of opinion lies, of course, in his strong ambivalence of feeling about race. He welcomes being a Negro and he rebels against being a Negro. He wants to be a special human being with distinctive characteristics, including color, but he also wants to be a universal human being who is able to rise above the limitations of a particular status. He rejoices in the primitive strength and hedonism of his group while despising their weaknesses which prevent serious group cooperation. His emotions turn somersaults between pride and shame, hate and love. From the white group he receives many of his severest wounds and some of his greatest blessings. Out of varying circumstances he finds it impossible to pluck any single emotional response or any airtight attitude about the problems of race. A complex personality, he manages to hold the whip hand over his warring elements.

Certainly his conflicts never seem to hamper his enjoyment of multiple experience. The big yeses quite outweigh the little noes he gives to life. Opportunities to know more, think more, and feel more he is quick to seize and quick to appreciate.

Thus he is borne along on a tide of enthusiasm for many of the countries he visits. In 1922 Russia draws him like a magnet. Like thousands of others he is "stirred by the Russian thunder rolling round the world." As "a social-minded being and a poet" he longs to see first-hand "a vast upheaval and a grand experiment." He pictures this land in the romantic afterglow of revolution. As early as 1920, John Reed had written him in London inviting him to represent the Negroes before the Communist Congress. When he finally reaches Russia, Lenin is still alive. He meets Trotsky, Karl Radek, Zinoviev on the political front, Pilynak, Mayakovsky, Meyerhold, and Lunacharsky on the artistic front. These are the days when Petrograd was soon to become Leningrad, when the famine had ended, the business revival policies of Lenin were flourishing, and the people were beginning to feel the release of new power and happiness.

He comes at the right psychological moment to share in the upsurge. Claiming that he was the first Negro to arrive after the revolution, he thinks that he must have served as a symbol of good luck. "From Moscow to Petrograd and from Petrograd to Moscow I went triumphantly from surprise to surprise, extravagantly feted on every side. I was carried along on a crest of sweet excitement. I was like a black ikon in the flesh." He is stimulated by his contacts with the great titans of the revolution, he enjoys both the fame and the money which his position as a literary celebrity brings him, but, most of all, he revels in his popularity with the masses of people everywhere. "Never before had I experienced such an instinctive sentiment of affectionate feeling compelling me to the bosom of any people, white or colored. And I am certain I never will again." It is in the nature of a "miraculous experience" which he accepts without being able to explain.

He likes the Russian people as a people. "Curiously, even Russian bourgeois persons trusted me." Feeling instantly at home everywhere, he never loses sight of this human side. "Bureaucratic control" leaves him cold even while he recognizes that, without it, the "mighty moving energy of the people" would be futile. He can work up "no enthusiasm for official ritual, however necessary, whether it be red or pink or black or white." He makes it clear that he is no member of the American Communist party and has no affinity for the Russian Communist party. As he explains to his Russian hosts, he comes to visit as a writer and not as an agitator, since he is "temperamentally unfit" to be a disciplined member of any party. Refusing to be a tool of political purposes, he will not assure the Russian people that the American revolution is just around the corner and prefers, instead, to participate with them in the nonpolitical pleasures of the moment.

Next to the people the cities lay a spell on him. Always sensitive to atmosphere, he seeks to put a finger on the contrasts. With Moscow he associates "color and mazy movement and life compact with a suggestion of Oriental lavishness, rioting and ringing upon the senses like the music of golden bells." But Petrograd seems more somber and brooding at first. It bears the scars of the revolution. It stands "poised and proud, with a hard striking strength like the monument of Peter the Great, and a spaciousness like the Neva." In time, however, he finds new aspects as its "great half-empty spaces became impressive with a lonely dignity and beauty." Each fresh discovery about these unique cities pleases him as if it were a personal gift.

France is the next favorite on his list. Its dissimilarities from Russia only enhance the flavor. In Paris he thrives in the tolerant and congenial company of "esthetes" and "cosmopolitan expatriates." It is a novel and restful change, "like taking a holiday," after keeping up with the pace of the New Russia. In the seaport towns and the provinces he mingles pleasantly with sailors and peasants alike. Again a feeling for the land permeates his feeling for the people. Brittany, especially, tugs at his heart, with its "quiet green and subdued grays and browns." The tall-masted boats in the green waters, the brown fields and rugged coasts, and the gentle rain blend into a harmony. While the English seem to him "a strangely unsympathetic people, as coldly chilling as their English fog," the Bretons retain a quiet friendliness throughout the dampness of their continual rainfall.

From the lyricism of provincial France he swings quickly over to the bright splendor of Africa. So enraptured is he that he finishes his novel, *Banjo,* and goes "completely native" there. In Morocco he feels as if he is "walking all the time on a magic carpet." The bazaars with their strange wares are "like an oriental fantasy." The beautiful mosaic becomes "a symbol of the prismatic native mind." The whole environment affects him "like rare wine."

Nor does Claude McKay lose America in the shuffle. Even the country which he associates most with race prejudice looms into importance for him. "For I was in love with the large rough unclassical rhythms of American life. If I were sometimes awed by its brutal bigness, I was nevertheless fascinated by its titanic strength." Its architectural and engineering feats impress him. New York City is a source of perpetual wonder, this "pragmatic metropolis" with its surging bigness of expression, its "baroque difference from the classic cities." By day and by night he likes to explore, to ride the ferries, to walk under the elevated tracks with the trains roaring overhead. He is exalted by the "epic proportions" and "monster movement" of the crowds, and by the "clean, vertical heaven-challenging" skyline seen from the harbor. Both in close-up and perspective he studies this dynamic city and manages to read significance into the least details. Even the clothes hanging outside the tenements appear "endowed with a strange life of their own."

America means Harlem, too. *Home to Harlem,* the title of one of his novels, seems to reflect some personal sentiment. For he tells us that it is good "to be lost in the shadows of Harlem again," to loiter down Fifth and Lenox Avenues and to promenade along Seventh Avenue. Familiar faces and familiar food beckon to him. "Spareribs and cornpone, fried chicken and corn fritters and sweet potatoes were like honey to my palate." Here he has a sense of belonging.

Yet we wonder if Claude McKay belongs to Harlem any more than to Brittany, to Brittany any more than to Morocco, and if, in belonging to all of them, he really belongs to none of them. The author drops many clues to lead to the conclusion that he is rootless, and that his final loyalty is only to himself. The same inner drive which has kept him from being confined by race, movements, or organizations and which has made him drop a marriage relationship because he wanted to be "footloose," is bound to send him like a rolling stone through the maze of nationalities and cultures. He will adapt and absorb everywhere, but settle nowhere. He will receive but never give entirely.

It is the poet in his nature which he is most anxious never to betray.

He undergoes his greatest unhappiness whenever he loses "the rare feeling of a vagabond feeding upon secret music singing in me." Into this reality he sends down his roots and is thus self-contained. Nobody can shake his assurance. Once Bernard Shaw tells him that it is tragic for a sensitive Negro to be a poet, that he would have more chances for success as a pugilist, that poets remain poor "unless they have an empire to glorify and popularize like Kipling." Claude McKay replies simply that he had not chosen poetry as a profession, but that poetry had chosen him. With this lead, Shaw avoids any discourse on world politics or race relationships and turns the conversation unexpectedly to cathedrals.

The subject is not as remote to this pagan listener as one might expect. Shaw counts on the fact that the poet can transcend the pagan sufficiently to glimpse the poetry in cathedral spires and arches. His insight is correct. In the years to come, Claude McKay spends "hours upon hours meditating about modern movements of life in the sublime grandeur of cathedral silence," and admiring the "concrete miracles of the medieval movement of belief and faith." He seems, indeed, a long way from skepticism among the Jamaican hills, "a long way from home." But this freethinker is not a dogmatist against religion either. Nothing which adds to the sum total of his sensuous experience is rejected. Beauty, whether of women or of cathedrals, of landscape or of skyscrapers, in ideas or in materials, waits on all sides to be perceived. It is a universal principle which a poet is able to discover at his convenience. It has meaning only in so far as this poet is sensitive enough to respond fully. In a certain sense then, as long as he feels this secret power, Claude McKay can never be far from home, because he carries his home within him.

The final impression which this autobiography leaves with us, therefore, is of a man who prizes his capacity for genuine poetic experience. We do not know many facts about his life, including details of his boyhood. Nor are we provided with much information about his training and career as a professional writer. Like Zora Hurston, he refrains from making his book a chronological record of his literary production. He has no interest in piling his achievements into a monument to Negro progress. What he does want to show us is the stuff of which one person is made, the raw materials of his creativeness. To facilitate this purpose the author supplies us with more opinions than facts, with more observations about places and people than self-analysis. The presentation is haphazard and impressionistic, and yet manages to convey the sweep of a panorama. Without the careful self-probing of Braithwaite or Elizabeth Adams it gives us a broad if superficial acquaintance with the man, his tastes, his temperament, and his views. We must take his word for it that his poetic impulses are more important to him than the casual pleasures of his life and stand their ground before the rush of activities inseparable from a man of the world.

Sharing Zora Hurston's and Taylor Gordan's enthusiasm for gaiety and the bright lights, their scorn for convention in any shape or form, and their wanderlust for new trails, he has greater intellectual sophistication. More of a thinker and a theorist, he sees many complications to the problem of living fully and freely. Consequently, he goes more thoroughly into the race question and is less able to dismiss it lightly by any consistent and simple attitude. However, although his conflicts are stronger, his will to live is correspondingly strong. By believing in his destiny as a poet of the world he has developed a mechanism for raising the individual above the clamor of race. It is evident that he does not wish to be remembered primarily for his militant and bitter racial sonnet, *If We Must Die,* but for his collection of odd bits of beauty on every highway and byway. His fingerprints can never be duplicated.

American Daughter

ERA BELL THOMPSON

IN spite of the accident of color, Era Bell Thompson could rate as an "American daughter" more than she herself realizes. Her autobiography corresponds to a life-pattern which is pleasing to the average American. There is nothing sensational about her behavior or her opinions to frighten the solid citizen. The pranks and predicaments that tag her footsteps have the tang of the typical American whose schoolboy mischief is legendary. No touch of genius, no sign of bohemianism, no hint of radicalism mark her off from the common lot. She is neither antireligious nor feminist. Any criticism of existing institutions falls outside her ken. Unaffected, completely herself without attempting to impress her audience, she generates a warmth in her book which appeals to the affections. Relying on material that invites sentimentality, her story is too robust and too genuine to succumb to this danger. The emotional undertone of pathos, harnessed safely to normalcy, should soften American readers, but the good-natured wit and flashes of earthy humor should endear her to them unreservedly.

Viewed in terms of the wider American population, this Negro writer is definitely "one of ours." Her voice comes to us from the western prairies. The cosmopolitan atmosphere of Paris, London, and New York drops away like a glittering opera cloak. Era Bell Thompson wears the simpler dress of the small-town and the rural areas, and has no interest in adding costume jewelry. She never seems urban even when she finally settles in Chicago. She carries with her a pristine love for that open country of North Dakota where she spent her childhood. Somehow this bestows on her the quality of being rooted in good American earth. She knows the land and the folk so intimately that she becomes an unconscious exponent of regionalism.

The background and personality of the father held no inkling of such a development in the daughter. Her name goes back to the Thompson plantation in Virginia where her father was the child of the owner's son. In spite of his blonde hair the small boy was not allowed to attend school and had to rely on the teaching of his white half-sisters. By the time he was ten, however, he was teaching adults how to read and write. He had a touch of the entrepreneur about him. Married three times, the last time to Era Bell's mother, he learned "to let bygones be bygones—especially female bygones," moved from Virginia to Iowa to North Dakota, and tried his hand as a cook, politician, farmer, and shopkeeper. In Des Moines, Iowa, he rose to the occasion of bringing the first Negro family into the East Side neighborhood by following a program of "continuous improvements." He planted flowers and shrubbery, sodded the lawn, and painted the house so that there could be no talk of property devaluation. By the time his little daughter was born he owned his house, was the proprietor of a restaurant, and served as a solid Baptist and a community leader.

His real forte was the city. He could function as an expert cook or as a suave employee in politics. His growing and unruly boys, literally living up to their names of Tom, Dick, and Harry, prompted him to try farming in North Dakota where he had a Negro half-brother. But he was always as lost and confused on the farm as his daughter sometimes felt away from it. In 1916 North Dakota politics offered him a way out. The Non-Partisan League of farmers swept the state; the new governor, Lynn Frazier, remembered meeting "Tony Thompson" on his campaign and made him his private messenger. "It was Pop, the city man, who brought a bit of country to the farm administration, for he was sworn in, still clad in his sheep-skin suit and his sheep-lined boots." One newspaper reporter exclaimed "Shades of reconstruction!" and wondered where he hailed from, but the new messenger was in the height of his glory here in Bismarck, the state capital, and proceeded to relay much valuable information to the new farmer-politicians who had often never "held an office above township level" or been inside the capitol. "Even the governor was among those grateful," and years later, as U. S. Senator, invited him to Washington.

Era Bell Thompson lives with her father at the end of these days of excitement for him. By this time her mother is dead, her older brothers have scattered, the farm is sold, and she is ready for high school. But this city of 10,000 does not appeal to her as it does to him.

Certain childhood impressions have cut too deeply into her nature to disappear.

She will always recall the early years in that "strange and beautiful country" so big and boundless that she could "look for miles and miles over the golden prairies and follow the unbroken horizon where the midday blue met the bare peaks of the distant hills." As a child of ten or eleven, she liked the loneliness and the silence, broken only by the clear notes of the nearby meadow lark or the honk of the wild geese far above. Sunsets brought a lonelier beauty, with the purple haze of the hills meeting the crimson blur in the west. Even the severe droughts were an occasion for observation rather than dread. As the dry, hot wind scorched the crops, she noticed that it "dried up the little slough until stiff alkaline rings formed a chalky mosaic in the hard, cracked bed." She noticed that on motionless days, when not even the grass stirred, people also were quiet. "You hated to break the prairie silence, the magic of its stillness, for you had that understanding with nature, that treaty with God." Words were unnecessary and inappropriate. "The silence wore hard on those who did not belong."

She belonged so intensely that each season took on indispensable features. Early fall meant the end of the intense heat and the beginning of soft breezes so that the grain fields became "hills of whispering gold." The spell was "so warm, so tranquil" that the little girl was tempted to stretch out on the brown, dry earth beneath the prairie grass. Later came the threshing and long rides in the bright autumn sunshine or in the twilight after the day's work. Sometimes she "stood down in the bottom of the deep wagon, drinking in the full glory of white sage against purple shadows, watching gold-streaked heavens turn blue with approaching night." At other times, in the dark, she listened to "the slow rhythm of tired horses," "the muffled rattle of the harness," and "the hayrack creaking under its burden." As the wagon moved across the prairie "in the shallow road of our making," she was filled with a mood of "sacredness" and "inner happiness." Still later came hunting and the cold rains. She kept a sharp watch for migrating birds and was rewarded by glimpses of brown-flecked teals and "big green-necked mallard ducks with their gray coats and white dickies." High overhead the squadrons of wild geese flew southward unaccompanied by her envy.

For she did not want to run away from winter. Creeping inside her was "a delicious, exciting fear that welcomed the storm and the cold and the unknown." When the tumbleweeds were lifted high in the shrieking winds, when the snow fell for three days in the middle of October, she accepted both the savagery and the still, white beauty. December blizzards which enveloped the barns, the windmill, and then the house, while the mercury dropped to 40° below and the wind traveled at sixty miles an hour, failed to spoil her Christmas. Heavy snow meant no school, tunnels from the house to the barn, baths which offered "a choice between cleanliness and pneumonia," and each novelty added something to her expectation of high adventure. There were sleigh rides across the trackless sea of snow to friendly neighbors. There was even the thrill of danger when she lost her way in a sudden blizzard. While her mother reached back towards the green hills of Virginia and the lush valleys of Iowa, and while her father and brothers pondered on the more congenial life of the big cities, she alone was "happy on our land, content to call it home."

In the aliveness of spring she could count on her family's thawing out. The sting left the morning air, the prairie grass acquired a tinge of green, and her heavy winter coat felt "like a suit of armor." Along with spring came "the excitement of the birth of living things." New farm animals entailed new responsibilities which she was eager to assume. She curried and brushed her pony for hours at a time. The proud possessor of a dog and a pet pig as well, she was "happy beyond the realm of people." When the family circle stifled her she was free to go roaming with her dog or pony across the warm and sunny prairie, searching for Indians and finding prairie roses and purple crocuses.

Years later, enchanted by spring elsewhere, she is still faithful to this first love. At the State University she enjoys the green velvet lawns and hedges, the robins and the lilac bushes, but grows homesick for the sage, the buffalo grass, and the delicate wild flowers. The verdant spring of Iowa offered her strange birds and flowers. But the ebony-feathered martins, the honeysuckle vines and the pale white sweet peas did not lead her to prefer the rich soil of Iowa to the endless prairie grass.

Her endorsement reaches out to include the climate, the landscape, and the rural life which was organic to them. In those impressionable years between nine and thirteen she makes up her mind so thoroughly that her narrative beyond this point is interspersed with nostalgic flash backs. As a high school graduate, working in a busy city, she suddenly feels desolate: "I was willing to give all the beautiful flowers in St. Paul for one ragged tumbleweed, all the beautiful lakes in Minnesota for one alkaline slough." As a mature woman, traveling on vacation from her government work in Chicago to the West coast, she observes the North Dakotan scene from her train window with a rush of emotion: "Familiar things, the towns, the highways, red elevators, windmills with spangles gleaming in the sun, burned firebreaks, discarded railroad ties, grazing stock in endless pastures, farmers grouped around the cream cans at tiny stations, waving at the train. And blue sky stretching out to purple bluffs and distant buttes." Certainly no professional regionalist of the great American plains area could offer a more heartfelt testimonial.

But it would be a mistake to conceive of these childhood years as an idyll. In fact, family and personal trials were so overwhelming that her enthusiasm could flourish only because it was a hardy plant. Migrating to North Dakota, the family had no home or land for the first few months, were unwelcome guests with relatives and then penniless lodgers in the bare and drafty hotel of a town with one hundred inhabitants. During the first year of farming father and sons had to contend not only with poor machinery and poorer land but with their gross inexperience. When the threshing crew descended upon them, Era Bell saw her parents making "pathetic efforts at hospitality." There were prairie fires and grasshopper plagues to battle. Horses got the mange or froze into stiff corpses.

Era Bell knew what it was to encounter cold, drought, hunger, sickness, and death. Alone with her mother when she died unexpectedly, the ten year old girl was afraid to touch her and took a reckless ride across the plains for her father. Afterwards she had to endure her father's "halo of grief," her brothers' discontent, and her own serious case of smallpox. Motherless, she was forced to adjust to some rough treatment at the hands of older brothers who were well-meaning but untrained to care for a small girl and who had too many personal problems to cultivate patience. Perhaps the greatest sorrow came, however, from watching the family break up after her mother's death. In 1919 one brother went to war, not long afterwards the other two deserted the farm for the city, and Era Bell found herself alone with the self-pity of her father and with the unpleasantness of domestic chores. Small wonder that the author recalls these incidents as a "cycle of calamity."

There are more cycles ahead. In fact, they seem to recur quite often during the next twenty years. After her father's political post is finished, he is reduced to making a living by running a secondhand shop. With no money forthcoming for her college education, Era Bell tries to earn enough, but arrives at the State University with only $30 for tuition and $30 for books. Her efforts to work her way through are stymied by sickness, first scarlet fever, and then pleurisy and pneumonia. She is told that it will no longer be safe for her to participate in running, hockey, and the other active sports she relishes. Not until she is twenty-four is she able to return to college and complete her education. Meanwhile her old father has died and she has spent months running his store and paying off every debt. Poverty never leaves her much rest. Even after her college degree she must face the job scarcity of depression years which entails some uncongenial servant work in Chicago and often no work at all.

Also on the debit side of her experience stands a large item connected with race. As she grew up trouble occurred more often in the schoolroom than in the community. On the North Dakota farm neighbors were curious but friendly, and frankly surprised at the "brownness" of the Thompsons. In the state capital of Bismarck, less than twenty of the 10,000 population were Negroes. In Mandan, across the Missouri river where Mountain Time and the "real West" begin, no more than two or three Negroes had lived at one time. Most of its 7000 inhabitants were Russian-German, seldom spoke English, and seemed like transplanted bits of the Old Country with "scrubbed wooden benches" leaning against "light-blue and pale-green houses," and earthenware jugs standing by the doors. They were kindly disposed to the Negro father and daughter, and willing to patronize their secondhand furniture store. The novelty which surrounded Negroes in North Dakota seemed to attract attention but little antagonism.

But curiosity sometimes went beyond bounds in school. Placed in fourth grade, Era Bell ran the gamut of her teacher's questions about her family and background until she had to "blink hard to keep back the tears." She and her brother, "two studies in brown," did not correspond to the pictures in funny papers and geography books, so the pupils stared and snickered and examined the white palms of her hands until she tightened her fists. She was relieved that they could not see her feet "where the color ran out." When she was called "nigger" she longed to be home in the comfort of her family but could not confide her hurt to them. "I was ashamed that others should find me distasteful." For the first time she wondered about the meaning of her color.

High school in Bismarck continued her state of confusion. Her textbook informed her that "Negroes were black folks with kinky hair and a thick skull that education could not penetrate," but her test grade turned out to be a 97. "The pupils wanted to know which was wrong, the book or I, and the teacher was in a spot until some bright kid remembered there was an Aryan in my family closet, so the white curse of intelligence remained on my dark shoulders accounted for and excused." Assembly speakers and songs were equally embarrassing. "Old Folks at Home" might be followed by a "darky" story in which case the student body would turn to see how she was taking it. She learned to confound them by turning to look, too. At the university the Dean of Women evinced little interest in her housing problem until she "made good" and was something of a campus celebrity. The sororities showed plainly that they didn't consider "Jews or Negroes or dogs." Once when she consulted her father about the vagaries of prejudice he answered that prejudice was a curious thing, that "it ran every way but out."

Even in the comparative isolation of the west Era Bell Thompson receives intimations of the wider scope of the race problem. Contact with other Negroes is rare but revealing. As a child she does observe some hard feeling, due to color differences, among relatives. Her Uncle John has more Negro heritage than her father because he is the son of their mother by her colored husband. However, he is married to a white woman, and father and brown daughter line up against mother and white son. In another colored family Era Bell notices that one man is proud of his "fat, black, and sassy" children who eat well and laugh heartily, whereas the lighter skinned brother, trained at Tuskegee and married to a schoolteacher, speaks in precise sentences, owns the only library in the township, and has a daughter, "who was full of 'yes, mamma,' 'no, mamma,' instead of turkey and ice-cream." At one house the Thompsons feast and relax, at the other house they have "a quiet night and an inhibited breakfast," with an Episcopalian blessing and "beautifully served but limited food." Thus ends Era Bell's first lesson in the intricacies of intragroup friction, color snobbery, and class-within-caste distinctions.

Occasionally comes news of lynching and riots from the outside world. Her soldier-brother sends home a copy of the *Chicago Defender* and for the first time she sees "the lifeless body dangling from the tree" and learns to hate and fear the South. "I wanted never to leave my prairies with white clouds of peace and clean, blue heavens, for now I knew that beyond the purple hills prejudice rode hard on the heels of promise and death was its overtaking. And I wondered where was God." She begins to understand that the antagonism between light and dark-skinned Negroes springs out of a society which puts a premium on white. She clings all the more to the satisfaction of that childhood Christmas when fifteen Negroes, four per cent of the state's colored population, gathered together in solidarity and generated a feeling of "race consciousness." "For the last time in my life, I was part of a whole family, and my family was a large part of a little colored world, and for a while no one else existed." But she knew even then that time could not grant her immunity forever.

Years afterwards, in Chicago, she must sort out these earlier impressions in relation to broadened experience. As a result, her theories on race form a conglomeration. While deploring intragroup snobbery, and "a color line within the color line," she finds herself "hating the common Negro" migrating from the South to the Black Belt of Chicago. His "loud, coarse manners," "flashy clothes" and "display of superficial wealth" irritate her especially because she knows that other Negroes will be condemned and segregated for them. This gives her a certain sympathy for Negroes who escape the onus by "passing" as whites. She believes in interracial friendships and is indignant at manifestations of Negro prejudice against whites. Landladies who bar her white friends are anathema. Yet she will not go so far as to countenance intermarriage. The idea never enters her head as a course for herself. When she likes white boys, she automatically avoids them if she sees danger signals. "Our side of the family didn't believe in miscegenation" and that was the end of it. Her original belief in race solidarity has not worn entirely thin in the big cities.

To balance her feelings of shame about "low-class" Negroes she accumulates in Chicago a fund of information about Negro leaders and artists she had never heard about before. In the late '20's she reads the books of the Negro Renaissance writers. She is impressed by the poetic prose of Dr. Du Bois. "Much of his writing was over my head, but I liked the feel of it. His words sang, giving off a haunting cadence, a mystic something that set him on a separate hill." A Jewish stenographer first introduces her to the singing of Marian Anderson by means of phonograph records. Even Joe Louis adds to the belated knowledge about her group which this girl from the western plains is seeking. A feeling of pride in race achievement seems to reconcile her to her chosen policy whereby she refers to "your people" and "my people."

Yet why can she not forgive black Chicago for not welcoming her white friends? Once again we see a case of conflicting emotions, an ambivalence which often leaves her stranded and helpless: "I was fighting the world alone, standing in a broad chasm between the two races, belonging to neither one."

In order to comprehend fully her strong attachment to the white group, we must bear in mind that the author is able to match almost every instance of cruelty with one of kindness. Eclipsing her tormentors in fourth grade was Jewel Nordland of the golden hair. "Her name was like a poem and her voice was like music." Old Gus, the drunken bachelor, helped her brother tame the horses. Carl, the good German neighbor, brought sacks of food, unsolicited, when the family flour barrel was empty. Other neighbors contributed pigs and chickens to give the Negro "greenhorns" a start. Era Bell's best friend in Bismarck was the Jewish Sarah Cohn, in Mandan, the German Elsie Wagner. High school seniors spoiled her. Her sociology teacher at the university made learning pleasant. "When I found out he was from Tennessee, it was too late. I already liked him." Her staunch friend there was Dora Gordan, a nonconformist with a "love for the underdog." The community at Mandan rallied to her aid when her father died, even to the point of chaperoning her solitary life. Their strict discipline of her comings and goings was protective, not malicious.

But the chief protagonist of white virtue was the Riley family. A red-haired Methodist minister with a temper about the right things, Dr. Riley paved the way for Era Bell's return to college by raising money for her tuition, breaking down the race prejudice of his wife, and making the Negro student a part of his own household. His five year old son had been converted to the idea by an appeal to his sympathy so that he was all prepared for "a poor little orphan who couldn't help being what I was." The result was as embarrassing as it was effective, but his solicitude soon tapered off into genuine affection until the Negro girl and the white child became inseparable. The family routine was haphazard but delightfully informal. Assigned tasks had a way of changing hands. "Soon Dr. Riley was involved in the Friday wash, and on Saturdays Glen scrubbed while I typed Susan's thesis." Such rearrangements suited the undomestic Negro student and made her feel that "it was our house now, not theirs; we, not I." So thoroughly did she become a Riley that the head of the family accepted the Presidency of a small Methodist college in Iowa on the condition that she should be accepted too. It was in this friendly atmosphere that Era Bell Thompson finished her college course. With the status of president's daughter, she blossomed into popularity among the six hundred students.

Let it be said to her credit that this popularity was no synthetic product. For it is plain on every page of her book that Era Bell Thompson had a genius for making friends. Dr. Riley gave her the opening with his family and the college community, but she had always possessed a knack of walking into people's affections and establishing herself there.

In fact, it is this trait which is basic to her whole pattern of adjustment to society and which enables her to relegate race troubles, along with family, health, and economic troubles, to a minor role. For, in spite of any or all logic to the contrary, this individual feasts on happiness. In the direst circumstance she spies a rift of blue sky, and neither blizzards, debts, nor insults can tame the spirit of a girl who gravitates towards friends as unerringly as towards western suns. Early deprived by circumstance of a connection with any Negro group, even an intimate family circle, she must needs exert her powers in a white world. In theory separated from whites as a Negro, in practice linked with them as a friend, she resolves the conflict by dropping the problem and picking up the compensations waiting for her as an individual.

It is not difficult to imagine some of the techniques of group adjustment she evolved. When she changed schools and again faced the ordeal of being called "nigger," she neither retorted nor ran away, but simply pushed the swings higher and ran faster than the others until she won respect. To achieve the title of good sportsmanship usually silenced the sharpest tongues. Furthermore her small size played a part in eliciting the protection of the softhearted.

Her resiliency and good humor under fire paid dividends. In addition, she had a spontaneous capacity for fun which proved irresistible and drew boon companions to her. She could "giggle over nothing," play practical jokes on teachers, and engage in daredevil adventures about town. In Bismarck two young teen-agers, Negro and Jewish, explored the city on their bicycles; visited without favoritism the library,

Capitol, and penitentiary; begged free rides on the ferry; and played precariously on the ice floes of the thawing Missouri river. At the university, Era Bell's English professor was the surprised recipient of a garter snake while her chemistry instructor was baffled by her trip outdoors with a shovel when she needed ice for an experiment.

Her sense of humor is the type which is no respecter of its owner. The author is objective enough to laugh at herself as the university freshman who signed up only for athletics and music appreciation courses, on the grounds that the latter would serve as relaxation after a strenuous day of sports. Or again, there was the Barb club, an anti-sorority organization with two members, Era Bell and her nonconformist white friend. The study of Latin proved a stumbling block to her graduation which only President Riley's dinner invitation to her teacher removed. Further back in high school days was an attempt at social reform which miscarried. Writing an article for a Negro newspaper in which she opposed the Garvey "Back-to-Africa" movement, she decided, on the basis of the scorching replies she received, to adopt the pseudonym of "Dakota Dick" and confine herself to the local color of the "wild and woolly West."

It was not merely the contagion of her personality which assured the Negro girl's success. Her humor and originality were fortunately associated with real talent. Her creative writing drew favorable acclaim throughout her school days so that she was often accorded special columns in student publications. With some experience in a Chicago magazine office, she finally edited her own little newssheet on the job, and circulated it among her fellow-employees. The response she always elicited must have been a rich compensation for her "cycles of calamity."

Behind the outer manifestation of talent lay an active mind which eagerly seized upon new ideas. Art and science alike attracted her. She learned to read "the ancient language of the fossils," listen to "the splendor and cadence of Bach and Wagner," and see "rare landscape and fresh color" in paintings. Under the tutelage of the Rileys her desire to learn grew healthily: "New worlds, these, unfolding before me, worlds like caverns so vast that each was a lifetime, and I must live again to explore each cavern, to travel each separate vista." Such an attitude towards knowledge must have expedited her way in academic life and at the same time provided still another green pasture in her uphill struggle.

This college student obviously is seeking an education for its intrinsic rewards and not for the prestige it may give her. Instinctively she has always avoided "cultured" people. She senses that her rural background and humble upbringing away from centers of culture make her feel "remote, apart," even inferior to many girls she meets in Chicago, yet she prefers to retain her love for the "foreign peasantry" of North Dakota than strive towards the "quiet luxury" of a manner of living which she "could admire, but never touch." She never fails to prize genuineness. She chooses to board with a "swearing lady" who has befriended her in need than to move to more refined homes when her merit is tardily granted. Essentially democratic, essentially earthy in her human sympathies and social aspirations, this young woman is free to be an aristocrat in her intellectual goals.

Certainly by the time she reached maturity Miss Thompson must have recognized clearly that her talent went hand in hand with a general ability and an intelligence of a high order. For many years she held her own in competition with white employees on government projects and ultimately was rewarded with the responsible position of an interviewer with the United States Employment Service. As people of varying national, racial, and religious backgrounds came to her desk for advice and as she utilized her resources of personality, experience, and intelligence to guide them, she must have had the satisfaction of feeling that, in her own case, she had pinned prejudice to the ground.

As the author draws her account to a close near the end of World War II, she is in her middle thirties with the years still stretching before her. We gain the impression that she asks only one privilege of the life ahead, the privilege to be an "American Daughter." This does not hinge upon any weighty solutions of the race problem. She does not profess to be a social analyst. In fact, we can almost feel the headaches when she touches upon the subject. Irreconcilables bother her, so she retreats to her province of personal reminiscence and records on her pages both her dislike of the migrating low-class Negroes and her preference for natural, ordinary folk. Outgoing and friendly herself, she has none of the complexity of make-up to fit her for a patient sifting of the intricacies of democracy. She would rather assume that American society is somehow moving in the direction of more light: "For castles are shining things, and in the blinding sun at the top of the hill color is neither black nor white." To live and let live seems so simple to her that she must conclude her book on a note of hope. "The chasm is growing narrower. When it closes, my feet shall be on a United America."

If her belief seems governed by wish, her life emphasis must be remembered. If a regionalist could also be an American, why could not a Negro also be an American? Distinctiveness should not mean exclusion from the wider realm. A prairie childhood and a dark skin should be considered as particular aspects of the individual, adding variety, not imposing limits. Therefore it is up to the individual, she seems to say, to act accordingly; to minimize hardships and concentrate on all the resources available for contentment. If he insists on approaching society in this mood, society will ultimately reciprocate.

Thus this last book in our third group of autobiographies stands in contrast to the last book in our second group. Mary Church Terrell stresses her forced apartness from white society by her title, *A Colored Woman in a White World*. Era Bell Thompson stresses her identification with white society by her title, *American Daughter*. From a background of greater opportunity, education, and achievement, Mrs. Terrell asserts her race pride and race consciousness. One of the people, Miss Thompson has no spectacular career or distinguished acquaintances to point to. She has no contribution to add to the annals of Negro progress. She thinks of herself primarily as a free agent, responsible only to herself, and regards even her writing as a private matter.

Perhaps the basic differences in the point of view which these two women reflect can be seen in their reactions to their writing. While Mrs. Terrell wishes to utilize her talent in the cause of the Negro group and is embittered by the prejudice which curtails her efforts and recognition in this field, Miss Thompson writes for the fun of it. She tells us that, as a young girl, she cherished the dream of becoming a "paid writer." Later she notes that this dream has not yet materialized but without the slightest reference to racial factors as a possible deterrent. Whereas Mrs. Terrell labors the point in her correct but stilted sentences, Miss Thompson skips lightly over it and bounds along in her lively style to other matters. Mrs. Terrell represents the serious vein in the older generation of Negro protesters, Miss Thompson the younger generation's distaste for problems in any shape. Ironically enough, her autobiography will measure up to the standard of entertainment for hundreds of readers who will make no effort to prevent dust from collecting on the heavier book. Without straining as much, she may be the one to achieve more success as a "paid writer."

Whether she succeeds or not, Miss Thompson does not clutch all her treasures tightly in one hand. Some are stored away in a thousand memories, some are scattered freely for others to pick up. A few are buried where she has marked the place and where she can return at will. For in an inner sense she possesses security and a home. She knows what it means to turn her footsteps towards a beloved spot, to anticipate "the little granary gleaming like a mystic castle in the blood-red glow of a surrendering sun." It is an individual prerogative which makes living, on any terms, a blessing.

Summary

FLIGHTS TO HAPPINESS

SURELY it cannot be disputed that our authors in this third group all manage to find life singularly worth-while. In so far as they can avoid the weight of the race problem, they do; in so far as they can't, they quickly lay the burden down. Each man for himself, they seem to proceed on the theory that the short cut to happiness is best negotiated alone and unimpeded. With few exceptions, they have little time to spare for maligning the white man.

This does not mean that they are unaware of the illogic and inhumanity of prejudice. They are moderns of the last two decades who have imbibed the current information about race, who thus have scientific support for rejecting the myth of "white superiority," and who are far removed in time and circumstance from the conditions fostering a "slave mentality." Their general level of intelligence and ability is high so that it is an elementary affair for them to sense the mechanisms of power in group relations and to refute the suggestion of inferiority by the dominant group.

They are not driven by the inner furies of early conditioning to assert their individual worth in order to reassure themselves. In most cases childhood experiences bolstered their egos in regard to race more than they undermined them. As isolated Negro children in white communities—Montana, California, Massachusetts, North Dakota—they were measured by white standards and not found wanting. Mixing with white children daily, they had ample opportunity to see their faults and to refrain from associating any magic with the word *white*. In addition, their conspicuous roles undoubtedly brought welcome along with unwelcome attention, especially when their quick minds or unique personalities could furnish the credentials for approval and even popularity.

They soon learned that in spite of textbooks or whispering campaigns they could always qualify in their white environment as exceptions to the notions of Negro incompetency. Claude McKay's Jamaican background and Zora Hurston's Florida all-Negro town produced the same effect by different means. Color lines were fluid in the British colony so that many Negroes rated higher socially than lower-class whites and caste discriminations never materialized for the young boy. When Zora Hurston was accustomed to see Negroes—including her mayor-preacher father—in positions of authority and leadership she could not suffer any shame in being a Negro. None of these Negro children, with the possible exception of Juanita Harrison about whose childhood we know nothing, was subjected to the early, daily discipline of a Jim Crow regime. They were not forced to accept separate and unequal accommodations as a fitting order of things. Meeting insult and discrimination as they still did away from the Deep South, they nevertheless must have realized from the start that they had a fighting chance to "make good." In their efforts they were not hindered overmuch by a psychology of no-accountism.

Nor do later circumstances conspire to break their spirits. They find many compensations in their surroundings. Practically all of them can claim at least moderate success as artist or writer. It takes only a quick reading of this group of autobiographies to recognize the superior quality of writing in comparison to the first two groups. The general standard of education of the authors—whether academic or self-acquired—is better; the general background of reading, travel, and knowledge of the world in which they live is broader. More conscious than their predecessors of the complexities and contradictions of their society, living in a period of greater flux, they are more inclined to throw overboard the old values, the traditional precepts of morals and religion. Claude McKay's aestheticism seems as foreign to Booker T. Washington's ethics as Miss Hurston's hedonism does to Mrs. Hunter's stern call to duty. Personality becomes more important than character. New experience awaits.

They do not wish to win the praise of white people by conciliatory, "good" behavior, nor by special achievements. Neither awed nor unduly antagonized by whites, they refuse to let them fill their mental horizon and strive to initiate ways of life independent of their yoke. Emancipated not only physically but intellectually from older patterns of group interaction, they take pioneer strides towards a new feeling of mobility, of freedom in choosing their values.

This consciousness of freedom extends to their relation to Negroes as well. Chafing under the mere thought of responsibility to group welfare, these Negro authors show that they are not afraid to apply to their own race the new realism which they acquire as moderns. We find very little sentimentality about "my people" in their pages, few references to superior racial traits, little boasting about Negro ancestry. Most of them go out of their way to comment on weaknesses within the Negro group, from Mr. McKay's diatribe against the intellectuals to Miss Thompson's condemnation of low-class Chicago Negroes. If the condition of being white is not sacred to them, neither is the condition of being brown or black. They do not believe in disowning the racial identity which has been thrust upon them, but they do insist on qualifying their loyalty to the point of claiming that no special virtue resides in any kind of complexion. Often ambivalent in their feelings about race, their reason asserts that only individuals, on whichever side of the race barrier, should occasion love or hate, respect or scorn. Consequently, they have no axe to grind for the group. In contrast to those in the last section who also stressed the individual but protested in the name of the race, our present writers believe in digging for the pot of gold in their own back yards. Their accommodation is not marred by resentment or shame but is merely a quest for happiness in a crazy world.

There is another side to their realism about race. While convinced that all stereotypes about groups are false, they seem equally convinced that society will not embrace such advanced views for years to come. Practically speaking, then, they accept the fact of naked power regulating race relations. Although they live in an age when the new science is proving that there is no rational foundation for race prejudice, they know that it is also proving that folkways and mores change slowly, that wrong emotional conditioning is a vicious circle which perpetuates wrong behavior. Thus a mood of fatalism about rapid progress for the Negro group is bound to affect them, directly or indirectly. Not articulate about such questions, they believe stress on race pride to be futile. Less optimistic than their forerunners about the possibilities of "uplifting" their group, they would be less inclined to dedicate their own achievements and apprentice their own abilities to any lost cause. In this way philosophical hopelessness supports their natural distaste for dabbling in schemes for improvement. Undoubtedly writers like McKay, Gordan, and Hurston, who experienced the intellectual ferment of the Negro Renaissance and were fully awake to their own powers, regarded themselves as born long before their times, and felt that the only service they could possibly render to race relations was in the capacity of advanced agents for a new culture. This could be done best not by preaching but by living fearlessly according to their personal creeds.

By whatever road, we are brought back again and again to the basic fact of their individualism. Every author is alive with it, every book enshrines it. Although we have to guess at their social views and deduce their realism about the race problem partly from external evidence, we meet their personal views and are struck by their romantic attitudes in each chapter. Not one of them fails to give the impression that he or she clings to a citadel of self, inviolable to misfortune and defeat. Within these boundaries, each is a monarch and rules according to whim.

The test of their optimism about their personal lives can be gauged by their reaction to economic factors. Without exception, these authors record firsthand acquaintance with poverty and the necessity to work for a living, often at an early age. Even Miss Adams and Mr. Braithwaite, coming from more protected middle-class homes, knew what it was to shoulder adult responsibilities prematurely. Taken as a whole, these Negroes are the children of World War I and its depression. As in Miss Thompson's and Miss Adams' case, they are frequently subject to greater job maladjustment because of race. Yet all these facts receive slight attention in their autobiographies. They seem to feel that poverty is part of the game and that there is as little profit in dwelling on it as on race injustices. Instead of becoming more disposed to cultivate the good graces of white employees in order to alleviate the harshness of want—a tendency we noted in our first group—they go blithely on their way. Even Claude McKay gives no indication that he tried to make himself particularly agreeable to his white patrons. Instead of holding long discourses on the special hardships which the depression brought to the Negro group, they turn to the cultivation of their private interests.

As we have seen, it is at this point that they part company. Naturally the devotees of individualism could never be true disciples if they followed the same course. The travel talk of Miss Harrison would have no appeal for Miss Adams. The tastes, language, and habits of Mr. Gordan would disturb Miss Thompson. Mr. Braithwaite and Mr. McKay could not even discuss literature together peacefully, while Miss Hurston could reassure all of them that happiness is like the classic bluebird, only safe in the heart of the beholder.

Variation of personality and point of view can be explained more readily by complex psychological influences than by mere economic status or geographical location. Parental dominance played a greater part in Miss Adams' personality than unemployment. Separated by a whole continent from Mr. Braithwaite, she could share more interests with him than with her Western contemporary, Mr. Gordan. Their preference for quiet beauty traces back to the ideals of a middle-class gentility which had little to do with cash income. Similarly, Mr. Gordan's distant Montana background does not deter him from sharing a spicy and robust sense of humor with Miss Hurston, a native of Florida. Different circumstances knocked them about until they toughened to meet them.

Fully to understand why these individuals think and feel as they do would require more information about formative influences in their human environment than their accounts yield. But the authors do encourage two generalizations, that happiness defies standardization and that freedom is a state of mind.

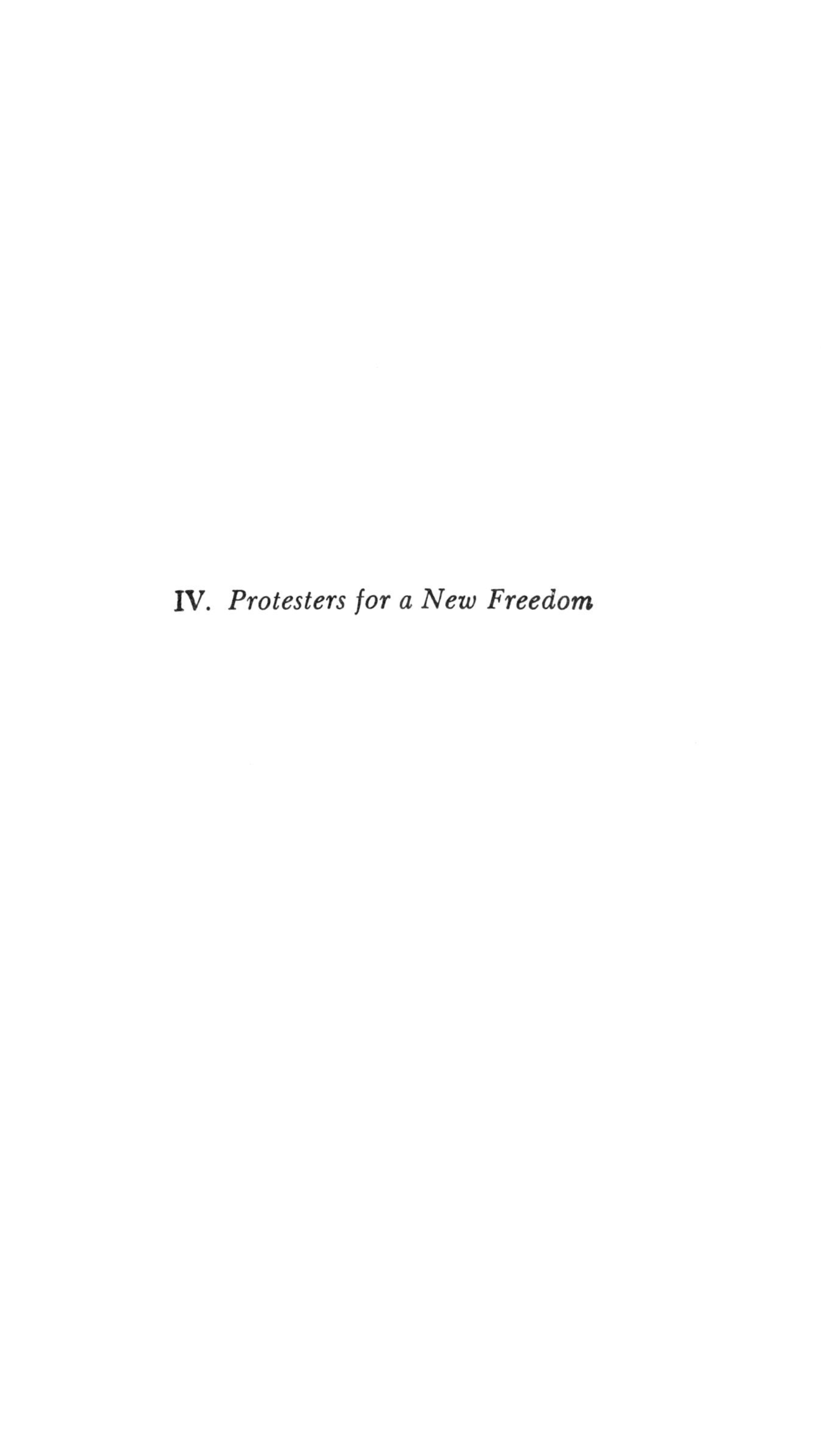

IV. *Protesters for a New Freedom*

PROTESTERS FOR A NEW FREEDOM

Our fourth and last group of autobiographies stands in marked contrast to the others. Also published during the 1930's and 1940's, these books share nothing else in common with those we have just considered. Although their authors have been subjected to similar trends of the time, to World War I, the depression, the new science of race, and a period of flux for Negroes, and although they have fully as much claim to be regarded and to regard themselves as distinct individuals in spite of societal ills, they voluntarily subordinate their individualism to the larger race problem.

These are the social thinkers. They are not content merely to relate the personal incidents of their lives as ends in themselves. Inevitably they connect up their stories with social implications. Probing and analyzing, they reach out towards the edges of a wider framework. Conscious of group responsibility once more, they differ from the Booker T. Washington school in their independence from repressive white attitudes, and in their motivation for aiding Negro causes. None of them is a professional race leader by intent, although some of them have leadership thrust upon them. There is little effort to curry favor with "their people" for the sake of job and prestige. Nor are they tempted to gloss over the faults of many Negroes in order to gain a blanket endorsement for all. Race pride is never featured in their pages, partly because they are cognizant of the new theories upsetting the old concepts of race, partly because they are too honest observers of the complex American scene to be satisfied with oversimplification, and mostly because they reject the psychological need to resort to such devices for their mental health.

These men radiate a breadth of vision and a maturity of judgment which put them in a category apart from their predecessors. Viewing the history of race-relations from the close of the Civil War to the present, they see much to encourage and much to discourage hopes for adjustment. They do not stack the cards one way or the other in terms of ultimates, but generalize from the observations and facts of experience and study with enough calmness and detachment to convey authenticity. Thus their autobiographies could belong just as aptly to sociology as to literature. The authors aim for a sociological realism, a psychological insight, and a scientific objectivity which become second nature to individuals with good minds who are forced by circumstance to examine their relation to society.

Stress on a reasonable approach does not exclude an emotional appeal, and sometimes an emotional bias. But when this element appears it is not directed towards sympathy for the author, but expanded towards the dilemma of all Negroes. No sentimentality is wasted on the plight of the individual. Even the most personal of this group, Richard Wright's *Black Boy,* quickly becomes symbolic of the fate of thousands of such boys growing up in the Deep South, and, with all its touches of bitterness, bears the stamp of a detached case study. Angelo Herndon, one-time communist, projects a strong plea for communism, but saves his story from propaganda by his real grasp of the actual problems of working-class Negroes, and by his analysis of the roots of exploitation. As a poet, Langston Hughes has a precedent for retiring into the aesthetic pleasures of his own world yet grows increasingly sensitive to social and economic issues in the surrounding environment. Neither W. E. B. Du Bois, James Weldon Johnson, nor J. Saunders Redding can treat the racial hurts and frustrations of youth aside from their meaning in the struggle of a whole group.

Skillfully blended with objectivity is a very pronounced militancy in regard to racial injustices. Compromise and tact are no longer employed as steppingstones to interracial harmony. Because of their awareness of social process, these writers feel qualified to drop pretence and to speak their minds openly on controversial subjects.

They have inherited the mantle of Frederick Douglass rather than of Booker T. Washington. In a modern setting, each in his own manner, they express the same spirit of fearless challenge which characterized that pioneer for Negro rights in the Emancipation era. Fugitive slave, self-educated man, co-worker with the Northern abolitionists, this heroic and dramatic figure became the mouthpiece for the aspirations of his group in a manner which was to outlive the aftermath of Reconstruction and send out vigorous new shoots into the present century.

To those who wished close acquaintance with the evolution of his ideas, Frederick Douglass left a detailed and complete autobiography. Expanded from the small narrative of 1845 to *My Bondage and My Freedom* in 1855, finally revised and completed as *Life and Times* at the close of his life, his account has long ranked as a classic among those who know the field of Negro-American literature; as both a valuable social document and a work of art outstripping Booker T. Washington's *Up From Slavery*. Although, strictly speaking, it does not fall within the scope of the twentieth-century autobiographies we are considering, in light of its perennial importance we can well profit by remembering some of its salient features.

✓✓

Life and Times of Frederick Douglass

✓ ✓ ✓

EVEN as an illiterate slave child, Frederick Douglass never temporized with the idea of slavery. "I had hardly become a thinking being when I first learned to hate slavery." At nine years of age he was so convinced of its "unjust, unnatural, and murderous character" that he could only conclude that it was "man-made, not God-ordained." He dismissed as contradictory the two notions handed to him that God had made the present order and that God was good. Sharply observant of the hypocrisy of pious but cruel slaveholders, he early branded "the blending of prayer with punishment" as inconsistent. This led him later to battle against the "sham religion" of white people, and the ignorant, emotional, superstitious response of too many black people which only perpetuated their bondage.

The rebellious conduct of the boy continually asserts itself in the social philosophy of the man. The thirteen-year-old had stubbornly learned to read, in spite of orders to the contrary. The sixteen-year-old had resisted the beating of a white man, thus discovering his manhood: "When a slave cannot be flogged, he is more than half free." The same disregard of current mores in favor of a higher morality made him advocate abolition, then citizenship, then enfranchisement for Negroes. He was a force not only behind the Fourteenth and Fifteenth amendments, and such civil rights for Negroes as nonsegregation, but also behind woman suffrage. His pride in being dubbed a "Woman's rights man" reflected his belief that freedom is indivisible, "that the liberties of the American people were dependent upon the ballot-box, the jury-box, and the cartridge-box." To him no group is innately inferior and all individuals are educable and worthy of fair treatment. His second marriage, to a white woman, is compatible with his attempt to live rationally and courageously: "The way to break down an unreasonable custom is to contradict it in practice."

By sheer force of intellect and purpose, this Negro leader achieved widespread fame. But he never bartered in exchange his right to independent thinking. Moving like a giant among great men, he did not hesitate to criticize them at times. William Lloyd Garrison, John Brown, even Lincoln he openly disagreed with on points of policy and procedure towards a common humanitarian goal. Throughout his distinguished career as public speaker, editor, writer, politician and diplomat, appointed Minister to Haiti, U. S. Marshall, and then Recorder of Deeds of the District of Columbia, Frederick Douglass thought through the issues which he faced with the same forthrightness and the same desire to see the total picture evinced in his boyhood.

Perhaps the most remarkable characteristic of his early thinking—aside from its precocity—was its objectivity. Bitter as his lot was, he sensed that slave-holders were also victims of the system, "of the circumstances of birth, education, law, and custom." Long before he could read and long before science had popularized such ideas, he was an environmentalist. Concerning one mistress who, ignorant of the taboo, started teaching him to read only to turn against him later, he remarked, "Nature made us friends but slavery made us enemies."

He looked around at his limited world and analyzed each aspect. He understood why slaves were encouraged to sing and not read, to feast and get drunk on holidays. "To make a contented slave, you must make a thoughtless one." Necessary for the preservation of order are "safety-valves, to carry off the explosive elements." Underneath the apparent "benevolence" of the master was "fraud" and self-interest. Yet he recognized the kind deeds of a few individuals, the white boy who protected him against older children, the white woman who secretly fed him extra scraps when he was hungry. The fact that he could stop for fine distinctions in his state of misery indicated the caliber of his mind. Flashes of insight guided him through the darkness of ignorance, without parents, isolated in a self-contained master-slave community, to a new concept of society: "There are thoughtful days in the lives of children—at least there were in mine—when they grapple with the great primary subjects of knowledge, and reach in a moment conclusions which no subsequent experience can shake."

Deeply convinced and yet dispassionate, the mature Douglass believes that "we must fight to win the prize" but has "no heart to visit upon children the sins of their fathers." The basis of his hope is that people—white and black—can improve conditions by mutual respect and cooperation: "To find valuable qualities in our fellows, such qualities must be presumed and expected." There is no room in this setting for anyone to feel inferior or to accept inferior treatment.

Frederick Douglass considers his special role to be that of "a witness and an advocate" for an inarticulate and oppressed people. His autobiography is an integral part of this plan. It does not seem to be prompted by self-glorification or self-expression: "I write freely of myself, not from choice, but because I have, by my cause, been morally forced into thus writing." The details of his own struggle are recorded "not in order to exhibit my wounds and bruises and to awaken and attract sympathy to myself personally, but as a part of the history of a profoundly interesting period in American life and progress." The description of his successes is given to awaken self-respect and ambition among Negro readers. Yet his tone is not moralistic. Nor does he preen himself on his virtue in dedicating his efforts to less fortunate brethren.

Too realistic to be duped either by himself or others, he seems to hold himself on the even keel of his purpose throughout a long and productive lifetime. Modest about the dent he has made, he is buoyed up by the dignity of his ideal: "It has been a part of my mission to expose the absurdity of this spirit of caste and in some measure help to emancipate men from its control." In his own phenomenal rise above the restrictions of caste he never forgets those who are cowed and caught by its tentacles. As a result, he cannot conceive of happiness for himself except as a by-product of social responsibility, of a task well done.

We must wait several decades before we encounter once more in Negro-American autobiography this tone of high seriousness, and this mood of indignation tempered by perspective. Faced with different issues, writers like Du Bois, James Weldon Johnson, and J. Saunders Redding clasp hands with Frederick Douglass across the years to push the race problem to the forefront. Titles like Angelo Herndon's *Let Me Live* and Richard Wright's *Black Boy* suggest the simple, unadorned facts about the present status of Negroes with which the authors wish to challenge society. On the whole, this last group of autobiographies brings us up to date and leaves us at the crossroads of race-relations.

Dusk of Dawn

W. E. BURGHARDT DU BOIS

THE name of Du Bois has become a household word in thousands of American homes during the twentieth century. It has stood for brilliance of mind, for eloquence of expression, and for noncompromise of social philosophy. It bears connotations of New England accent and manner, of European polish, of academician turned agitator. For his bitter opposition to Booker T. Washington, for his original research in race relations, for his dynamic editorship of *The Crisis,* and for his extensive publication of both fiction and scholarly works, Dr. Du Bois deservedly won widespread recognition and centered on himself the loyalty and the opposition, the hopes and fears of countless people, white and dark complexioned, who were sufficiently informed and aroused to take a stand on the race question. For many years there was a tendency to be either for or against Du Bois, a tendency prodded by the force of his personality and of his ideas.

Puncturing at many points the legend around his name, Dr. Du Bois explains himself frankly in his autobiography. Published in 1940, when the author was seventy-two years old, *Dusk of Dawn* stresses the evolutionary development of a complex person. The stereotype of a dogmatist gives way before the truer picture of a man who came to his convictions painfully and gradually, who was not afraid to modify his opinions with increased knowledge and experience, and who had to work against elements in his own nature to assume his active role. Only one constant he always had, and that was a faith in his own mental acumen. Given a set of circumstances and sufficient time, he believed that he was able to penetrate through confusions to the core. "Perhaps above all I am proud of a straightforward clearness of reason," in part a "gift of the gods," but also due to "scientific training and inner discipline."

The outer events of Du Bois' life readily confirm any claims he may make to superiority of mind. Born in Great Barrington, Massachusetts, he was the first one of his relatives to finish high school. He excelled among his white classmates and was consequently shunted into a college preparatory course by a wise principal who realized that he would be a misfit in a vocational course directed towards the limited opportunities for Negroes as day laborers, farmers, or servants. Orphaned after high school, he nevertheless continued his education by winning scholarships to Fisk University, then to Harvard University where he received both his B.A. and M.A. degrees, finally to Berlin University. With a background of European study, a mastery of the German language and culture, and a Ph.D. degree, he entered into a period of productive teaching and research between 1894 and 1910. Two years at the small denominational college of Wilberforce where he taught Negro students Latin, Greek, German, and English but felt too circumscribed to remain and one year at the University of Pennsylvania (where he received only $600 as an assistant instructor but published his original study of the Philadelphia Negro and spoke at the meeting of the American Academy of Political and Social Sciences), were followed by thirteen fruitful years at Atlanta University.

During this long stretch Du Bois had the satisfaction of being an innovator. Under his guidance, Atlanta University became "the only institution in the world carrying on a systematic study of the Negro and his development" in business, the school, and the church, with attention to urbanization, crime, and mortality. In addition, he published, in 1903, his provocative book, *The Souls of Black Folk,* which made him the official spokesman against Booker T. Washington. In 1905 he initiated a call to a conference for "aggressive action," historically referred to as the Niagara Movement and instrumental in the formation of the National Association for the Advancement of Colored People.

Inevitably this type of activity drew Du Bois away from the secluded field of scholarship into the world of affairs. From 1910 to 1930 he devoted his energy to the editorship of *The Crisis* and the program of the N.A.A.C.P., with his headquarters in New York. In five years he built up the circulation of *The Crisis* from 1000 to 100,000, made it self-supporting, and used it as a medium for encouraging Negro writers. He mixed in practical politics and took the measure of Presidents and would-be Presidents, of Taft, Theodore Roosevelt, Wilson, and Hughes. He was behind the legal fights to overthrow the Grandfather clauses, abolish residential segregation, and pass the Dyer antilynching bill.

Postwar interests occasioned several European trips. He visited France in connection with the Treaty of Versailles and his efforts to establish a Pan-African Congress; Geneva in the early days of the League of Nations; in 1923 and 1924 Spain, Portugal, and Africa; in 1927 and 1928 Germany, Turkey, and Russia. His third Pan-African Congress was held in London, with the support of well-known liberals like Harold Laski, H. G. Wells, Lord Olivier, and Beatrice Webb. In 1936 came a world tour, finishing with the Orient.

Resignation from the N.A.A.C.P. signaled a return to his natural habitat of scholarship. It involved another period at Atlanta University, the initial work on a comprehensive Encyclopaedia of the Negro, contributions to the new university magazine, *Phylon,* and continued publications. "In a sense I returned to my ivory tower, not so much for new scientific research, as for interpretation and reflection; and for making a record of what I had seen and experienced." Certainly his final record, by the time he wrote his autobiography, was impressive, with over a dozen solid books to his credit over a period of forty years. He had proved conclusively by this time that he was an intellectual of the first water. The final touch of conviction, if needed, rests in the autobiography itself, the product of a seventy-two-year-old man whose capable grasp of prose and incisive treatment of ideas defy any disintegration of age.

But we would miss the whole point of Dr. Du Bois' book if we regarded its purpose as a chronicle and final proof of his intellectual achievements. The author specifically states otherwise. He devotes only minor attention to the events of his career, and ignores his marriage and family life. In terms of space, comparatively few pages are taken up with biographical details except in so far as they illuminate his views of race. This illumination, by all possible means, is his main intention. Not idly, therefore, does he give as his subtitle, "An Essay Toward an Autobiography of a Race Concept." Instead of dismissing his discussions about "the white and colored worlds" as lengthy digressions from his personal history, we are exhorted to take his personal history only as illustrative material for his larger racial thesis. "My living gains its importance from the problems and not the problems from me." To elucidate them "in terms of the one human life that I know best"; to explain society through "one of its rejected parts," constitutes an opportunity and a challenge to this thoughtful writer. For he considers race "the central problem of the greatest of the world's democracies and so the problem of the future world."

Actually, it is this aspect of his autobiography which calls forth the intellectual fire of the author. As he goes over each stage of his experience with a fine-tooth comb, as he dissects and appraises his immediate and his wider environment in relation to race he acquaints us with the inner workings of his mind in a way which makes the outer happenings of his life seem tame by comparison. His ability to stand outside himself and study his racial reactions and their significance in the total social pattern of America makes his acknowledgment of high intelligence seem as natural and objective as the statement of a disinterested scientist.

New Englander

Looking back on his boyhood, he sees it as a period of relative stability. The English, Dutch, Irish, and German population of the Berkshire valley directed no marked hostility towards the few colored families, most of whom were old settlers and intermarried among themselves. In fact, the Irish received their share. "It was a matter of income and ancestry more than color."

The boy had reason to be casual about color. His own ancestry was mixed. On his mother's side he was Dutch and African, with a very dark grandfather, a light complexioned grandmother, and a brown mother. His paternal great-grandfather was a white man, a French slaveowner in the Bahama Islands with a brown slave common-law wife. Their son, Alexander, white in appearance, was sent to an Episcopal school in the United States, but was classified as a Negro after his father's death. This Alexander "did differently" from Alexander Hamilton who came from the West Indies and married into the white group. He married into the colored group, but had a son, Alfred, who was "a throwback to his white grandfather." This olive-skinned handsome "play boy" grew up to be the father of our author who describes himself as a mulatto.

Early a widow in her native town, his mother, together with her people, exerted the decisive family influence in his younger years. "I absorbed their culture patterns and these were not African so much as Dutch and New England." Thus he felt at home in the community. He loved the countryside with its mountains, lakes, orchards, caves, and green fields. Early contacts with playmates were "normal and pleasant." Benefited by a regular ten months of schooling each year and by attendance at the same school, he received a solid foundation in his subjects.

He had little ground for feeling different and apart from other children. Although he did odd jobs to help his mother, they were the usual lawn-mowing, furnace-tending type open to small-town boys, and did not signify extreme poverty. In spite of the fact that it was an exception for a colored boy to go through high school, discrimination was lessened by the absence of fraternities, dances, and social life generally, and by his high ranking as a student. Actually, in taking the college course, he was thrown in with the young people from the best homes which protected him so that he "had little contact with crime and degradation." Since the main delinquency of this placidly religious town was drunkenness, and since he had promised his mother never to enter a saloon, he was evidently not in great danger of suffering a moral lapse.

Years later he can write: "I am glad that the partial Puritanism of my upbringing has never made me afraid of life," but certainly at the time he was a solid citizen with the best of them. Along with the religion he took at one stride the Republican politics, the sex mores, and the democratic institution of the annual town meeting. Underneath ran an economic philosophy to which he ascribed wholeheartedly: "that all who were willing to work could easily earn a living; that those who had property had earned and deserved it and could use it as they wished; that poverty was the shadow of crime and connoted lack of thrift and shiftlessness." Even in temperament he became a thorough New Englander. It was not good form "to express one's thoughts volubly, or to give way to excessive emotion."

Dr. Du Bois draws the outline of a boy who was somewhat of a prig, and definitely an avowed egotist. Whatever of racial feeling he encountered, as he was bound to occasionally, acted on him like a tonic. It "exalted" him and gave him a chance to excel. Confident that he could outdo any white rivals, he concluded that "they were the losers who did not ardently court me, and not I." Yet below the surface lay sensitive feelings and "inner withdrawals" from real and imagined discriminations. Thus his self-assurance hid his introspective tendencies. His pattern of New England reserve was reinforced by an emotional need, by "the habit of repression."

This combination of pride and reserve, so successfully masking his inner feelings, was to "plague" him in the future. The author recognizes that it handicapped him in making friends of strangers, in being a natural leader. While he knows that his temperament has antagonized people he wastes no futile regret over a condition which was the result of social forces beyond his control. The positive side remained in that his self-assertion carried him out of the narrow rut of his familiar surroundings into the wider, competitive world.

Race Enthusiast

Consciously he conformed and felt adequate in his home environment. It was as if he forced himself away from any implications of inferiority. But unconsciously he felt uncomfortable. To a certain extent, then, it was a relief to find himself at Fisk University among Negro students who were at the same time on his intellectual plane. His imagination was captured by these hundreds of young people, of rich and variegated skin color, "bound to me by new and exciting and eternal ties." Eagerly he developed a loyalty to a "closed racial group" with its own history and philosophy. The fact of race was faced openly, equality with whites asserted, inferiority denied. Dr. Du Bois describes this stage in his development as imbued with a romantic spirit which we might well liken to *Sturm und Drang*. He was swept along with the students in a "glorious crusade" to match their mettle against the cold white world. No longer was he an outsider who must be included because he was an exception. This young Northerner in the South nurtured a race pride which was almost chauvinistic. In his enthusiasm he embraced voluntary segregation and opposed amalgamation. Afraid of "inner racial distinctions" which would harm the unity of the Negro group, he "resented the defensive mechanism of avoiding too dark companions" for the sake of convenience in public.

Observing violence for the first time in the South, horrified by the facts of lynching, he determined to help the real emancipation of the Negro by means of the "scientific conquest" of his environment. His graduating subject was Bismarck, the strong hero. He did not question the values his hero stood for, nor the ideals in general of white society. Extremely interested in international political developments, he accepted the current ideas of optimism and progress and objected only because Negroes were excluded from their benefits. "It was as though moving on a rushing express, my main thought was as to the relations

I had to other passengers on the express, and not to its rate of speed and its destination." Ignorant of economics, he hailed the Industrial Revolution and imperialism without seeing the relation to the slave trade and exploitation in Africa. All that Negroes needed in the present was the strength of united effort.

He carried his pride with him to Harvard, willingly remaining outside its social life, counting only on the teachers and the library. He sang *Fair Harvard* only because he liked the music. "I do not doubt that I was voted a somewhat selfish and self-centered 'grind' with a chip on my shoulder and a sharp tongue." As in high school, an element of inferiority was present. "I was desperately afraid of not being wanted; of intruding without invitation; of appearing to desire the company of those who had no desire for me." Yet he did not let his lack of popularity spoil his enjoyment or break the guard of his conceit. He had his "island within," and, above all, his studies where he still had the mastery.

Systematically, he began to fill in the gaps in his knowledge. Distinguished teachers like William James, Santayana, Royce, Palmer, Kittredge, and Charles Eliot Norton helped him. He turned from philosophy and history to economics and social problems. What he finally achieved was a course of study as close to sociology as was possible in that day. The point of view taught him, however, was a cautious one. Strikes and organized labor were frowned upon more than trusts and monopolies. There was an instinctive defense of wealth and capital in this venerable university. The young Du Bois progressed far enough to write his master's thesis on the suppression of the slave trade, but it was not until years later, as a teacher, that he tied economics and politics together and saw "the fundamental influence of man's efforts to earn a living upon all his other efforts." The sociological approach to the study of man still lay ahead of him.

Meanwhile he relaxed for awhile in Europe. Shaking off the aggressive habits acquired in white America, he absorbed the quaintness and beauty of his surroundings. Lightheartedly he described Holland as "an extremely neat and well-ordered mud-puddle, situated at the confluence of the English, French, and German languages," while relishing the smell of clover and the glimpses of black and white cows. In more serious mood he appreciated the symphonies of Beethoven, the colors of Rembrandt and Titian, and the arch, stone, and steeple of cathedral architecture. Dr. Du Bois tells us that this period abroad profoundly modified his outlook: "I had been before, above all, in a hurry. I wanted a world, hard, smooth and swift, and had no time for rounded corners and ornament, for unhurried thought and slow contemplation," for the possibilities of beauty and elegance in life and manners.

Social Scientist

However, the respite from problems was short-lived. He soon lay down the cane and gloves of his German student days to do some more spadework in his chosen field. Learning through teaching, he finally grasped the concept of "a changing developing society rather than a fixed social structure," and with it, the greater complexity of race relations.

He decided to collect facts about Negroes through research. Behind this move was a youthful idealism: "I regarded it as axiomatic that the world wanted to learn the truth and if the truth was sought with even approximate accuracy and painstaking devotion, the world would gladly support the effort." His subsequent studies revealed the Negro group as a symptom and not a cause, as a part of a long historical development and not an isolated, static phenomenon in American society. At last he felt equipped to join together all the pieces of his knowledge into an over-all picture. He still saw modern history centered in imperialism, but by 1910 its glories no longer obscured its evils: "the domination of white Europe over black Africa and yellow Asia, through political power built on the economic control of labor, income and ideas." In America this industrial imperialism had involved "the expulsion of black men from American democracy, their subjection to caste control and wage slavery." Race prejudice was merely the convenient tool, the rationalization of economic gain.

He remained hard-hitting with his facts and definite in his point of view, even when he lost his illusions about the warm reception his research would be accorded, and discovered that pressure had been put on Atlanta University to get rid of him as "dangerous." But more and more he found it distasteful to be a detached scientist while Negroes were murdered and starved. Understanding the reasons for racial tensions as he never had before, he felt that he was prepared to become an informed "master of propaganda." "Stepping, therefore, in 1910, out of my ivory tower of statistics and investigation, I sought with bare hands to lift the earth."

By this time, caste segregation had acquired a more deadly aspect in his eyes. At the end of the nineteenth century the young intellectual had believed that the Negro race could and would make a unique contribution to civilization. Fifteen years later he felt that the main heritage Negroes shared was the negative social heritage of oppression, that there was no clear and fair opportunity for their competitive achievement beside white people. The adventure of race dissipated before the dangers of race. While a scientific definition of race became impossible, its "absurd assumptions" remained to ruin men's lives by a white "monopoly of economic and physical power, legal enactment and intellectual training." The psychological effect of caste was paralyzing to its victims. They felt entombed, imprisoned behind "some thick sheet of invisible but horribly tangible plate glass." Agitated by such thoughts, Dr. Du Bois found it necessary continually to haul his soul back and say to it, "All white folk are not scoundrels nor murderers. They are, even as I am, painfully human."

Direct Actionist

Both Negroes and whites must be saved from the tragic consequences of their "spiritual provincialism" about race. In this mood Dr. Du Bois took up the cudgels against the leadership of Booker T. Washington. As early as 1903, soon after the publication of Washington's autobiography, he had articulated the organized opposition of young Negro intellectuals, for the most part educated in the North. (It is worth speculating whether Washington, if Du Bois' chapter on him in *Souls of Black Folk* had antedated his own autobiography, would have been goaded into an answer to his critics after all.) In 1905 he had followed up his divergence by starting the Niagara Movement with its "aggressive action" program. From 1910 on he was in a position through the medium of *The Crisis* and the N.A.A.C.P. to direct the full battery of his convictions against the enemy. By 1940, with the advantage of perspective, he was able to summarize his disagreements without any softening of heart.

Some credit he was willing to assign to Booker T. Washington. His emphasis on industrial education and efficiency had encouraged the accumulation of Negro land, property, and income, and had made the South realize the Negro as a "possible man." Dr. Du Bois even went so far as to admit that Washington's belief in Negro leadership founded on wealth and economic status was "not absolutely contradictory" with his own belief in leadership springing from knowledge, character, and the higher education of a "Talented Tenth." In fact, he pointed out, Booker T. Washington sent his own children to college.

But the stumbling block between them was caste. Washington's idea of better understanding between white and black depended on it. During the post-Reconstruction reaction against Negroes and the subsequent curtailment of their civil rights, he excused white policy by referring to "short-comings" and putting the "chief onus" of the situation back on Negroes themselves. In line with this approach, he recommended "acquiescence or at least no open agitation." Consequently, Du Bois felt justified in charging, after Washington's death in 1915, that "we must lay on the soul of this man a heavy responsibility for the consummation of Negro disfranchisement, the decline of the Negro college and public school, and the firmer establishment of color caste in this land."

Du Bois explains Washington's caution partially on the grounds of his poor insight. It was not that he advocated "a deliberate and planned segregation" of Negroes by a caste system, but that he advised submission to the inevitable. By so doing, they might gradually elicit such sympathy and sense of justice from the powerful majority as to further the interests of both groups simultaneously. What Washington failed to take into account was the skepticism of the dominant group about mutual interests, and the apathy of the weaker group if it ceased to resist and thus grew to accept oppression as normal.

As an economic realist, however, Dr. Du Bois pushes his analysis much further. Behind everything else in Washington's philosophy he detects the opportunism: "that Mr. Washington's large financial responsibilities have made him dependent on the rich charitable public and that, for this reason, he has for years been compelled to tell, not the whole truth, but that part of it which certain powerful interests in America wish to appear as the truth." It was not just a question of his appeasing the South. To many white Northerners, capitalists, and employers the Negro problem had changed into a matter of business instead of philanthropy. The mass of black workers in the South could be used to restrain the demands of organizing white labor. Washington's program came "as a godsend" to them. Its individualism within careful racial lines forestalled any group solidarity with white workers, sanctioned the virtues of thrift, investment, and profit, and allowed for the gradual evolution of a Negro capitalist class which would in turn exploit labor.

It was quite natural, then, that these practical business men would be more than anxious to support the founder of Tuskegee. As he was feted at home and abroad by important people, as he received larger and larger sums of money, he acquired political power. The "Tuskegee Machine" operated smoothly and tolerated no freedom of expression among Negroes. Because of its "safe line," it was consulted by governors and congressmen, scholars and industrialists. For a period of years, Washington became "the political referee in all Federal appointments." Matters reached such a pass that his recommendation was essential to all fund-raising Negro institutions, and his "opposition was fatal" to promising careers.

Such conduct brought out all the rebel in Du Bois. He was now so positive that race prejudice was perpetuated by economic gain more than simple ignorance and ill will that he espoused forceful methods of handling it. Boycotts, protest parades, lobbying, lawsuits, and lynching investigations became commonplaces in his thinking. He looked at the world about him and did not find it good. More and more false idealism annoyed him. Although he had resigned from the Socialist party in order to be able to vote for Woodrow Wilson, he was sadly disillusioned. Under Wilson's administration came many anti-Negro bills, segregating colored Federal employees, advocating "Jim Crow" cars in the District of Columbia, forbidding intermarriage, and excluding Negroes from commissions in the Army and Navy. Black Haiti was seized in 1915. In the same year *The Birth of a Nation* was shown widely in movie theatres while the lynching rate increased. This is also the year of Washington's death and Du Bois' renewed attack against the stronghold of industrial imperialism.

World War I caught him in conflict. Still convinced that rival imperialisms were the cause of war, he was equally certain that German militarism, as he had seen it, should be checked. Hoping that the United States might fight for colored as well as white democracy, and not for war investments, he finally cast his hat into the ring and urged Negroes to forget their special grievances for the sake of the larger issue. Soon, however, the N.A.A.C.P. found itself fighting segregation in the army, and losing, only to be forced into the unpleasant position of having to advocate segregation in the form of an officers' training camp for Negroes. "The War Department squirmed. We had to fight even to be segregated." After all that, no rank above captain was allowed. But more important than the spread of injustice and violence at home was Du Bois' realization of the horror of war itself, and "its wide impotence as a method of social reform" for the world.

The author remarks in 1940, before Pearl Harbor, "I am less sure now than then of the soundness" of supporting World War I. He thinks that a German victory might not have turned out worse than the Allied victory, that perhaps the "passive resistance" of all Negroes might have been better than their participation. We are left to wonder at the close of his autobiography whether he was equally puzzled later about the correct attitude towards World War II.

Increasingly in the postwar period he has occasion to brood over the paradox of the average white American. As a Christian one can believe in peace, goodwill, and the simple life, as a gentleman in justice, exclusive wealth, and the police, as an American in power and patriotism, and as a white man in exploitation, empire, and war. It still remains possible for a man to be all these things, keep his sense of integrity, and "openly refuse to treat as a fellow human being any person who has Negro ancestry."

The author recalls the continuous changes in proof about Negro inferiority, the progressive rationalizations gleaned from pseudo science. While his early geography books described Indians, Negroes, and Chinese by their most uncivilized representatives and whites by their most distinguished looking philanthropists. Harvard used brain weight, brain capacity, and the cephalic index to support the theory of "lower" races. In his graduate days emphasis shifted from physiology to culture, and found the Negro race wanting in cultural history. When World War I brought the popular psychological tests, and Negro intelligence was discredited once more, Du Bois was impervious to a science which bowed down to caste. He notes that Odum, McDougall, and Brigham "eventually turn somersaults from absolute scientific proof of Negro inferiority to repudiation of the limited and questionable application of any test which pretended to measure innate human intelligence." He welcomes this change while doubting if it will have influence on popular prejudice already entrenched. His skepticism grows with age.

For Dr. Du Bois feels that even if the typical white American is told by the newest scientific research that dark Americans are not congenitally stupid or primitive and that statistics no longer favor the stereotype of rape and degeneracy, he will find some loophole for prejudice as long as his income is fattened thereby. For this reason, Du Bois considers the case of Negroes to rest in their own hands for settlement.

Social Planner

As Du Bois, the direct actionist, turns social planner he recommends mass solidarity as a prerequisite of Negro advancement. In a society organized against them, colored people cannot afford to indulge in color snobbery and rival class interests within their race boundaries. Granting that Negroes are not a homogeneous group, that instead of "one undifferentiated low-class mass" they contain an educated upper class group above the average of the whites, Du Bois still maintains that it is incumbent on Negro leaders to throw their lot in with the masses. Pragmatically, how can Negroes expect to set up a vertical class structure, from low to high, parallel with the whites? The white upper class holds its status by wealth and political power, not by a "superior" culture. Upper class Negroes "do not have the economic or political power, the ownership of machines and materials, the power to direct the processes of industry, the monopoly of capital and credit" to duplicate that success. Their best bet lies in dropping any false illusions of separate class interests in favor of cooperation towards racial gains.

Negro workers must have their eyes opened on this score, also. No panaceas like joining the Communist party should mislead them. American communism has ignored the fact of race, "cutting square across the economic layers" until white and black workers are further apart than white workers and capitalists. Du Bois grants that the Communist party in the United States had managed to minimize the color bar within its narrow confines, but maintains that this policy frightened off many white workers. At the same time, the Jim Crow practices of the large trade-union organizations like the A. F. of L., and sometimes the C. I. O., have constituted a dead-end street for black workers. Thus they must face the necessity of some sort of union organization of their own, with the backing of all groups of Negroes.

In his advancing years Dr. Du Bois did not hesitate to heap his scorn on the heads of bright college students who championed "the new scientific argument that there was no such thing as race." Certainly it existed, practically speaking, and no Aladdin's lamp was going to snuff it out quickly. Instead of minimizing it, he urged expanding it even beyond the borders of America. Genuine pan-African solidarity could make a virtue out of necessity. When critics charged that any such world movement of Negroes would repeat the present pattern by arousing race prejudice against the whites, he replied simply, "So long as we were fighting a color line, we must strive by color organization." Why brand a strategy mapped out for self-defense and survival as chauvinism? He interpreted it as a struggle for status of all Negroes everywhere, which did not involve the engendering of hate and the encouragement of further segregation but only the adaptation to conditions not of their own choosing.

Once they are imbued with a spirit of unity, what specific steps can Negroes in the United States take to improve their lot? This is the problem around which the thoughts of the older Du Bois revolve. He no longer anticipates substantial help from white people. He regards any geographical flight of Negroes as impractical, including the "grandiose and bombastic" Back-to-Africa movement of Marcus Garvey, inner migrations to Canada, the North, or the West, and the formation of a forty-ninth state. "Negroes have no Zion," no place, least of all Africa, where they can go without fear of exploitation. They must stand their ground in their native country, while not counting on biological amalgamation with the white group. The cultural escape out of caste of the talented Negroes remains an individualistic solution. Gradual acculturation of the masses into American society, so normal in the case of foreign-born groups, is blocked by color-caste. The only alternative left, according to Du Bois, is the organized strength of Negro consumers.

The author devotes generous space to his final plan of a separate Negro economy. He envisions an immediate program to raise the standard of living and make life bearable within caste. Negroes as consumers approach economic equality more closely than as producers. They spend one hundred and fifty million dollars monthly. By correlating production and consumption into a large cooperative movement, by taking over retail distribution, by eliminating unemployment, profit, and advertising, by socializing professional services and putting leaders on salaries, by resettlement and housing projects on a large scale, Negroes could succeed in building up an efficient cooperative commonwealth in the midst of the surrounding American economy. Such a system could only approximate independence. For example, Negroes must continue to buy from whites as long as natural resources are monopolized. Yet they could command better terms if they were in a position to buy in large quantities for cash. Gradually they could wrest from an inhospitable environment a good measure of economic stability.

Once more, when his Negro opponents shouted "segregation," Du Bois pointed to the existing segregation foisted on a majority of Negro Americans in schools, churches, the professions, housing, hotels, and restaurants, and recommended a wiser course of planned self-segregation. He insisted that his solution would be a means to an end, a method of self-preservation which did not exclude the continued agitation for equal rights but which gave Negroes a foothold until a better day.

To Dr. Du Bois there is a vast distinction between such organized use of power and sheer violence. As an old man he discounts violence in any form. In the first place, no direct assault by Negroes against white civilization could ever be successful when they are in the minority. In the second place, Du Bois is opposed to it in theory: "I do not believe in the dogma of inevitable revolution in order to right economic wrong." Poverty and injustice can only be abolished by reason and discipline, and not by bloodshed.

At the same time Du Bois defended many aspects of the Russian revolution. He visited Russia in 1928 and received a basic change in his "mental outlook." While he was sensitive to the failures of the Bolsheviks, he was also aware of their handicaps, the wars of intervention, and famines, which did not prevent them from facing frankly "a set of problems which no nation at the time was willing to face." In the treatment of the ragged waifs, in the new factories and art galleries, in the demonstrations of the Red Square he discovered "an unforgettable spirit upon the land" which stirred him strangely. The author does not condone the violence in this great social upheaval, but "we must admit that nothing that Russia has done in war and mass murder exceeds what has been done and is being done by the rest of the civilized world."

He was especially drawn to the theory of the new Russia. "It made the assumption, long disputed, that, out of the down-trodden mass of people, ability and character, sufficient to do this task effectively, could and would be found. I believed this dictum passionately. It was, in fact, the foundation stone of my fight for black folk; it explained me." Linked with this shared faith in the potentialities of the masses went his enthusiasm for Marxist doctrine. Karl Marx, one of the greatest thinkers, had put his finger on the truth when he taught that "the way in which men earn their living" determines the development of civilization. "And this conviction I had to express or spiritually die."

On the one hand, Du Bois recognized the universal tenets of Marxism, on the other hand, he felt that they could aid Negroes in the United States only if they were adapted to meet such special conditions as race prejudice. While American communists seemed too inflexible on this score, the N.A.A.C.P. seemed unrealistic about economic reform. In proportion as he felt that economic interpretations of history and economic weapons of combat overshadowed political factors, Du Bois grew away from the N.A.A.C.P., with its militancy expended in legal and political battles, and towards the development of his idea for a separate Negro economy. He did not feel too hopeless about its practical possibilities for the simple reason that he judged capitalism to be dissolving anyway. There is "impending change" in the air. Because the whole world faces new economic organization, Negroes do not need to feel too fearful of the huge industrial machine in the United States. Instead, they should take advantage of the inexorable social movements of history by shaping their own economic reconstruction. In this way they would also contribute towards ultimate world socialism, "common ownership and control of the means of production and equality of income."

Psychological Realist

The sense of urgency which Du Bois feels about Negro initiative springs from his matured opinions about the nature of prejudice. With all the wisdom of his seventy years of learning, he accompanies his economic imperatives to colored people with a new psychological slant on white people. No longer can be regard prejudice as a result of ill will, ignorance, or cupidity. Rather, it is rooted in the irrational nature of man, buried in his unconscious, perpetuated by the folkways and mores of a whole culture. It is "the result of inherited customs and of those irrational and partly subconscious actions of men which control so large a proportion of their deeds." Behind the economic exploitation lay "a racial folklore grounded on centuries of instinct, habit and thought and implemented by the conditioned reflex of visible color."

Du Bois concludes that new discoveries of "these vague and uncharted lands" of human consciousness call for new cures. Although his study of psychology under William James had predated the Freudian era, it had prepared him for it. He grasps the intricate motivation of the individual buttressed by "age-long complexes" of the group. The white man is, to a certain extent, a blind mechanism within his own culture patterns. He can be won to a creative view of race not by moral appeals and cold arguments, but by "planned and scientific propaganda" over a long period of re-education. Only through reconditioning his behavior in light of his unconscious hates and fears can he be freed of his compulsions to exploit his fellow man.

Du Bois, the realist, does not underestimate the time it will take for white emancipation. To be enmeshed in one's own limitations without realizing it is the most subtle form of tyranny. One victimizes, and is yet the victim. Meanwhile, Negroes must live while whites grope towards more self-knowledge. They must entrench themselves for a long siege against color-caste by such practical measures as he has formulated.

Du Bois is not too sanguine of the outcome. At the end of his busy life he seems to be an ameliorist rather than a pessimist about the future of race relations, but only by grace of inner discipline. He is too sensitively organized to avoid a great deal of vicarious suffering. In spite of his realistic interpretations he is a romantic at heart. In his people he sees "the spirit that knows Beauty, that has music in its soul and the color of sunsets in its head kerchiefs; that can dance on a flaming world and make the world dance, too." Every damage done to it is a damage against him. His aesthetic sense is pleased more by the varied colors of "bronze, mahogany, coffee and gold" than by "pink, gray, and marble," by the litheness of movement of Negroes compared to "Anglo-Saxon stalking." In cultural values his group ranks high with its cultivation of forgiveness and humor, of patience and unselfishness. Yet, for no sensible rhyme or reason, these warmhearted, beauty-loving people are the outcastes of their native country. To view the daily waste of human potentiality and yet to keep his sights ever forward require that effort of will and intelligence which would be impossible for a man of lesser stature.

So far does Du Bois combat his own despair that he refuses to settle for mere materialistic gain. It means a lot to him that he has "lived completely, testing every normal appetite," that he has "seen the face of beauty from the Grand Canyon to the Great Wall of China." Balancing his stress on economic welfare is his personal creed that "regardless of income, work worth while which one wants to do as compared with highly paid drudgery is exactly the difference between heaven and hell." Enough idealism has survived the crucible of racial experience to prompt his closing thought that economic justice and world peace will always remain chimeras without "discipline of soul and sacrifice of comfort." Thus this advocate of Marxism interprets it in its widest aspects and envisions a changing society in which "Negroes must live and eat and strive, and still hold unfaltering commerce with the stars." By the title of his book, the author seems to suggest that only in so far as Negroes accomplish this Herculean feat can they survive to watch "the dusk of dawn."

In reaching an ameliorist position, Du Bois has worked through many of the paradoxes which characterize the race question. Yet the conflicting views and the varied programs of his life and thought are held in equilibrium within his mellowed philosophy by one constant: whites are the sinners, Negroes are the sinned against. Even his psychological insight into the causes of white behavior does not alter his moral judgment. His accommodation to existing conditions has been made only under protest. Whatever apparent compromises he may have tendered as ways of meeting discrimination, he has never compromised on the basic issue that race prejudice is a crime.

As a thinker he has always believed in change. He points out that the program of 1910 is not appropriate for 1950, that "no idea is perfect and forever valid." A society in flux must be watched carefully and handled according to its symptoms of disorder. But underneath all the painstaking social documentation runs a deep personal conviction about the conditions for cure. To him, human beings are worthy of being treated as human beings. With all the forthrightness of a twentieth-century Douglass he condemns the white exploiters who have forced a "narrowed goal" upon colored Americans, and guarantees no health in the body politic until the devil is cast out. Like Douglass, he does not rely upon religious incantation to complete this process, but upon common sense, initiative, and the latest scientific techniques.

Let Me Live

ANGELO HERNDON

IN terms of international fame, none of our authors could compete with Angelo Herndon. Between 1932 and 1937 his case became a *cause célèbre* holding symbolic importance far beyond the borders of the state which charged him with insurrection. As his trial shuttled back and forth between the Georgia courts and the United States Supreme Court, as he was released on bail or placed back in prison again, all sorts of people watched the fluctuations of his fate and speculated about the shadow of the chain gang hovering over his head. The drama of the situation was increased by their knowledge that he had two counts against him, that by being both a Negro and a communist he had invoked the combined racial and political antipathies of the South.

His autobiography sustains this mood of suspense. Published in 1937 when the outcome of the last appeal is still uncertain, *Let Me Live* carries out its title by a plea to tip the scales of justice in the right direction. It becomes a tract for the rights of man against an oppressive society until every reader wonders whether the uneven struggle is doomed to futility or redolent of things to come.

That the book is dated is part of its particular strength. Although the informed reader knows that Angelo Herndon was freed shortly after his book was finished, and that today, in his middle thirties, he is no longer a Communist party member, this does not detract from the validity of his autobiographical impressions ten years ago. The author does not aspire to the heights of wisdom of threescore years and ten, from which vantage point Du Bois reviews the passing parade. Instead he throws all the resources of his thought and emotion into one faith, one course of action, one cause. Eliminating all extraneous material, the youthful writer gives us a detailed case study of the makings of a Negro Communist. What unmade him constitutes another chapter in his autobiography which Herndon may well write some day, but cannot impinge on the simplicity and sincerity of the present autobiography nor decrease its historical importance.

Those students of the American scene who regard poverty as the breeding ground of radical doctrine might take Herndon's life as a case in point. Born in 1913 in Wyoming, Ohio, one of several children, the boy was early introduced to the meaning of real want. As a miner his father was overworked, undernourished, and broken before his time, dying of miner's pneumonia. The small boy suffered from this death and the death of a brother in the same year, but, still earlier when he was six, had endured a severe and protracted illness himself. At that time he learned that medicine is a luxury the poor can ill afford. "I was not unaware of what was happening. Children of the very poor become conscious of the problems of their parents long before they should." No wonder that the sick child regarded his great grandmother of Indian slave heritage, who turned up with her small savings and her quiet efficiency to save the family from its "tragic plight," as a "marvelous and magnificent creature." Most of the time, however, miracles did not intervene while "we were all walking in a blind alley, resigned to our fate," and barely surviving physically. "Absurdly young as I was, I already began to feel a share of the general responsibility," to look at the world "with new and troubled eyes."

At nine he delivered groceries. When his mother was widowed and working long hours as a servant to support the children, Angelo worried about finding a job to help out until he became morose. At thirteen, with a brother three years older, he bummed his way on freight trains to Lexington, Kentucky, where they found work as coal loaders in mines with no legally specified age limit. Negro miners were segregated, given the poorest food and the hardest work, cheated on their pay checks, and indebted by loan sharks and credit stores. Along with the bad safety conditions they shared with white workers they had the special handicap of job limitation. Better-paying jobs such as check weighmen, steel-sharpeners, and electricians were not available to Negroes. Only once did Angelo complain of unfairness, and when the foreman shouted obscenities at him and suggested that he wouldn't receive better treatment elsewhere he felt the uselessness of protest. "I decided that I could do nothing about it."

At fourteen he was fooled by a labor agent in Birmingham, Alabama. On the promise of $40 a month and board, he consented to go in a truck to an unknown destination. When it turned out to be a work camp, under guard, with no pay, to construct a dam, he escaped by swimming the river at night. Yet his next job of construction work for the Goodyear Rubber Company offered little improvement. Heavy work, bad food, and army discipline broke his spirit. When the men were not paid according to agreement, they rushed the guards, but were met with clubs, black jacks, and drawn guns. "A burden of weariness" settled on the young worker prematurely. "I began to be overwhelmed with the painful certainty that all the world was a prison and that man was born to suffer, suffer endlessly from the day of his birth to the day when they return him to the earth." Back in the mines again, he worked fourteen hours a day instead of the legal eight hours. This confirmed his drift towards pessimism. "I became a veteran in endurance and in suffering. The world looked evil to me. As for myself, I felt like a leaf in the wind, without a will to guide my own destiny."

Yet a spark of vitality flickered. Something prevented his sinking to the low level of his fellow workers who were apathetic to their own degradation. "The life I led might have brutalized me, were it not for the terrific resistance I offered against the influence of my environment." Sharing the common lot, he stood apart from the others in his ability for critical evaluation.

The root of his apartness lay in his loyalty to family training. He remembered that he had been "the family's choice" for the honor of an education. His work-worn father had shown "touching solicitude" for his progress and had encouraged him to write his name by imitation thirty or forty times a day before starting school. His mother worked Sundays and holidays to keep him in the public school. While his parents could barely read and write themselves, it was the familiar story of projected ambition. The young Angelo rose to meet their expectations by a quick response to learning. With the help of a sympathetic Negro teacher he overcame his shyness in school and was well launched on his studies when poverty abruptly cut them short.

From his parents also had come religious influence. They tried to alleviate their daily trials by the consolation of faith. Angelo's father was a devoted church member, and bore the hardships of his job with meekness. His mother took tender care of him during his long illness, prayed, and told him stories of Jesus. When the boy ran headlong into the race prejudice of white boys whom he beat at marbles and was as confused by their epithets as by their stones, his mother counseled humility. "As I listened to her, a deep sense of guilt came over me. To be sure, I must be a sinner too, and the fact that the white boys called me 'nigger' must have been the will of God. Already I felt as if by this act alone, by being humiliated in spirit and bruised in body, that I was expiating for the pride and the vanity which my mother charged against our race." The inevitable next step was conversion and baptism. Given the picture of the Day of Wrath, he was made responsible for his own sins. At the same time he was taught to believe in the essential good of man. As a result, his tendency during the dark days of his job experience was to rationalize away the evils of his immediate environment before his consciousness of his own imperfections and his vague hopes in the larger world outside.

It took the realities of "Jim Crowism" to sting him to action and to discard his Christian teachings. Daring to fight a foreman who hated Negroes and forced them to work overtime without pay and to inform the superintendent that his partner was electrocuted as a result of this foreman's negligence, Angelo Herndon learned that he had to stand up for his rights. When a white conductor aroused a sleeping Negro, accused him of shamming in order to escape paying his fare, and beat him severely, the fifteen-year-old spectator was horrified that the other Negroes accepted the act without protest. Daily observation piled on to his growing information about lynchings to convince him that the Christianity of his parents was inadequate to the situation Negroes faced. "The spirit of rebellion" churned inside until "my thoughts streamed into one mighty torrent of bitterness and hatred toward white men and their cruelty." He turned from the ideal of forgiveness with contempt and saw the example of Christ, the Saviour, "as a trap and as a distraction" from the true state of affairs. A new course of conduct appealed to him: "my own moral code now was to return two blows for every blow I got, to take two eyes for one taken from me, to defend my rights as an upstanding man, to defend the elementary dignity of the human being in me against all aggressors." All that was needed to execute it was will power.

At sixteen, however, he was still confused about the ways and means of winning rights for himself and other Negroes. He entertained many "ridiculous ideas" such as becoming a detective for his "role of deliverer," or organizing a secret armed society against the Ku Klux Klan. Not only was his aggression unchannelized, but it was thwarted by depression unemployment. Always he had preferred the hardest work to forced idleness and futile efforts to find work. "I look back with horror at the anguish, the suspense and the humiliation which accompanied my job-hunting." Depression conditions magnified this unpleasantness until the young Negro was in an emotional turmoil of frustration and bitterness within the confines of the urban South.

By June, 1930, it is safe to conclude that he was ripe for the revelations of communism. A chance handbill of the "unemployment council" drew him to a joint meeting of Negro and white workers and showed him "that not all white people were enemies and exploiters of the Negro people" but only the wealthy and powerful whites. The war he had anticipated, complete with long sword, gold tassels, and bands, now took on the form of a class struggle against oppression. So moved was he by the talk of white and black workers keeping together in a common cause that he wasted little sorrow over the lost vision of himself as a returning hero.

At one stroke he had discovered a program and a philosophy. Just as the political activity of the party provided an outlet for his resentment of injustice, so did the theory of Marxism plant other values in the vacuum left by Christianity and nourish his long-starved desire to learn. The old fears and regrets dropped off. "I felt like a man from Mars entering into a new world." In the beginning much of the instruction was difficult for his untrained mind to grasp, yet each meeting of the unemployed council "became a classroom" from which he garnered "enlightenment and culture." Eagerly he read about the lives and ideas of Marx and Engels, Lenin and Stalin, and established a contact point with his own experience. In place of the innocence and illusions of religion, "I had found something more satisfying, a realistic recognition of the world and the rational plan of scientific socialism with which to create order and harmony out of the human chaos." With every question set at rest, young Angelo entered unreservedly into this fresh way of life. "Like a man who had gone through some terrible sickness of the soul I miraculously became whole again."

So certain was he that his feet were now set on the right path that no amount of dissuasion could affect him. Warned that communists were foreigners and reds who were misleading and exploiting Negroes for selfish purposes, Angelo Herndon remembered the evidence of his own senses: their equal treatment of Negroes without condescension or patronage, their tireless effort to improve conditions of the unemployed, their courageous resistance to police and employer brutality. The net result was that the seventeen-year-old convert joined the Communist party and became a union organizer in and around Atlanta.

Although he now entered into a period of mistreatment which exceeded his past record, he no longer felt depressed by the evil of the world. Every time he talked to the miners about organizing and was arrested on the trumped-up charge of vagrancy he saw a pattern and a purpose in his continued effort. "Every time I went to jail, every time I was brutally tortured and given the third degree, I felt myself bound closer and closer to the communist movement." When he was placed on the black list of the mining companies, when he was in danger of a lynch mob for speaking to share croppers, when he was locked up with the insane and the degenerate, he sensed a kinship with the early Christian martyrs. He could not regard his life as wasted as long as he believed that there were thousands like him, "fighting resolutely for a new world order."

These thousands were his class brothers, not his color brothers. Angelo Herndon now recognized a closer tie to white workers than to "self-appointed" Negro leaders like Du Bois who "lined up on the side of the capitalist class" and who only "pretend to fight for Negro rights." To the young communist, the whole concept of separate Negro rights seemed false. What stimulated him most was the idea that he was enlisted in the struggle of the common man everywhere.

He needed all his resources of courage and faith for the coming events. In the backwash of the depression the lines of cleavage between "the haves and have nots" sharpened. By 1932 Atlanta was one of the principal cities for the Fascist order of Black Shirts as well as for the Ku Klux Klan in full regalia. "A reign of terror against all Negroes was begun by the city authorities at the instigation of the coal and steel magnates." Seventy Negroes were killed in the course of a month, and many more, including our union organizer, who was well known to the police, were seriously injured. 1932 was the year of communist campaigning for Foster as President and Ford as Vice-president, and the enforcement of the high poll tax by the state of Georgia to disqualify radical voters. It was also the year of the relief crisis which precipitated Herndon's personal crisis.

The author carefully reconstructs the background of events which led to his fateful arrest. No illegal acts, no violence occurred on the part of the workers. When officials stated that they must drop twenty-three thousand families from the unemployment relief rolls because of shortage of funds, they agreed to let those in need present their grievances in person. The response alarmed the city. One thousand colored and white workers—the largest gathering of its kind ever to have taken place in the South—met at the court house in a peaceful and orderly demonstration. "In vain the police tried to provoke us,—we maintained an iron discipline." For Angelo Herndon's part in distributing leaflets and encouraging the unemployed in such demands as a minimum of $4.00 weekly, he was arrested, cross-examined, held eleven days incommunicado in spite of a habeas corpus writ for his release, and finally indicted for insurrection.

In their haste, the authorities indicted him on July 22 for attempting to incite to insurrection on July 16, even though he had already been almost three weeks in jail. "And what was the law upon which the indictment was based? It was the anti-slave insurrection law of 1861 which the State Legislature of Georgia had passed to crush all slave rebellions." It provided the death penalty for circulating any paper for purpose of exciting revolt or resistance among slaves, Negroes, or "free persons of color." Although Herndon surmised that the charge against him was incidental to the real purpose of crushing the new labor and share-cropper organizations which threatened the status quo of the South, this insight did not whisk him away from the reality of Fulton Tower where he awaited his trial in the cell-company of confessed murderers and robbers. He knew that, by fair means or foul, the machinery of the state had been set in motion to crush him.

Six months later, as his trial started, the defendant followed the proceedings closely and studied the manner in which the case was stacked against him. Out of his new fund of realism he sized up the prosecutor: "In his august person he represented the majesty of the law, the might of the National Guard, and the sanctity of the Methodist Church." When this man concluded that the issue was not between the State and its unemployed citizens, but between the State and Communism, that the trial was not merely of Herndon but "of Lenin, Stalin, Trotsky and Kerensky, and every white person who believes that black and white should unite for the purpose of setting up a nigger Soviet Republic in the Black Belt," the prisoner knew that reason would be hard put to withstand such emotionalism.

He noted the judge and the jury nodding heads in agreement. He observed the presence in the court room of Atlanta's best citizens, "social registrites" whose curiosity had prompted them to turn out for this "Roman holiday." The two principal witnesses against him seemed to be the assistant prosecutor and the chief jailer, as if his crime had been committed after his arrest. Taken together, these farcical elements added up to tragedy: "This was one of the worst vaudeville shows I had ever seen, and yet the most interesting to me, for this particular vaudeville show happened to hold my life in the balance."

Admiring the technique and spirit of his Negro attorney, Herndon sensed that even he had little hope for winning an acquittal. Obviously he was making as many exceptions as possible with an appeal to the higher courts in mind. He argued that the anti-insurrection law was unconstitutional, that the indictment was too vague, that Negroes were excluded from jury service, and that his client could not possibly receive a fair trial because of the obvious race prejudice throughout. But his audience was impervious to cold logic. It preferred the frenzied language of the prosecutor, sprinkled with Biblical references: "blood and piety, these are the two principal ingredients of boasted Southern civilization." As the time drew near for the verdict, the young defendant fortified himself with a "strange sort of optimism" which consisted in eliminating suspense and anxiety by expecting the worst. When the verdict was guilty, he saw the hollow mockery of the recommendation for mercy. Eighteen to twenty years on the chain gang could only mean a living death.

In light of the fact that five years of his young manhood were consumed by this case, it is not surprising that the author devotes almost half of his autobiography to the details of his arrest, trials, prison terms, and releases on bail, and that he includes transcripts of decisions by the various courts. But he does not allow his account to become either a propaganda sheet or a dry historical document. Through his genuine troubles and his keen perceptions, the reader is alerted constantly to the human equation.

Even the technicalities of his case make considerable sense to the layman who is shown the flesh-and-blood issue beneath the legal terminology. It is not hard to imagine the feelings of the prisoner as the courts disagree on everything except his claim to freedom. The

State Supreme Court in 1934 decided that he was indicted not for distributing circulars "of a more or less harmless character," but for spreading "insurrectionary" communist doctrine, according to circumstantial evidence which is allowable to protect the state. It claimed further that the fact that the Communist party had been allowed to print the names of candidates on the official ballot did not legalize its dangerous doctrines. It insisted that it was enough for guilt if the offender hoped to foster an insurrection against the state at "any time" in the distant future, thus rejecting the whole emphasis of the original trial court on the direct evidence of "clear and present danger" at "any given time." Oblivious to the possibility that it was suggesting an unconstitutional restraint upon the historical liberties of free speech by extending indefinitely the time when revolt might occur, the State Supreme Court devoted most of its attention to analyzing the race radicalism in communist literature and its ultimate threat to the public safety. After the sound and fury subsided, Angelo Herndon saw that the practical upshot for himself remained unchanged.

The prospect looked even more bleak in 1935 when the United States Supreme Court decided, in spite of the disagreement of Justices Brandeis, Cardoza, and Stone, that the Herndon case was out of its jurisdiction. Back in prison, with forty days between him and the chain gang, Angelo Herndon felt justified in his cynicism about the due process of law. It was a dramatic rightabout-face when his lawyer, as a last resort, argued for a writ of habeas corpus before Judge Dorsey of the Georgia Court of Appeals on the grounds that the anti-insurrection law was unconstitutional, and when Judge Dorsey sustained this contention. One hour later the famous prisoner was out on bail, with the way open at last to a reconsideration of his case from a less biased starting point.

But Herndon's quota of suffering was not exhausted in the court rooms. In his description of prison life he reveals the lowest point of hardship. Trials came and went, but the misery of his daily existence was always with him. It was not alone the poor food, the unpleasant companionship and the rough treatment which bothered him. As a realist he was prepared for the unvarying round of card-playing, fist fights, and sex perversion among the men and for the taunts and curses of the guards.

But, as earlier in his mining days, he was prevented from merging with the others into their environment by his more acute sensitivities.

As a highly organized personality he had no callousness to fend off the insidious forms of torture. He was depressed by intangibles like atmosphere, by "an indefinable air of something slimy, monstrous and unnatural" hanging over the entire prison. At another time the darkness in his cell bothered him. Shut off not only from the light of the sun, but from artificial lighting, he felt buried alive, as if he were the chief actor in some melodrama. Sometimes noise jarred on his nerves. His hatred of "the whirring motors as they ceaselessly throbbed" was matched by his hatred of the men who deliberately operated the laundry above him night and day. His jailers were inventive. "Their cruelty was raw. It hurt like an open wound." If they could think of nothing else, they allowed water from the laundry or sewage from rotting pipes to drip down into the cells below.

Yet his worst enemy was time itself. Temperamentally unfit for idleness, he often feared for his sanity as the days dragged by. During one stretch of twenty-six months "every minute became an eternity of suffering." As the only recourse from disintegration "I painstakingly studied the weird patterns of mud and discoloration on the walls and ceilings." He had to fight against the feeling that he was living in a "hermetically sealed universe."

Surely this young communist has been exposed to sufficient punishment for his convictions to make him question their wisdom. Ironically enough, however, it is the very possession of these beliefs which offers him his only solace. He remembers that first court room where the "respectables" hoped for his sentence but where his "class brothers" feared for his fate. He is deeply moved by the ex-slave who speaks to him afterward of the joy he experienced in seeing a black man stand up for his rights in a white man's court: "Son, I feel as if a new day is coming for the Negro. We have waited for it long enough." The old man's "dreams of redemption" glow in the heart of the young radical as well. During the leaden hours of his captivity, Angelo Herndon recalls passages from Marx and Lenin and reminds himself that at least his mind is free to soar above the bestiality of his surroundings. "The moral duty of acting in the light of my Communist convictions" spurs the flagging spirit. When hope for freedom is running out like the last sands in an hourglass and he is shut in the death house with thirty-five condemned prisoners, he organizes classes in Negro history, trade unionism, and fascism. Instead of brooding over his fate, he marvels at the eagerness of these lost men to learn about the society they are leaving. To touch the essential decency of humanity in such circumstances challenges him to polish his values until they shine.

Purposefulness outweighs despair in proportion to his opportunities to serve his cause. When he is suddenly discovered by the working class and becomes "a symbol of its embattled aspirations," when he at last feels "warmly and intimately associated with hundreds of thousands of invisible well-wishers and friends," he is enabled to transform his "little hideous world" behind steel bars by this "terrifying but beautiful feeling." It alleviates his pain to realize that a wide public compares his case to the Dreyfus affair in France and the Sacco-Vanzetti scandal in Boston, and reads in all of them "a conflict between reaction and free ideas." But the greatest triumph comes when his supporters effect his release on bail. Faced with the necessity of raising $15,000 in twenty-three days, a cross-section of the public rallies to the crisis. Liberals, intellectuals, business men, religious and professional people contribute large and small sums until the goal is achieved.

Herndon's journey by train from the Atlanta prison to New York is somewhat in the nature of a triumphal procession, with many dramatic high lights. There is rumor of a plot to lynch him en route. Theodore Dreiser telephones Governor Talmadge and asks for police protection. At every stopping point Herndon is greeted by crowds of sympathizers. The demonstrations are "spontaneous and moving."

To be in touch with nature again seems a rare privilege to the released man. Everything takes on symbolic meaning. As he walks out of Fulton Tower he notices the magnolia trees in the quiet summer breeze: "And there they were standing now, the same as I first saw them, but even fresher and greener. A great joy welled up in me. I, too, had struggled hard and had succeeded in keeping my spirit fresh and green and full of undying hope." On the train he is stirred by the sight of the sun as it rises over the horizon. He drinks in the loveliness of the landscape: "The fields were green and golden with ripening crops and glistened with dew in the soft morning light. I felt tired, very tired in spirit. But the purity and the peace in nature flowed into me like healing balm."

But above and beyond his relation to nature is his relation to his fellow man. There can be little doubt that this is the deepest source of his healing and of his strength. Originally he is frightened at the thought of readjustment to life outside of prison: "I was gripped by an unreasonable desire to hide myself somewhere in a cell far more secret than the one in which I had spent almost two and a half years of my life." Yet once again symbolic interpretation of his place in society helps him master his fear. As he travels northwards and feels the enthusiasm of the people, he realizes that his freedom is an expression of their "collective will." His tension eases and he achieves an "emotional release." The warm breath of all these experiences takes the chill off of the tedious days of waiting still ahead.

In his sense of dedication to the people Angelo Herndon has not avoided the race problem. His communist-inspired class-consciousness is merely a wider concept than race consciousness. Because he estimates that the majority of Negroes are held down into the lower class, he feels justified in considering their special problems, but only in the larger framework. Not their racial characteristics, but their low status concerns him. He has no patience with the niceties of argument about superior and inferior races. As a thorough-going environmentalist, he assumes that the only injustice is lack of opportunity and the only solution a struggle for power between oppressed and oppressors of all colors. He writes as a Negro, and shows no inclination to escape identification with Negroes, but he also writes as a man, as a human being who wishes to extend his aid to those bound to him by more profound ties than complexion.

At the opposite pole from Du Bois in background, training, and experience, Herndon shares with him a desire to move and act within a framework of social responsibility, and a courage to tell unpleasant truths if need be to the dominant white group. From the people, and of the people, Herndon himself would be the first to deny kinship with that intellectual and aristocratic Negro leader. Yet neither the Harvard-trained spokesman of an older generation nor the Southern worker of a younger generation minces his words about the sins of white monopoly and exploitation. While Du Bois hurls invective at imperialism and Herndon at fascism, both fear entrenched wealth, and seek for weapons against it. Disagreeing on ways and means, they cherish somewhat the same vision of a society of free men. Their egoism, their strong feeling of their own importance, is dissolved into this larger purpose. Their personal achievement is deliberately manipulated for social ends.

Angelo Herndon sees freedom as a strange word with many meanings. "But to me it means only one thing: a world which will not reduce men to the level of vile beasts, which will not drive them by need and a corrupt environment to rob and kill and deceive and commit every other sort of infamy." It is indicative of the burden of his experience that the concept should be thus phrased in negative terms. Certainly no matter what his detractors may say about the impractical nature of his communist theory, none of them can deny that his uncompromising protest against cruelty has a foundation in the hard facts of his life. However naïve his philosophy or his solutions to problems may appear, his firsthand acquaintance with many social abuses qualifies him for the rank of realist.

The Big Sea

LANGSTON HUGHES

OUT of the pages of *The Big Sea* steps a well-rounded personality. The author reveals to us so many moods and views, and alternates intimate pictures with objective judgments to such an extent that he creates a multidimensional effect. Behind the warm, human touches which enliven this autobiography, we can discern a mind ceaselessly at work. Obviously Langston Hughes is a poet—as the singing prose attests—but he also has the capacity for perspective on himself and on the strange world which provides him experience. Perhaps the measure of his talent lies in the aptness with which he could be called poet-sociologist.

There are tantalizing contrasts in Langston Hughes which add to the impression of depth. His naïveté is disarming. Only slightly older than Angelo Herndon, he has in common with him that simple directness and scorn of social polish we have come to associate with youth today. Yet he does not lack the intellectual sophistication of a Du Bois. As one of the most talented writers of the Negro Renaissance, Langston Hughes knows his way around in any group and can talk the language of the best of them—if he chooses to. In his autobiographical journey he is never too serious-minded to neglect humor, never so engrossed in his subjective reactions to forget the lightning shafts of satire. He participates while he observes, and observes while he participates. In love with the miracle of individuality, he responds to the needs of the group.

It is evident that his autobiography is not written as a memorial to his talent but as an expression of his broad view of the human enterprise. Although his medium is literature and not science, poetry and not politics, just as much as Du Bois or Herndon he is concerned with swelling the sum total of human wisdom. It is equally impossible for him to overlook or to wish to overlook the race question. Not in any sense a social reformer, as sensitive to aesthetic experience as Braithwaite or McKay, he nevertheless has a fund of social realism about race relations which brings him to heel constantly. This insight, added to his gift of sympathetic identification, clips the wings of any latent escapism. Langston Hughes writes as a Negro with much of the burning indignation against restrictions on all Negroes that we would expect of a latter-day Douglass.

The springboard of his book is pride in being a Negro. On one of his first pages he states categorically, "You see, unfortunately, I am not black." This is only one way of asserting his independence from false standards. If the darker one is, the more he is subjected to humiliation, then Langston Hughes would voluntarily pick the hardest lot and find the glory in it. His tendency is to start at the bottom and work up. He wants to reverse the popular notions and hold up the potentialities of the lowly and the despised.

This emphasis is part of a pattern. As he grows up, the young poet finds himself fighting increasingly for the right to be himself, unadorned and unashamed, fighting against sham, respectability, and snobbery in any form or shape. Thus it is appropriate that his account opens with a description of his state of mind at twenty-one, the traditional age for taking stock on the threshold of maturity. The picture we are given is of a young man starting out as a sailor towards unknown ports, and throwing his college textbooks into the deep sea. Academic education has depressed him. He has no desire for its laurels of prestige. He wants to know about real life, not literary life, to make a fresh start free of the sterile ideas of scholars. "It was like throwing a million bricks out of my heart" to get rid of those books. They symbolized the stale values that had been passed on secondhand. But now, freed of old associations, "I felt that nothing would ever happen to me again that I didn't want to happen."

From this dramatic beginning, the skilful craftsman, by use of the perennially effective flashback technique, reconstructs the events of his previous life which have forged his values. In family and community relationships, in work and travel experiences, we can see the developing personality. On the one hand is a considerable amount of social mobility counteracting the paralyzing effect of caste, on the other is an unstable family situation generating insecurity and rebellion.

Born in Joplin, Missouri, in 1902, Langston Hughes spent much of the time until he was twelve with a grandmother in Kansas, lived with his mother in Cleveland through high school, and stayed with his father for a long visit in Mexico. His parents disagreed sharply on their way of life and separated when their only child was a small boy.

In the father's ancestry was a slave trader and a Scottish distiller. His mother's paternal grandfather was Captain Ralph Quarles of Virginia, related to the Jacobean poet, Francis Quarles, who had colored children by his slave housekeeper. In his mother's maternal line was a Cherokee Indian mated to a French trader. Their descendants had free papers during slavery, and the maternal grandmother who raised Langston went to college at Oberlin and married a freeman who was killed in John Brown's raid. Her second marriage was to Charles Langston, who also believed "people should be free," who went into politics instead of trying to make money, and whose distinguished brother, John Mercer Langston, was a Congressman from Virginia, U. S. Minister to Haiti, and first Dean of the Law School at Howard University. The young Langston admired this Indian looking grandmother with the long black hair because she was proud and strong for freedom. There was something about his grandmother's stories which taught him "the uselessness of crying about anything."

His mother was "olive-yellow," his father a darker brown. While the son does not attempt to draw connections between their differences in color and their views of life, the fact remains that the father was more ambitious in a worldly sense than the mother. He preferred to live in Mexico in order to escape discrimination, make money faster, and achieve solid middle-class success. Langston's mother chose what seemed to be the easier and safer way in Kansas, was willing to work to support her child, but was not so concerned about saving that she missed the opportunity to live a little along the way. She took the eager boy to a variety of plays, from "Uncle Tom's Cabin" to "Faust," and started him on his imaginative experiences. Always struggling against poverty, forced to work in service in Cleveland when her second husband could no longer stand the strain of the steel mills, she apparently never regretted the break with Langston's "successful" father, and gave her boy something as valuable in its way as his grandmother's ideal of freedom.

Through these years with his mother and grandmother the boy was forming opinions with a certain maturity. There was little of the dogmatist about him. When he attended a white school he paid due attention to the fact that one little white boy always stood up for him. "So I learned early not to hate *all* white people. And ever since, it has seemed to me that *most* people are generally good, in every race and in every country where I have been." He was disposed towards the same tolerance about religion. When his grandmother died and he was taken temporarily by friends he decided that "both of them were very good and kind—the one who went to church and the one who didn't. And no doubt from them I learned to like both Christians and sinners equally well."

Basic to his tolerance was a capacity for appreciation. He enjoyed people—he also enjoyed animals, food, movies, books, and whatever came his way openly and freely. In the country he set the hens, drove the cows, and relished the fresh garden vegetables, hoecake, and molasses. In the city he was enraptured by the silent films of Mary Pickford and Charlie Chaplin and by the road shows of Sothern and Marlowe. And always there were stories, even before the novels of Edna Ferber, Harold Bell Wright, and Zane Grey. Very early he "fell in love with librarians—those very nice women who help you find wonderful books." He liked the silence inside the library, the chairs and long tables, "the fact that the library was always there and didn't seem to have a mortgage on it." It is not surprising, then, that even before he was six "books began to happen" to him.

In his Cleveland public high school there were favorable conditions for growth. He had several good teachers, one of them the daughter of Charles W. Chesnutt, pioneer Negro novelist. His English teacher introduced him to Carl Sandburg, Vachel Lindsay, Amy Lowell, and Edgar Lee Masters. Under this stimulus he began to write not only Negro dialect poems but poems without rhyme on a modern note.

Because of the variety of racial, religious, and national backgrounds, a natural democracy flourished in the school. The children of the foreign-born tended to be more democratic than the native-white. Often when there was a religious deadlock, between Catholic and Jewish groups, for example, a Negro student would win an election. Langston Hughes was a scholarship student, a member of the track team, editor of the yearbook. His best friend was Polish. A Jewish girl took him to his first symphony concert. With schoolmates he heard Eugene Debs and celebrated the advent of the Russian Revolution. "From the students I learnt that Europe was not so far away, and that when Lenin took power in Russia, something happened in the slums of Woodlawn Avenue that the teachers couldn't tell us about, and that our principal didn't want us to know." During this period of high intellectual excitement and dawning political consciousness the young Negro broadened his racial views as well. He concluded that "lots of painful words can be flung at people that aren't 'nigger.' 'Kike' was one; 'spick' and 'hunky,' others." Negroes had no corner on suffering.

The total effect of his high school experience was to stretch his imagination beyond his immediate little world. He was ready for new ideas in every field. No longer satisfied with westerns, he read Schopenhauer, Nietzsche, and Dreiser. One night, while reading a story in French by Guy de Maupassant, he suddenly felt "the beauty and the meaning of the words in which he made the snow fall" and decided that he wanted to write stories, too, "stories about Negroes, so true that people in far-away lands would read them—even after I was dead."

Up to this stage in his life Langston Hughes had endured plenty of disadvantages. He had no stable family life, he belonged to a minority group in society, and he was exposed to the insecurity of poverty. Working at odd jobs himself, he was sensitive to his mother's efforts to make ends meet. In fact, his sympathy with the Russian experiment at the end of World War I, when he and his high school friends were beginning to wonder about American democracy, was not the result of idle theory. "The daily papers pictured the Bolsheviki as the greatest devils on earth, but I didn't see how they could be that bad if they had done away with race hatred and landlords—two evils that I knew well at first hand."

But the important point to bear in mind is that these realistic factors had not dampened his enthusiasm for life. Perhaps the peculiar alchemy of his temperament unconsciously influenced him to draw on the opportunities of his environment. In any case, as he neared the close of his high school days, his ambition was unclouded. His outlook on the future was certainly more romantic than the actual conditions of his existence could support. Even the injustice of society tended to fade away before the vague idealism of his revolutionary ardor.

It remained for his father to give him his first rude push towards pessimism. In customary fashion, the boy glamorized this distant father and anticipated his first visit to him. He took no stock of his mother's epithet, "a devil on wheels." "In my mind I pictured my father as a kind of strong, bronze cowboy, in a big Mexican hat, going back and forth from his business in the city to his ranch in the mountains, free—in a land where there were no white folks to draw the color line, and no tenements with rent always due—just mountains and sun and cacti: Mexico!" The contrast between this idyll and the actuality was so extreme that the disillusioned boy became ill.

It was true that the landscape lived up to his expectations. But the strong cowboy turned out to be small-souled, mean-minded, and "tough like a jockey." A typical American businessman, interested only in making and saving money, he regarded his ranch only as property investment and encouraged no largeness of life around him. With middle-class standards of success, he put great pressure on his son to become practical, learn accounting, study to be a mining engineer. Worst of all was his snobbery, directed indiscriminately towards Negroes and native Mexicans. He scorned the ignorance of the natives and thought "it was their own fault that they were poor." His conversation was punctuated with derogatory remarks such as "Mexicans steal," "Never give an Indian anything. He doesn't appreciate it." The son, observing, concluded that his father "hated himself, too, for being a Negro."

Chafing under the meager diet and restricted regime of his father, Langston Hughes was often bored and lonely, and always resentful. Toying with the idea of suicide, only the thought of what he might miss later calmed him down. After all, he still had not seen the top of a volcano or a bull fight, graduated from high school, or married! Yet his father's typical "hurry up," his favorite expression in Spanish or English, finally built up the boy's irritation to such an extent that he could no longer eat, and became ill with a high fever. Even at that time Langston Hughes recognized the psychological nature of his disturbance: "I was sick because I hated my father."

It is therefore problematical whether Langston Hughes' father contributed anything to his development. Whatever it was can best be stated in negative terms. The role of reaction was predominant. Rejecting violently all the values upheld by the father, the son cultivated a new loyalty towards Negroes, and specifically lower-class Negroes. "They seemed to me like the gayest and the bravest people possible—these Negroes from the Southern ghettos—facing tremendous odds, working and laughing and trying to get somewhere in the world." While the father wanted him to acquire polish by travel and study abroad, the son longed, above all, to see Harlem, "the greatest Negro city in the world." It is symptomatic of his aroused race consciousness that, on his way back from Mexico, he answered, when asked, that he was colored, not Mexican. He preferred the discrimination involved to betraying his basic integrity.

For a period, too, Langston Hughes lost the thread of his earlier ambition. Soured on the efficiency of his father, he tended to associate all ambition with the narrow aims of middle-class life. Although he had received his father's support for a year of study at Columbia University, he did not respond to it. The author mentions two counts against it, that the University was too large, and that there were too many instances of race discrimination. But unconsciously he was probably motivated by a continued counter-suggestibility to his father. Conventional education in any shape or form smacked of the respectability and worship of success which made him ill. Choosing to be self-supporting, "remembering the smell of the sea," and desiring to make up his own mind about the world on his own terms, Langston Hughes left the cloistered classrooms, and became a worker and a vagabond of sorts. Overboard with his books went his father's way of life and his own more serious intentions.

At twenty-one, then, Langston Hughes was in an experimental mood. Before him lay several years of free-lancing. In Africa, Spain, France, and Italy he alternated between unemployment and hunger on the one hand, and a variety of odd jobs and romantic adventure on the other. When his passport and money were stolen, he was stranded as a beachcomber in Genoa. Sometimes he worked as a sailor, sometimes as a doorman, cook, or waiter in Paris night clubs. Once he fell in love with an English-African girl, "a soft doe-skin brown," whose cultured and well-to-do African father disapproved of him. The young people wandered through the Paris springtime, dipped strawberries in cream, and felt "very 'tristes' and very young and helpless, because we could not do what we wanted to do—be happy together with no money and no fathers to worry us."

Or again, in Italy, there was "a marvelous time in that postcard village by the too-blue-to-be-real lake" with picnics in ancient olive groves amid the friendliness of a people curious about the rare sight of a Negro. He appreciated Venice under the guidance of Dr. Alain Locke, the distinguished Negro scholar with "a cultured accent and a degree from Oxford" who knew Venice like a book, and "who seemed to me a gentleman of culture, happy to help others enjoy the things he had learned to enjoy." Occasionally, when he grew weary of palaces, churches, famous paintings, and English tourists, he slipped off to visit sections not mentioned in the guide books. "And I found that there were plenty of poor people in Venice and plenty of back alleys off canals too dirty to be picturesque."

Africa also held romantic-realistic experience. Predisposed to regard Africa as his motherland, the young traveller anticipated the Africa he had dreamed about, "wild and lovely, the people dark and beautiful, the palm trees tall, the sun bright, and the rivers deep." Some of all this he found, but he also found natives "baffled and humble" before the missionaries and especially the traders "who carry whips and guns and are protected by white laws, made in Europe for the black colonies." The bitterness of this discovery far outweighed his personal chagrin over the ironic fact that the Africans would not believe he was a Negro because he was brown, not black.

On the whole, his "Grand Tour" paid dividends so in excess of the original capital invested that even his father could have found little grounds of complaint. Arriving in Paris with seven dollars, staying many months abroad, he landed back in New York with twenty-five cents and thus claimed that the total trip had cost only six dollars and seventy-five cents! Fortunately, his nonmaterial gains were correspondingly great. With the dust of his past life shaken off, with a fresh set of observations made within a wider world, Langston Hughes felt prepared for the sober task of earning a living and finding a way of life in his own country. Already he wanted to return to college, "to study sociology and history and psychology and find out why countries and people were the kind of countries and people they are." Now that he had tasted of knowledge directly, he saw the necessity of book knowledge as a supplement. Most of all he envisioned education once more, as in his high school days, in terms of training and background for his writing. His intentions of becoming a writer burned brightly again.

Between 1924 and 1930 Langston Hughes had a succession of experiences to help him towards his goal. The first was his job maladjustment which, fortunately for art, made him so unhappy that he became creative. In Washington, D. C., his efforts to find the type of work that would enable him to save for his college course were fruitless. "Folks! start out with nothing some time and see how long it takes to work up to something." Impatient with the qualifications, influential connections, and endless waiting a good position seemed to require and down to his last cent, he finally took a job in a wet-wash laundry. "I didn't like my job, and I didn't know what was going to happen to me, and I was cold and half-hungry, so I wrote a great many poems." According to the poet's own analysis, he always wrote his best poetry when he was feeling the worst. Thus spontaneous expression marked his development.

But he was not to be disappointed in his college ambition either. Receiving a scholarship to the Negro college of Lincoln in 1926, he returned to his books and was graduated in due course. That this period was not unproductive is evidenced by the publication of his important novel, *Not Without Laughter,* a great portion of which he wrote during this time. It would be hard to say, however, whether the academic training he gained was any more essential than the financial backing of a wealthy white patron. To be freed from the enervating struggle for food and shelter in order to study and write was an unexpected boon.

Yet perhaps the most formative influence of all turned out to be his dynamic connection with the Negro Renaissance movement. It was more than a matter of winning several literary prizes offered by the Negro magazines, *The Crisis* and *Opportunity*. He responded to the spirit of encouragement among Negro intellectuals, to those people like his earlier friend, Alain Locke, "who midwifed the so-called New Negro literature into being," who were "kind and critical—but not too critical for the young," and who thus "nursed us along until our books were born." It is consistent with our impression of Langston Hughes that his sensitivities did not allow him to take his sudden success for granted, but prompted him to seek contributing factors outside of his own talents and to give credit wherever it was due.

It seems plausible that the young writer's open-mindedness and lack of egotism enabled him to draw the utmost from these years of high literary endeavor and wide social contacts. In his autobiography he not only speaks glowingly of "the generous 1920's," but documents his opinion with pages of description. No other author has reconstructed more intimately and faithfully the atmosphere of that period when Negro and white intellectuals, artists, and celebrities of all kinds first found a common meeting ground. Centered in New York and featuring Harlem, this Negro Renaissance offered that re-evaluation of the Negro in positive terms for which Langston Hughes had long been prepared.

His pithy commentaries illuminate scene and character. He attended a variety of parties ranging from solid respectable to bohemian; he contacted a conglomeration of personalities, including Rebecca West, Somerset Maugham, Fannie Hurst, Carl Van Vechten, Alfred Knopf, Louis Untermeyer, Waldo Frank, Hugh Walpole, Jascha Heifetz, Salvador Dali, and Rudolph Valentino. And always he was taking mental notes. At the home of James Weldon Johnson, outstanding Negro writer and diplomat, he had gumbo suppers and met "solid people like Clarence and Mrs. Darrow." At the home of Jessie Fauset, novelist of Negro middle-class life, he found "literary soirees with much poetry and but little to drink," and "serious people who liked books and the British Museum." Here there were few white guests since Jessie Fauset wished to avoid the tourists and the faddists. At A'Lelia Walker's, on the other hand, there was plenty of easy conviviality. This hair-straightening heiress, "joy goddess" of the 1920's, gave expensive, crowded parties for Negro singers and poets like Taylor Gordan and Countee Cullen and for foreign princes. Walter White, Negro executive of the N.A.A.C.P., proved to be a jovial and cultured host with "a sprightly mind" as well as a beautiful wife.

The natural center of the bohemian circle was Wallace Thurman, "a strangely brilliant black boy, who had read everything, and whose critical mind could find something wrong with everything he read," who liked and disliked solitude, gin and bohemianism, "who liked being a Negro but felt it a great handicap." In contrast to his bitter paradoxes stood the amusing personality of Zora Hurston. It was almost superfluous for her to write books "because she is a perfect book of entertainment in herself." Occasionally wealthy white people "simply paid her just to sit around and represent the Negro race for them, she did it in such a racy fashion. Hand in hand with her naïveté went cleverness and real ability. But the wittiest of the younger set seemed to be Rudolph Fisher, Negro doctor, short-story writer, novelist. "He and Alain Locke together were great for intellectual wise-cracking. The two would fling big and witty words about with such swift and punning innuendo that an ordinary mortal just sat and looked wary for fear of being caught in a net of witticisms beyond his cultural ken."

Moving from group to group, learning a bit here, enjoying a bit there, Langston Hughes reflected that temperamental appreciation balanced by mental reservations which always characterized him. In 1927, on his first visit to the South, he felt a tolerance for the people of New Orleans applicable in principle to his reception of the Negro

Renaissance. The author states it simply: "The non-Creoles said that the Creoles were a very dangerous people, given to the use of knives, and the Creoles said the same about the others. But I had a good time with all of them." If there was any knife-throwing going on this young observer was realist enough to recognize it, while refusing to let it affect his pleasure in people.

With his chronological years closely following the years of the century, Langston Hughes approached his thirties with a rewarding apprenticeship of writing behind him. To his credit stood two acclaimed volumes of poetry and his novel, *Not Without Laughter,* which received the $400 Harmon award in 1931. Without pausing long at the crossroads he plunged down the road towards professional writing. He did not underestimate the difficulties in making his living this way. But, after all, he had always been poor, never earning more than $22 a week at a job. At least he might as well be poor doing what he liked to do, and devoting his whole time to it. The "generous twenties" and the day of scholarships and subsidies were over, the depression was starting, and the author knew that his future lay in his own hands. The results justified his hope and his determination: "Shortly poetry became bread; prose, shelter and raiment. Words turned into songs, plays, scenarios, articles, and stories."

The meaning of the title of his autobiography is now explained: "Literature is a big sea full of many fish. I let down my nets and pulled. I'm still pulling." But the author does not do full justice to his own figure of speech. For life has also been for him a big sea with teeming treasures. No other autobiographer in our series so vividly presents the unity of literature and life. Only by exploring life fully did Langston Hughes become the writer he did.

He is a special kind of writer, with a special philosophy behind his words. He is a special pleader for democracy, genuine democracy, the kind that stops at nothing to complete itself. Later experience reenforces his earlier sympathy for the lower-class Negroes, and from them for all exploited people. While Herndon, the southern coal miner, identified himself with workers by circumstance, Hughes, northern reared, with formal education, exposed to middle-class attitudes, identified himself with the lower class by choice. His poverty was sometimes voluntary, as attested by his break with his father. From the evidence of his autobiography there can be little doubt that opportunities for climbing into a secure middle-class niche awaited him if he had been willing to conform. But he had an integrity with which he didn't want to tamper.

Critical of all smugness and pretension, he did not exempt Negroes from examination. With the same intensity he had shown in opposing his father's standards he attacked colored society in Washington, D. C. Originally he had been disturbed by the "ghetto life" for colored people there, by segregated residential districts, exclusion from theatres and restaurants, by all the "strangely undemocratic doings" taking place "in the shadow of the 'world's greatest democracy.'" But then he bumped into the "rigid class and color lines" within the Negro group itself. The upper crust of government workers, professors, doctors, lawyers, and politicians had no use for Negroes who worked with their hands, were dark in complexion, or had no degrees from college. They lived in comfortable homes, gave formal parties, and drank Scotch, but seemed "altogether lacking in real culture, kindness, or good common sense." Not really rich because of the restrictions of a white-dominated economy, standing so close to the poorer Negroes that many of them had relatives working as redcaps and porters, this colored society clung all the more tenaciously to middle-class respectability. "Their snobbishness was so precarious," explains the poet-analyst, "that I suppose for that very reason it had to be doubly reinforced."

After observing this pretentiousness, the young man found the free and easy life of Washington's Seventh Street a "sweet relief." "Seventh Street is the long, old, dirty street, where the ordinary Negroes hang out, folks with practically no family tree at all, folks who draw no color line between mulattoes and deep dark-browns, folks who work hard for a living with their hands." Back in 1924 they sang the blues, told tall tales, ate watermelon, and dared to laugh out loud within view of the Capitol dome. The poet began to write some of his best blues as he vibrated to this "gay and sad" atmosphere with its rhythm, strength, and earthy humor. To such people who instinctively practice the art of living he allied himself gladly.

He maintains this loyalty even under fire. In one way he is objective enough to sympathize with those Negro critics who resent his writing. "In anything that white people were likely to read, they wanted to put their best foot forward, their politely polished and cultured foot—and only that foot." They had seen their race caricatured by the Octavus Roy Cohens and abused by the Thomas Dixons until they had become sensitive. Therefore they naturally preferred the attractive tableaux of

Jessie Fauset's novels to his backstage portrayals. In another way, however, he thinks that they have been distracted from the fundamental issue. To Langston Hughes personal sincerity and artistic sincerity are inseparable. He can only write about what he feels, believes, and knows most. Middle-class colored people striving towards upper-class status were not only alien to him, but froze his creativity. "I knew only the people I had grown up with, and they weren't people whose shoes were always shined, who had been to Harvard, or who had heard of Bach. But they seemed to me good people, too."

With equal firmness he withstood the pressure put on him by white people who had still different ideas about how he should live and write. His white patron, in particular, tried to dominate him. She was an aristocratic old lady of culture and wealth who meant to be kind but had the technique of the ruling class. "She possessed the power to control people's lives—pick them up and put them down when and where she wished." The conditions of the depression so affected him that he felt uncomfortable eating dinner on Park Avenue with freshly cut flowers within and falling snow without. But when he began to write realistic poems of unemployment she was displeased.

She spoke of the mystery, harmony, and spontaneity of the Negro soul which should not be contaminated by the cheap and ugly "white" civilization of the western world. Her conception of his duty as a writer was to translate this primitive heritage. "But, unfortunately, I did not feel the rhythms of the primitive surging through me, and so I could not live and write as though I did. I was only an American Negro—who had loved the surface of Africa and the rhythms of Africa—but I was not Africa. I was Chicago and Kansas City and Broadway and Harlem." The disillusionment of discovery that she had liked him for her particular purposes and not for his real self made him as physically ill as in the old days of conflict with his father. The break to independence was inevitable.

Langston Hughes' autobiography bares the outline of a free thinker. He does not think in this way in order to shock or to be in style, but simply because he has an inner need to be himself. He has no great respect for established institutions or conventions when they kill the spirit of truth. When he was twelve years old he had waited in vain to "see" Jesus and had finally stood up because he was ashamed to keep everyone at the meeting waiting. But afterwards he had cried over his hypocrisy. Organized religion never had any further power over him.

The same attitude characterizes his approach to Negro-white relationships. Convinced that discrimination is undemocratic, he sees no excuse for giving lip-service to its polite existence, for flattering, lying, and "Uncle Toming" in order to secure concessions from white folks. At Lincoln College he was shocked to find an all-white Board of Trustees and faculty. He realized that this fact alone fostered an inferiority complex in the Negro students—presumably in training for leadership. So he promptly wrote a survey suggesting that there must be at least a few Negro graduates capable of teaching there. One successful graduate, who felt that he had built up a "great institution" for his race, pointed out that a Negro never got anything out of whites by telling them unpleasant truths. Such an incident goaded Langston Hughes into framing his definitive philosophy of noncompromise.

He admitted to himself that "the old grad has his buildings just as Booker T. Washington had Tuskegee," and that they would probably stand a long time "on their corner-stone of lies." At the same time, "how heavily the bricks of compromise settle into place." Although at first the young man, who had not thought much before about the nature of compromise, felt confused and unhappy before the problem and wondered "for bread how much of the spirit must one give away," he quickly found his bearings. He sighted those intangibles which supported the only values he knew and put him in the company of the glorious rebels. "I began to think back to Nat Turner, Harriet Tubman, Sojourner Truth, John Brown, Fred Douglass—folks who left no buildings behind them—only a wind of words fanning the bright flame of the spirit down the dark lanes of time."

By his own avowal, then, Langston Hughes belongs in the Douglass camp. But we would not need his direct statement to place him there. All the evidence of the autobiography bespeaks an individual who loves freedom so much that he cannot enjoy it apart from the Negro group and who is too sincere and courageous to follow the beaten path of acquiescence to white superiority. Conscious of the maladjustments of society on a wide scale, like Du Bois and Herndon, he, too, seems to feel that Negroes bear the consequences unduly. Equally disturbed with them at the undemocratic class distinctions among Negroes, he too seems to feel that the condition is fostered by the unhealthy caste barriers erected by white people.

He sees little sense to race, in theory. "When we get as democratic in America as we pretend we are on days when we wish to shame Hitler, nobody will bother much about anybody's race anyway." He is prepared to look for the good in all individuals irrespective of color and to cut across race lines to put in a word for all exploited people. But, born a Negro, the circumstances of his life throw him back to a special loyalty towards a doubly exploited Negro group. Essential to his philosophy of freedom is his ability to combine respect for his particular status as Negro with respect for his universal status as man.

Along This Way

JAMES WELDON JOHNSON

THE longest of all our autobiographies by Negro Americans, *Along This Way,* published in 1933, already rates as an American classic. Although its author was killed in an accident a few years later he had already reached his sixties when he finished his book, and could thus cover a broad sweep of experience. But the length of the book does not depend so much on the number of years which it includes as on the quality of those years and their meaning for himself and others. One of the most respected of the elder Negro statesmen, James Weldon Johnson has both a varied career and a fund of ideas to elucidate. He does full justice to each, so that the four hundred pages of his story leave us with a sense of completion about a personality and an era, and the way in which one mature American has met the problem of race.

Born only a few years after Du Bois, James Weldon Johnson resembles him in general achievement and stature. A college-trained man, professor, writer, United States consul to Venezuela and Nicaragua, he also displayed intellectual caliber of the first rank. The style of his autobiography reflects the serious academic training in the humanities at the turn of the century. The periodic sentence, the Latinized vocabulary, the lavish adjectives bespeak an age when leisure, not efficiency, was the handmaiden of culture. His administrative powers had outlet not only as diplomat, but as school principal and as field secretary of the N.A.A.C.P. for fourteen years. Yet like Du Bois he was temperamentally inclined towards the contemplative life. But for the exigencies of the race problem, both men might normally have led comfortable middle-class existences, unperturbed in their pursuit of the ideal of the gentleman and the scholar.

Again comparable to Du Bois' experience is his late introduction to the race issue. Not until his college days does its urgency occur to him. Although he was born in Florida at the opposite end of the Atlantic seaboard from Du Bois and attended an all-colored instead of an all-white school, family background and standing in the community gave him a certain immunity from direct contacts with prejudice. The author cannot stress the importance of this fact too much. Postponement of the problem until near-maturity enabled him to face it more objectively: "As an American Negro, I consider the most fortunate thing in my whole life to be the fact that through childhood I was reared free from undue fear of or esteem for white people as a race; otherwise the deeper implications of American race prejudice might have become a part of my subconscious as well as of my conscious self." Perhaps this explains why his utterances on the most controversial aspects of race relations always sound so dispassionate while adhering to firmness of principle.

Both by example and precept the parents induced self-respect and emotional stability in their two children, James Weldon and Rosamund. The mother grew up in Nassau, capital of the Bahama Islands under British rule, came to New York as a young girl, but returned to Nassau during the Civil War. Her father, of French and Haitian parentage, had risen high in the political and public life of Nassau, as Assemblyman for thirty years, Chief Inspector of Police, Postmaster, churchman, and bank trustee. Her mother, of African descent, was strong-willed and always remained a royalist and British subject throughout her later years in Florida. She herself had such a feeling of freedom from her girlhood that she never knew her "place" in the South and tended to be a nonconformist. Intelligent and well-educated, she encouraged her sons' musical training, read Dickens and Scott aloud to them, and was the first colored woman in Florida to become a public school teacher. Her artistic nature bestowed beauty and harmony on the home life.

Although James Weldon Johnson knew little about his father's background except that he was born a freeman in Virginia he was appreciative of his character traits. This "light bronze" man had fallen in love with his future wife when he heard her sing in New York, had pursued his courtship in Nassau, and had prospered there as a headwaiter. In entrepreneur fashion he brought his family to Florida at the close of the Civil War. Although it was many years before Jacksonville became a boom town, he foresaw the possibilities in the crude settlement, built and painted a new house, and acquired the headwaiter position in the new hotel. With all his industry and commonsense, he was quiet and unpretentious, inclined to be unsociable. Self-educated, he became a preacher when he was past fifty. Yet he was not too strait-laced for flexibility. Volunteering to go and pray for a dying prostitute, he sometimes claimed that he was never *compelled* to associate with bad people until he joined the church in middle age. In his free time, he took his boys swimming or taught them to play the guitar.

James Weldon Johnson soon sensed the community approval of his parents. Long-time residents and early settlers, they had contributions to make to the growing town and were respected by both white and colored groups. The father's thrift, honesty, and dependability were so well known that a word from him was enough to secure a loan for the son as a young man. In his home town the son could always speak his mind rather freely on race injustices because white men remembered who his father was. James Weldon Johnson traces back to his father's influence his own self-control and desire to finish what he started, which held in check a more adventurous streak. As the author reviews his life, he realizes clearly for the first time that "in the deep and fundamental qualities" he has grown more like his parents all the time.

The author has many nostalgic memories of the pleasant and normal boyhood so taken for granted at the time, but so carefully insured by his parents. The Victorian parlor, with its typical whatnot, contained photograph albums, sea shells, stereopticon slides, and a piano to hold the interest of the child. At school there were marbles, tops, and later baseball in which he excelled. Always there was the congenial companionship of his younger brother, and then, at fourteen, the added interest of a colored Cuban boy in the household. In due time came the thrill of independence through his first jobs as brick carrier, driver of a cart, newsboy, and then helper in a newspaper office when the field of journalism began to hold a strong fascination for him.

During these years he had, if anything, "an unconscious race-superiority complex." Restricted in play, he encountered for the most part only friendly white neighbors and companions who did not suggest grounds for inferiority. Besides, the small boy noticed that it was colored men who did the most interesting work, drove the teams, built the houses, painted the fences, unloaded the ships. His parents not only taught him nothing directly about the facts of prejudice in the world outside, but refrained from delivering "a dash of cold water on any of my dreams." His early ambitions to be an important person some day were accepted naturally. The author comments that while the colored child of less sensitive parents is likely to have the information thrust on him from infancy that special obstacles will block any future success, his parents belonged to the school which believed in sparing "the bitter knowledge" until the last moment. With detachment the author adds: "And no Negro parent can definitely say which is the wiser course, for either of them may lead to spiritual disaster for the child." Yet this conclusion about the "serious dilemma" facing all Negro fathers and mothers does not rob him of his assurance that in his own case the particular decision was the correct one.

Unhampered by fear, the young boy's mind expanded to include many ideas and tastes beyond his immediate little world. When he was twelve years old, a trip to New York awakened his "love for cosmopolitanism." He later decided that he was "born to be a New Yorker," that one is either a cosmopolitan or is not, and that he was among the select. Everything about the bustle and atmosphere of the big city attracted him, from the chugging ferry boats to the mixture of peoples. Shortly after, a Spanish-speaking companion awakened in him an enthusiasm for foreign languages and cultures.

Perhaps his most conspicuous point of divergence from the folkways of his Florida community lay in his independence about religion. His maternal grandmother wanted him to be a preacher and took him to Methodist revival meetings, which were distasteful to him. At the age of nine he fell asleep on the mourner's bench, was carried home while feigning that he was still asleep, "awoke" and recounted a vision of a scene of heaven remembered from his reading. Although receiving the desired attention, he was later not only ashamed of his deception but chagrined at the fruits. For some time he managed to live up to expectation, be a model convert, and attend all religious services until the saturation point was reached.

Years later his emotional rejection was re-enforced by his reading and study. Not only the writings of Thomas Paine and Ingersoll but the systems of thought of many of the world's great philosophers led him to question the tenets of orthodox Christianity. Already at the time of his entrance to the preparatory school of Atlanta University in his middle teens, he was a free thinker along religious lines. "I now recall with some amusement how my agnostic reasonings left most of my fellow students aghast—there was only one other student in Atlanta University at that time who confessed similar views."

Although James Weldon Johnson as a new student had a "prestige entirely out of proportion to my age and class" because of his accomplishments and cosmopolitan air, and although he could jolt the other students with his well-informed arguments against religion, he had much to learn at Atlanta University. It was a strict school with "petty regulations and a puritanical zeal," which required of its men students a pledge against the use of alcohol, tobacco, and profanity and which cultivated in them a "Sir Galahad" attitude towards the women students. Yet it joined high standards of scholarship to high ideals of service. Students were given social ideas as well as information. The function of education was conceived to be the maturing of thoughtful adults rather than the production of "go-getters." Specifically, the ideal of service to his own race emerged for the young man. The other students talked "race" all the time and were obviously far enough ahead of him in this field of knowledge to jolt him in turn.

The student was now able to piece together into a pattern his scattered bits of personal observation of race relations. On the way to Atlanta University he had had his first Jim Crow experience, his "first impact against race prejudice as a concrete fact." Unknown to him, Florida had just passed its law separating the races in railroad cars. Traveling on first-class tickets, he and his Cuban friend discussed the matter in Spanish when the conductor insisted on moving them, only to find that they impressed him into silence. Thus it became apparent to James Weldon Johnson that, "in such situations, any kind of Negro will do; provided he is not one who is an American citizen" or appears to be an American citizen. With this initiation he began his "mental and spiritual training to meet and cope not only with the hardships that are common, but with planned wrong, concerted injustice, and applied prejudice." He saw his relationship to America in a new light, conditioned by "the peculiar responsibilities due to my own racial group," by the need to implement American democracy for Negro citizens.

The visit of the famous Frederick Douglass to Jacksonville took on fresh significance in retrospect. The boy had read his autobiography in advance with "feverish intensity" and "intellectual interest," and had been impressed by the "tall, straight, magnificent man with a lion-like head covered with a glistening white mane." But now, under the stress of his own experience, James Weldon Johnson must have found that deeper identification with Douglass' noncompromising approach which never left him, and which stimulated him later to refer bluntly to "the limits of utter asininity to which race prejudice can go."

Coming into a fuller comprehension of the race problem tends to be a narrowing as well as a deepening experience, "so narrowing that the inner problem of a Negro in America becomes that of not allowing it to choke and suffocate him." From this danger James Weldon Johnson freed himself to a remarkable extent. Never allowing himself to slip into a rut vocationally, alternating between the poor pay of idealistic work and lucrative employment, between serious-minded purpose and frivolous interlude, he continually replenished his life energy and renewed his vision. Starting as a summer teacher in the backwoods of Georgia during his undergraduate days, ten years after he left Atlanta University in 1894 he was nearing a consularship in South America. At the beginning of the century, when Booker T. Washington was publishing his autobiography imbued with his own idea of service, James Weldon Johnson was a celebrity on Broadway.

The episode in Georgia marked his "psychological change" from boyhood to manhood. He was thrown on his own resources to deal with those social forces which "constituted the complex world in microcosm." Hedged in by white prejudice so that it was not safe for him to travel the country roads at night, he organized and conducted his little school for the Negro farm children. Yet greater than the satisfaction of his development as a teacher was his appreciation for his first direct contact with the masses of Negroes. "I had in the main known my own people as individuals or as groups; and now I began to perceive them clearly as a classified division, a defined section of American society—what Black and White meant stood out starkly." While understanding their handicaps, he grew to admire these simple people. Admittedly this early experience gave him an immunity to any later snobbery.

At twenty-three, the college graduate had the honor of being principal of his old school in Jacksonville, with a thousand pupils and twenty-five teachers under his direction. Attacking the job vigorously, he studied the methods of the white grammar school, promoted the philosophy that three quarters of the art of teaching lay in arousing interest, and continued teaching his graduating eighth graders until a high school course for Negroes was a *fait accompli* without town opposition. In this period he also ran a Negro newspaper for several months, studied law, and gained admission to the bar in a gruelling open examination against white opponents.

Meanwhile, however, he had begun to feel the pull of New York. The restrictions of prejudice he could now see tightening around him, coupled with the pettinesses of small-town life, disposed him towards a change. But the motivating force was his brother, a talented and Boston trained pianist, who had already sampled the musical possibilities of Broadway. In this instance James Weldon Johnson decided in favor of his adventurous side and resigned his principalship to enter wholeheartedly into the cosmopolitan type of existence he had earlier dreamed of.

The productive partnership of the Johnson brothers and Bob Cole made musical history in the early years of the century. James Weldon Johnson, who had previously tried his hand at Negro dialect poetry, now wrote words for the songs which were the musical hits of that day, introduced on stage and in vaudeville, and sung and played all over the country. With the Marshall Hotel as their headquarters, the three men became the center of an artistic set which included both white and colored. Harry T. Burleigh, Will Marion Cook, and the famous comedians, Williams and Walker, were among those who created the gay and zestful atmosphere of the dining room at midnight, after show time. Ziegfield of Ziegfield Follies fame recognized the talents of these artistic Negroes and dared to give them opportunity. His wife, Anna Held, sang one of their most popular numbers, *The Maiden With the Dreamy Eyes.* It was quite an exhilarating experience for James Weldon Johnson to be recognized as a "Broadway personality," to be pointed out as the composer of such lyrics as *Under the Bamboo Tree, My Castle on the Nile,* and *Nobody's Lookin' But the Owl and the Moon.* He and his co-workers rode the crest of the wave and earned as much as $12,000 in royalties alone in the course of six months. Expensive food and fashionable clothes added pleasure to social intercourse. In surroundings where it would be hard to imagine the scholarly Du Bois, James Weldon Johnson proved to be a good mixer.

Yet the author informs us that his phenomenal success on Broadway never went to his head. It never seemed quite real to him. He had a recurring dream of taking an all-important examination and waking before the result was announced. The author comments that "a psychoanalyst could, I suppose, tell the significance," without relating it to the basic insecurity it seems to indicate. Even life in New York could not relieve the tension of competing in a white-dominated society. On tour, the shifting sands on which their situation rested became more obvious to the three Negro musicians. Treated like "outcasts and pariahs" in Salt Lake City, for example, they could find no decent place to eat or sleep, and faced once more "a lot which lays on high and low the constant struggle to renerve their hearts and wills against the unremitting pressure of unfairness." The practical difficulties of self-segregation in this case were apparent. There were too few Negroes in Salt Lake City to allow for the operation of a Negro hotel. To expect it would be as unreasonable, according to the author, as expecting Negroes to own their own opera house for grand opera, or their own railroads for Pullman travel.

The musical trio probably felt a more unqualified welcome in Europe than in their own country. When James Weldon Johnson listened to the first London performance of his brother and Bob Cole, he underwent that typical "pain and pleasurable reaction," that strain of watching Negro performers who inevitably "become protagonists of the whole racial cause." But the ovation was so tremendous that he soon relaxed in his English environment. He learned to love London, which he decided was a grave city, not debonair and sprightly like Paris but with a spirit closer to the realities of life.

But, as with several of our autobiographers, James Weldon Johnson felt most free from consciousness of race in France. He forgot everything else in watching the Paris life eddying around him, in watching the people at every level, from the elite audience at the Opera House to the swearing fishmongers in the market place. Not interested in conducted tours and points of historical interest, he made an acquaintance with the romantic city on his own terms. He was able to enjoy every moment in France because he was never made to feel like an outsider. "From the day I set foot in France, I became aware of the working of a miracle within me . . . I recaptured for the first time since childhood the sense of being just a human being."

Perhaps that uneasy American-inspired dream in the heydey of his success can be more clearly understood in light of his reaction to France. The author is afraid that his attempt to describe his experience will be futile for his white readers and unnecessary for his colored readers. In any case, "I was suddenly free; free from a sense of impending discomfort, insecurity, danger; free from the conflict within the Man-Negro dualism and the innumerable maneuvers in thought and behavior that it compels; free from the problem of the many obvious or subtle adjustments to a multitude of bans and taboos; free from special scorn, special tolerance, special condescension, special commiseration; free to be merely a man."

The fact remained that he was an American citizen and felt called upon to work out an adjustment in his own country. The problems this involved could not be pushed aside indefinitely by the satisfactions of a Broadway career. The author explains his drift away from this musical life partly on the basis of changing fashions: "A vogue of that kind is a vogue, and is about as exempt from recapture as past time." But Rosamund Johnson and Bob Cole continued their musical specialties for some time after he left them. His explanation in terms of temperament sounds more convincing: "Being light enough for Broadway was beginning to be, it seemed, a somewhat heavy task." He grew tired of the "feverish flutter" and anticipated a little "stillness of the spirit." The full explanation is probably even more complex. The responsibility of being a Negro acted on his temperament in such a way as to make a swing back to more serious-minded endeavor the only solution.

Even before his Broadway days were over he had laid the foundations for serious writing. He had reacted to the whole idea of dialect poetry, its emotions limited to pathos and humor, its artificiality and exaggeration aimed to please an outside white group. Even his friendship with the great Negro dialect poet, Paul Lawrence Dunbar, had not changed this opinion. In contrast, folk art and folk poetry seemed genuine, creative expression, directed towards the inside group. James Weldon Johnson began calling attention to the beauty of Negro spirituals and pioneered the later concept of the cultural contribution of the Negro to America. The end result of his own interest was a published volume of poems in 1917, and his collection of prose poems, *God's Trombones,* in which he captured the primitivity of the old-time Negro sermon, its imagery, color, syncopated rhythms, and native idioms as well as its universality of wishful dream.

Accompanying his poetic development was an interest in prose. While still writing lyrics for popular songs he took advanced courses in drama under Brander Matthews at Columbia University. This professor's freedom from pedantry and catholicity of taste, even to the extent of liking musical comedy and comparing the plays of Weber and

Fields to the plays of Aristophanes, warmed his heart and formed the basis of a friendship between the two men. Encouraged by Brander Matthews, he began to write his first novel, *The Autobiography of an Ex-Colored Man,* which was published anonymously in 1912 and aroused much controversy over its frank treatment of "passing" and intermarriage and much speculation about the authorship.

As essayist about Negro literature, as anthologist of Negro poetry, James Weldon Johnson finally added to his own creative work in prose and poetry the role of literary critic. Concerned about sponsoring Negro creativity, he fell naturally into the mood and purpose of the Negro Renaissance years later. His parties in Harlem in the 1920's not only gave that solid encouragement to young writers described by Langston Hughes, but offered the contrast of serious purpose to the persiflage of his earlier Broadway days.

James Weldon Johnson's qualifications for leadership were not confined to his writing. In fact, the definite break with his musical partnership occurred when he accepted the post of United States Consul in Venezuela. Influential friends had persuaded him that his abilities needed a wider field and that his success would help Negro-white relationships. He applied himself to this work with the same thoroughness shown in his school principalship, refusing to succumb too much to the indolent manner of life prescribed by the tropical climate, adhering to his usual "abhorrence of 'spare time.' " Although the sentiment of the country was anti-American, it was not directed against him personally. Quietly he watched the repercussions of the political struggle between the rival dictators Castro and Gomez, carried out his official duties, and dispatched careful reports.

His appointment to Nicaragua followed in 1909. This time he took a more active part in internal affairs—in this case the insurrections connected with President Diaz. Realistically, he decided that the armed intervention of the United States was not so much for the given reason of protecting concessions and loans, but for the hidden motive of eventually controlling an interoceanic canal across Central America. As he studied the social patterns in Nicaragua he noticed that the Germans intermarried with the natives and thus gained an "inside advantage" over the English and Americans who hesitated to enter into the social life without many reservations and attitudes of superiority. The Negro consul adjusted easily to the native population and brought his American bride to the attractive home he planned with cool, green-woven furniture, a victrola, and water colors and prints on the walls.

But he knew that he was not exempt from race prejudice even in this country and in this position. Sometimes American whites did not know how to treat their own consul. Occasionally "race prejudice bumped into me. I mean to indicate specifically that I did not bump into it. In other words, I was not concerned with its stupid outbursts or with how it bruised its own head." Usually he let individuals alone to work out their own recovery from shock. When the time came, however, that politics and race prejudice joined forces to keep him from advancement to another post, he resigned from the diplomatic service of the United States.

By 1914 he was back in New York—this time in the new, rapidly growing Harlem—increasingly prepared for outspoken leadership towards Negro rights. Personal and public, domestic and foreign affairs united to inspire an indignant frame of mind. Although he had planned to practice law in his native Jacksonville, now a boom town, neither he nor his northern-raised wife could tolerate the southern attitudes. Even the refusal of a white man to tip his hat in the presence of a colored woman was more than the triviality it seemed to be: "this mere trifle declares that, actually, there is no common ground on which we can stand; and I shall, whenever it is possible for me to do so, avoid standing on any ground with him." It was superfluous for an old friend of his father's to advise James Weldon Johnson to leave this environment which had lost the protective coating of childhood.

On the eve of World War I he welcomed the opening for service as Field Secretary of the N.A.A.C.P. in New York. The political situation looked gloomy for democracy. On the one hand fair-minded government leadership was lacking: "My distrust and dislike of the attitude of the Administration centered upon Woodrow Wilson, and came nearer to constituting keen hatred for an individual than anything I have ever felt." He preached the self-determination of small nations, for example, and yet seized the friendly little Republic of Haiti where black slaves had liberated themselves, cut up the large plantations into small plots for all, and thus done away with peonage. On the other hand, Johnson was disturbed by the apathy of Negroes to such miscarriage of justice: "the race as a whole had adopted soft-speaking, conformity, and sheer opportunism as the methods of survival." In the "bitter feud" which had been raging between Booker T. Washington and Du Bois, and still farther to the left, Monroe Trotter of the *Boston Guardian,* there can be little question on which side Johnson's sympathies fell. With militant determination to arouse Negroes to action he shortly increased the number of branches of the N.A.A.C.P. from sixty-eight to three hundred and ten, with over one third of them in southern cities where organization had been considered impossible or dangerous.

For fourteen years James Weldon Johnson kept up the pace of direct race leadership. Through the channels of the N.A.A.C.P. he fought for practical reforms. Like Du Bois, during World War I he tried to direct public sentiment against the revived Ku Klux Klan, the East St. Louis massacre of Negroes, the race riots. He suggested silent protest parades of Negroes. He reminded white people that "in large measure the race question involves the saving of black America's body and white America's soul."

His supreme effort came in the postwar movement of liberal organizations to pass a Federal anti-lynching law. In connection with the Dyer Bill of 1921, he lobbied for two years, bringing to bear on one Congressman after another the full weight of his information and conviction. Although the bill passed the House, James Weldon Johnson could not win over Senator Borah, the key man, who claimed that it would be unconstitutional. The Republicans betrayed it in the Senate by stalling or not appearing for the vote until the Democrats had time to organize a filibuster. When the bill was finally abandoned, the Negro leader felt doubly embittered because his inside knowledge led him to believe that it would have passed if it had been brought to the vote. He wondered at "the thoughtlessness of people who take it as a matter of course that American Negroes should love their country." After all, America is "the only spot in the world" where systematic lynchings could occur without any legal check.

In spite of his militancy, there was nothing of the fiery radical about Johnson. With his urbanity and erudition he usually failed to antagonize even individuals with a conservative background. For many years he was an ardent Republican and always had plenty of "respectable" connections. In the 1920's the Rosenwald Foundation awarded him a grant for creative writing and the American Council of the Institute of Pacific Relations sent him as a delegate to Japan. At this conference he not only responded to the universality of the color problem, but enjoyed the companionship of the son of Ramsey MacDonald, the son of Lady Astor, and then the grandson of John D. Rockefeller. Immediately the Negro delegate respected the character of this inheritor of great wealth: "At first, it seemed not quite congruous that this modest, unassuming, almost shy young man represented such tremendous power. But under his quiet manner, earnestness and a sense of responsibility were steadily revealed." Such an observation, typical of his insistence on judging each person as an individual, showed that he had no bias against wealth as such, but only against its misuse by the wrong individuals.

In other words, James Weldon Johnson was radical only in the field of race relations. His autobiography reveals none of the preoccupation with Marxist doctrine which characterized Du Bois. Specifically, the author outlaws the possibility of communism, especially for Negroes. It would be idiotic "for the Negro to take on the antagonisms that center against it, in addition to those he already carries." Besides, political and economic revolutions do not change the hearts of men, but only the frameworks within which they operate. To this author, Negroes will still remain the exploited group until a moral revolution occurs. At this point his mental distance from Angelo Herndon is the span between two worlds.

With less daring and less concrete solutions for the race problem, then, than either Du Bois or Herndon, James Weldon Johnson is often more outspoken on the full implications of racial equality. He does not give an inch on what democracy involves for Negroes, even though he fails to see any one political or economic means to the end. Even during his later years, when he felt justified in retreating to that contemplative life one side of his nature had always longed for, his enthusiasm for his goal remained paramount. As a professor in the chair of Creative Literature at Fisk University he realized that he could still stay in "the pitched battle between justice and wrong" since his writing and teaching were also "fields on which causes may be won." In his classes with Negro students he hoped "to help effectively in developing additional racial strength and fitness and in shaping fresh forces against bigotry and racial wrong." It was with eagerness that he entered into this last phase of his life and began to articulate those matured and incisive conclusions about race which are interwoven into the structure of his autobiography.

A first step towards understanding the noncompromise of his final philosophy would be to start with that question which was once asked him in the spirit of insult and which he asked himself seriously—would he want to be a white man? The author states that his deepest introspection cannot produce an affirmative answer. He wants only to be himself, with the chance of equal opportunities. He can detect no buried admiration for the whites as a race, especially in light of the fact that no race could have made a "worse mess" of the areas of the world it controls. Being a Negro is part of being himself, and part of the privilege of belonging to a group whose potentialities he appreciates.

This appreciation is not directed towards the upper or middle class alone. It extends to share croppers or unemployed workers alike. He deplores the intragroup snobbery which underestimates the "technique for survival that the masses have evolved," which cringes from their easygoing traits and spontaneous laughter without recognizing their "slow but persistent movement forward." Actually, the deep laughter of the Negro in the backwoods of the South should be an "ominous sound" in the ears of the "grim white man." Similarly, Harlem needs to be evaluated below the exotic tourist surface. More advantaged Negroes can learn from the "commonplace, work-a-day Harlem" which contains "real tragedy, real triumphs."

Intrinsically, Negroes as a group have all the necessary prerequisites for happiness and success. The author sees no reason why they should envy any other group from this point of view. His race pride, somewhat analogous to that of Du Bois, asserts that "the perfection of the human female is reached in the golden-hued and ivory-toned colored women in the United States." Whenever he is asked whether he believes in amalgamation, he replies that his wish would be for the Negro "to retain his racial identity, with unhampered freedom to develop his own qualities." The desire to preserve his own identity is thus expanded to include the race.

The theory and practice of amalgamation, however, are two different matters. Ultimately, James Weldon Johnson foresees the "blending of the Negro into the American race of the future" through means for the most part not of his own choosing. With "elemental forces at work," and the lure of "the forbidden and unknown," sex will continue to cross the color line. Because the possessive maleness of the whites "is broad enough to embrace the women of other men" while it "brooks no encroachment on the women of the clan" and because it has the power to back up the taboo, intercolor relationships may continue to be largely confined to white men and colored women. The final result will be the same. The Negro "will add a tint to America's complexion and put a permanent wave in America's hair." The irony of the situation will lie in the fact that the Negro group as a whole, not the white initiators, must pay the price for this biological process by being deprived of "social equality."

According to the author the concept of social equality is vague, and used to justify every form of restriction against colored people. It is a term which "makes cowards of white people and puts Negroes in a dilemma." By endorsing Negro-white cooperation while rejecting social equality Booker T. Washington gave the excuse to his white listeners to leave "a very narrow margin, perhaps only a mudsill level of things on which to cooperate." From such a dilemma James Weldon Johnson promptly extricates himself by an unequivocal stand for social equality "on any definition of the term not laid down by a mad man or an idiot." He does not anticipate that it would lead to a mass invasion of white dinner parties by uninvited Negroes. Certainly there are both white and colored people he knows whom he would not have into his own house under any circumstances. Nothing can force social intercourse. At the same time, "there should be nothing in law or public opinion to prohibit persons who find that they have congenial tastes and kindred interests in life from associating with each other, if they mutually desire to do so."

Self-respect demands that a Negro, even if he has no wish to associate with any white people on any terms, should never put himself in a position of accepting the implication of social inequality "that he is unfit to associate with any of his fellow men." The individual choice should be his prerogative as well as the white man's. The fact that James Weldon Johnson feels personally oriented towards his own racial group does not weaken his principle or lead him into the temptation of wishing to influence the preference of others. If full social equality increases the rate of intermarriage it can be no more harmful to society than the present hypocritical and farcical state of affairs whereby a white gentleman may sleep but not eat with a colored person without risking his reputation. If there is partnership of any kind, it should be equal partnership.

The author believes that the denial to Negroes of their right to be human beings will leave them only one salvation. They must make a religion out of their forced isolation; they must cultivate hatred for everything white. Even though this process would destroy the best elements of their natures, it would grant them "a saving degree of self-respect" in the midst of abasement.

That society will be insane enough to allow such an eventuality does not seem probable to this Negro leader. Like Du Bois, he believes that what harms one segment of society harms all of society, and that eventually all people will learn this elementary lesson. Like Du Bois, he is an ameliorist in the sense that he thinks American society has a fighting chance for recovery before it is too late. He counts on the outcome sufficiently to enlist in the struggle, to dedicate his talents to group advancement rather than private enjoyment, to function as an agent of enlightenment.

In the last analysis it is difficult to determine what combination of circumstances led James Weldon Johnson toward his program and philosophy. He himself, in spite of the meticulous attention he pays to the details of his life, feels baffled by the problem of motivation. When he tries to isolate and trace back the forces which have determined his direction, he discovers that they are "so manifold, so potent, so arbitrary, and often so veiled as to make fatalism a plausible philosophy." Individuals are "far too complex" for complete analysis, and whatever steps are taken in this attempt often only rationalize the results of observable human behavior.

What remains unclear about motivation need not hamper decision and action. "What more can any of us do," inquires the author, "than struggle to converge the forces at work toward some desired focus?" It is clear that in his own case he has enough self-knowledge to surmise the general influences in his life, and enough wisdom to utilize them for constructive purposes.

It is true that he is not sustained in his efforts by any religious faith. The agnosticism of his youth carried through to the end of his life. "I do not know if there is a personal God; I do not see how I can know; and I do not see how my knowing can matter." Recognizing that religion is essential to many people, not wanting to deprive them of it, he just happens not to feel the need for it personally. He can conceive of no immortality waiting beyond the present world. "I do not see that there is any evidence to refute those scientists and philosophers who hold that the universe is purposeless; that man, instead of being the special care of a Divine Providence, is a dependent upon fortuity and his own wits for survival in the midst of blind and insensate forces."

Yet in a deeper sense the James Weldon Johnson of *Along This Way* is a religious man. He does not deny spiritual values but he derives them "from other sources than worship and prayer." A religion can be valid when and if it is rooted in decent social behavior. "I feel that I can practice a conduct toward myself and toward my fellows that will constitute the basis for an adequate religion, a religion that may comprehend spirituality and beauty and serene happiness." The teachings of Jesus contain "the loftiest ethical and spiritual concepts the human mind has yet borne" but the power to actualize them does not lie in the presence of some Divine Being but in the hands of humanity.

It is as a humanist, then, that James Weldon Johnson views the moving world around him and his particular relation to it. Although the universe may be purposeless, man's individual life is "charged with meaning." His sufferings, defeats, and aspirations are "just as real and of as great moment to him as they would be if they were part of a mighty and definite cosmic plan." It should be an even greater challenge to him that his ultimate fate lies in his grasp of present opportunity, that "each day, if he would not be lost, he must with renewed courage take a fresh hold on life." Our author has no intention of being lost himself. In his efforts towards winning justice for Negro Americans, he has neither time nor inclination for defeatism. The moral revolution he advocates needs the stoutest cudgels of the human spirit.

No Day of Triumph

J. SAUNDERS REDDING

IN *No Day of Triumph* a northern-born and educated author bears witness to the class-caste structure of society. Although a comparatively young author, J. Saunders Redding touches upon the American race problem with the sober judgment of a Du Bois or a James Weldon Johnson. His life, like theirs, is so interlaced with it that his autobiographical account also doubles as a social document. Publishing his findings in his middle thirties, he has already spent a large portion of his time and thought as a social observer of the American scene and has concluded that the Man-Negro duality forced upon Negroes is the most vital concern of his and their existence. He does not dodge his consciousness of race. His personal reactions to being a Negro in a democratic-undemocratic white society are recorded in the spirit of enlightenment for others instead of mere self-expression.

These pages do seem to offer a means of emotional catharsis for the author. Like others in this group, he is in great distress and puzzlement about the paradoxes of race, and turns to the search for answers to private difficulties first. But the measure of his responsibility to the group can be seen in the structure of his autobiography. While the first part deals exclusively with the particular circumstances of his youth, most of the book is occupied with his adult travels and studies of Negro-white relationships in the South. In 1940, with the support of the Rockefeller Foundation, he left his teaching position and went in quest of values he could share, "looking for people, for things, for something" which could throw light on the future of Negroes in the United States.

By this time he is well aware that the Negro problem is also a white problem, that society as a whole is in a dangerous condition. He is looking for stability "in a world that had been slowly disintegrating for a dozen years, and now, half of it at war, was breaking up very fast"; that had suffered a depression which was "a final paralysis before the death of a way of life that men had thought enduring." There is legitimate room for doubt in his mind what values would be preserved or worth preserving. But at least the author has now reached the point where he can be open-minded and objective in his analysis.

To have achieved such a stage of detachment is a real victory for the author. From the extreme introversion of his student days, out of a mesh of complexes and neurotic tendencies, he manages to pull himself together for a more extroverted approach to his environment. Instead of retreating before the shocks of his life, he learns to push them back on their heels and look them in the eye. His sensitivities become a means of psychological awareness. Here again we have a case of a participant-observer, of a writer who stands inside and outside his every experience.

J. Saunders Redding represents the psychological trend of modern writing. From his terminology to his explanations of human behavior we recognize that we are in the presence of a man who is well versed in the newer developments of psychology. Du Bois and Johnson sound old-fashioned in comparison, while even Langston Hughes, who shares the point of view, lacks the technical facility of Redding and his preoccupation with involved emotional problems.

As the author reviews his childhood, he sees much cause for early introversion. Family first, neighborhood and school next, made him conscious of the class-caste nature of his environment and conditioned him to frustration and withdrawal. By adolescence, uncertain of his role in society, he indulged in morbidity.

The young boy encountered the caste restrictions of white people indirectly at first. The color differences within the family circle he early learned to connect with class distinctions within the Negro group, and only later traced back the Negro attitudes to the pattern of white superiority. What dominated his consciousness at the start was that he had two grandmothers who hated each other, that one was "black" and the other "yellow," and that he himself was dark within the family's "indeterminate group of browns."

His black paternal grandmother invariably brought conflict with her on her visits. She was a real character, a woman whose strong will wheeled around her hatred of whites. In 1858, when she had attempted to escape slavery at the age of ten, she had been caught and punished severely. The broken ankle she incurred set permanently the hatred which "shook her as a strong wind shakes a boughless tree" so that she "limped defiantly to her grave." If white children ventured near her grandchildren, she would command them fiercely, "Git, you white trash, git!" In her presence calm discussion of the race problem was impossible. She injected "a kind of spiritual poison," some of which was absorbed by the members of the family.

In contrast, his maternal grandmother could afford to be lenient toward whites because of her own ties to them. Her father had been white, her mother part Irish, Indian, and Negro, her first husband a mulatto carriage maker with three generations of freedom behind him. Marked by no bitterness from slavery, she approved of white people and their ways. Very religious and given to frequent prayers even about trifles, she preached a strict morality—stretched to include a double standard in sex matters—and held to an optimistic view of the best possible of worlds. Her tastes and standards were "bourgeois," corresponding to white middle-class attitudes which, translated in relation to the Negro group, became upper-class. The whiter the better formed such a dominant element in her thinking that she symbolized it in skin color. Because she was an integral part of the household, she had the advantage of the other grandmother in impressing her views. As a result, "ours was an upper-class Negro family, the unwitting victim of our own culture complexes; deeply sensitive to the tradition of ridicule and inferiority attaching to color; hating the tradition and yet inevitably absorbing it."

Here was a strange situation—dislike of whites from one grandmother, dislike of blacks from the other grandmother. The family tried to resolve the conflict by ignoring it. There was a gentleman's agreement never to mention skin color: "In the careless flow of our talk, it was the one subject avoided with meticulous concern." The words "black," "yellow," "nigger" were taboo, the vaguer and more polite words "dark" and "light," substituted when necessary.

In the beginning the policy brought moderate success. In no conscious way did the children consider their Grandma Redding a lesser person than their Grandma Conway. A black skin was less beautiful but bore no badge of inferiority. Soot-black boys in school might be uncomely but their frequent ability to outplay and outthink the mulatto children received due recognition. The immediate members of the family were exempt even from this aesthetic judgment. The lighter-skinned mother, brother, or sister did not suggest to the darker-skinned father or boy that they were less attractive in appearance. The family was "a garrisoned island in that sea" of the surrounding white world.

Gradually, however, the grandson began to perceive the fuller implications of his mulatto grandmother's beliefs. A black skin was "more than a blemish" to her. "In her notion it was a taint of flesh and bone and blood, varying in degree with the color of the skin, overcome sometimes by certain material distinctions and the grace of God, but otherwise fixed in the blood." Although his family lived on a respectable street, attended a segregated service at the Episcopal church, maintained safe, conservative standards in politics, and believed "in individual initiative and in its fruits," the boy began to sense the struggle which had gone into this status.

He remembered the flight at night to their new home in an all-white neighborhood of Wilmington, Delaware. Their street was quiet and elm-shaded, but it was the last outpost of gentility. Not far away lay the corner saloons, the dirty grocery stores, and the blank-walled factories where poorer whites and darker Negroes lived. He recalled the tireless industry of his father who was up at dawn, painting and repairing the house, shoveling snow, never late to his work, and only giving in to illness once in fifteen years. His father was dark, and both doomed and determined to combat his feeling of inferiority.

What the boy sensed dimly the author analyzes in detail. His father's exertion became his answer to prejudice. He was driven by "more than the necessity" to provide for his family decently. Married to a lighter-skinned woman, surrounded by whites, he was goaded by "an intangible something, a merciless, argus-eyed spiritual enemy that stalked his every movement and lurked in every corner." Since every white man embodied this enemy, he was always self-conscious and cautious, and only won "defensive victories." He had tried to rise from the "spiritual ghetto," the "east side" of slavery. He had worked his way through Howard University, taught country school, been a waiter, run a grocery store, and finally obtained the security and respectability of a postal service position. But outer achievement gave him no peace of mind.

The mother had all the assurance he lacked. Also a Howard graduate, she was tall, good-looking, and poised. The son admired her pride which was not vanity but "a kind of glowing consciousness" of her worth. Race talk had little meaning for her because she had never had occasion to feel inferior. "She knew the speeches of John Brown and Wendell Phillips, the poetry of Whittier and Whitman, but not as my father knew them: not as battering stones hurled against the strong walls of a prison." Consciously she recognized no imprisonment.

But her self-confidence was based on the color snobbery which her mother, in turn, had so unerringly inculcated in her. The moment her exclusive position was threatened, she lost her emotional control. The first break in the family conspiracy of silence about race occurred on that day when another Negro family moved into the neighborhood. They were renters, had a pianola, and gave other indications of "vulgar taste." For the first time the boy saw his mother "in rage and tears" and overheard her heated remarks to his father which epitomized the difference between them. To his father's quiet reminder that the newcomers were "our people" after all, she made the bitter rejoinder, "yours, maybe, but not mine."

Events accelerated after this to remove forever the boy's illusions about the unimportance of color. Within a few months of his mother's anger all the white people had left their street and mulattoes had moved in, doctors or ministers who paid high prices for the houses. They, in turn, were seeking to escape the mass migration of southern Negroes to the northern city. In the tide of World War I this "leaderless mass of blacks," this "dark tide of migration" had inundated the poor residential areas and the public schools. By the time Saunders Redding reached high school in 1919 color prejudice not only in his family but among the Negro population of this Delaware city was out in the open and in full swing.

In school the lesson of black inferiority was driven sharply home. Mulattoes received the choice of the parts in plays, the first chance for the new books, the first places in contests even when they fell below the standard of darker competitors. The black children either dropped out of school of their own accord or were encouraged to do so. Often the high school student noticed that these boys became drunks and loafers. Attracted at sixteen to a "doe-soft black girl named Viny," he himself received a direct warning about color. His high school principal asserted that this girl would never get any place in the world and would be a drag on his prospects of future success. By innuendo he could gather that, although he was dark, he was neither black nor a woman, and, with his family background and ability, had the opportunity of "marrying light" and climbing far.

His college course provided no surcease to this problem. Thoroughly confused and depressed by the contradictions of race, Saunders Redding attended college as a matter of course, but with little relish for the future and no convictions about a career. By now, the virus of class-caste had so poisoned him that he could adjust neither to a Negro nor a white school. "I hated and feared the whites. I hated and feared and was ashamed of Negroes." His only desire at last was to be alone.

At Lincoln University in Pennsylvania he detected a difference between him and the other colored students. He reacted to their smooth ambition, their desire to possess "yellow money, yellow cars, and yellow women," their single purpose "unmixed with either cynicism or idealism." To him they were small-souled extroverts, too encased in smugness to feel the pricks of other values beyond material success. In contradistinction, he was stirred by strange "imponderables" and "incommensurables" which made him uncertain and restless: "I could not spin in a whirring cosmos of my own creation, as the others did. I could not create a cosmos; I haunted others. I could not even spin; I wobbled." Isolated and lonely, he strained for glimpses of truth by avid reading and then decided on a new environment.

But Brown University in Rhode Island seemed to make matters worse. It precipitated an acute case of race consciousness. The two or three colored students studiously avoided each other: "We took elaborate precautions against even the appearance of clannishness." Occasionally they came together in their rooms at night with the shades pulled down, but even in this privacy they refrained from discussing race, refused to acknowledge aloud the snubs and slights of white classmates. Only once did one of them protest against their stilted behavior and articulate their inner tensions when he burst out: "I'm sick of being casual! I want to be honest and sincere about something. I want to stop feeling like I'll fall apart if I unclench my teeth." But this removal of his mask was the signal for his leaving college and later committing suicide.

A less drastic handling of the problem seemed to be a series of temporary escapes. The few colored students from nearby colleges would hold gay parties in Boston and cement their "desperate bond of frustration" in forgetfulness. The wilder the parties the more they became "the measure of our tense neurosis." The maladjusted group deluded themselves into believing that they had the courage of doomed men. But, underneath, those with puritanical upbringing suffered from a sense of guilt over their moral lapses. No real happiness resulted. Rather, the author analyzes these episodes in terms of unconscious self-destruction. "In reality we carried on a sort of blind quest for disaster, for demotic and moral suicide outside the harbors of sanity." Subsequent events had the inexorable quality of classic tragedy. Out of this group of about fifteen students, five committed suicide in the interval of six years. The rest tended to be "spiritual schizophrenes."

In such a situation it is not remarkable that Saunders Redding went completely over to nihilism by his Senior year. His emotions were solely negative. Now the only Negro, he had a sense of "competitive enmity," of fighting singlehanded against the whole white world. Furthermore, he could conceive of no reason for pursuing any longer those intangibles which might give meaning to life. Their very existence seemed doubtful. Just as democracy and religion were hollow mockeries, so was truth a figment of the imagination with only subjective validity. Lost in a maze of thoughts which led nowhere and were "symptomatic of a withering, grave sickness of doubt," this college student welcomed no visitors and withdrew into a room "peopled by a thousand nameless fears."

The graduate was in no mood to look at the world beyond college walls with any rose-tinted optimism of youth. In 1928, when he assumed a teaching position at Morehouse College in Atlanta, his critical gaze found flaws everywhere. He was disappointed in the predatory students, the "flabby softness" of the faculty, and the spiritual decay which emanated from the whole "futile, hamstrung group." The administration, in response, wasted little love on him, catalogued him as a radical, and dismissed him after three years. Nothing about his manner invited tolerance. The author pictures himself as "a lonely, random-brooding youth, uncertain, purposeless, lost, and yet so tightly wound that every day I lived big-eyed as death in sharp expectancy of a mortal blow."

During the next decade, however, he grew out of his extreme neurosis. Although the process is not explained by the author, undoubtedly maturity and the responsibilities of family life had a normal stabilizing effect. Swinging away from nihilism, he adopted an ameliorist position about race and society comparable to other authors in this group of autobiographies. Values become essential to him again.

The author is explicit that emotional awareness of his difficulties and of his need for stability preceded his painful intellectual comprehension. Even back in his college days a Jewish acquaintance had tried to show him the common danger of denying some part or all of oneself, the common longing for a spiritual home, "not a place in space, you understand. Not a marked place, geographically bounded," but a place for belonging. Not only he but all individuals groped towards a way of life in which they could absorb and be absorbed, understand and be understood, and thus feel "completely free and whole and one." Perhaps this was the seed of Redding's later hope that mankind was eternally building as well as destroying, that he was both a Negro and an American, that he was above all "an atom of humanity, a man." He could not isolate himself from the struggle of countless others. Identification with family and race would assuage his restlessness, but beyond that awaited "a people and all their strivings; a nation and its million destinies." His earlier misanthropy lay in his failure to recognize "that we were all estranged from something fundamentally ours" which could only be recovered by mutual effort.

Emotionally prepared, then, for a constructive attitude towards society, he still ran into intellectual obstacles. The fact remained that Negroes were treated like Negroes and not like men. Where were the contact points between Negroes and whites that would loosen the stranglehold of class-caste? How could both groups find their common meanings and build a new culture from their common heritage before it was too late? "What validity? What reality for this dying world of men and Negroes?"

The mature man could no longer be satisfied with speculation about abstract truth. Rather, the inductive method of science offered a refreshing alternative. If there were any answers at all to his questions, he would find them in concrete situations, with flesh-and-blood people. New faces and new scenes could give him intimations of the truth about the state of the world. So, in this spirit of inquiry, the researcher headed his car southward one day, to a part of the United States unfamiliar to him and most likely to administer a concentrated dose of the race problem.

Although the author gives us a progressive report as he journeys from place to place at random, it might be well for us to classify the types of people he meets. From Maryland to Mississippi he talks with Negro farmers and workers, teachers and lawyers. A vagabond, a gambler, and an old grandmother hold his attention as closely as a landowner and a college president. Everywhere in the black belt he finds Negroes who have been defeated by the caste system and Negroes who profit by exploiting other Negroes. But he also discovers individuals whose minds are alert to the social processes at work or whose sense of values have helped them find satisfactions in living. It is a strange and varied pattern.

There is Leon, sitting at dawn on the courthouse steps, competing with other Negroes for scarce jobs, "knowing that he was black and the planning was against him." He is filled with stereotypes about race: that Negroes can't get together, that "white folks got us beat," that an unfriendly Negro "ain't no white folks." He accepted his lower status as an absolute. "Instinctively he resented any attempt to transgress that validity, for it brought order into his world." In limiting his choices, it gives him more peace of mind than rebellion brought to the author's distant relative in Kentucky. Spoiled by her family, but resentful of her lighter-skinned mother, brothers, and schoolmates, she had become jealous and domineering, started to lie and drink heavily, and finally turned so abnormal as to be considered psychotic.

The tired, sick woman in cotton Arkansas who is raising her grandchildren never questions her lot as a Negro. Her greatest wish is for a little pension money so that she won't have to be buried in the gumtree swamp. But her unthinking kinship with misery and poverty are no more pathetic to Redding than the apathy of those colored teachers whose education has not conveyed real self-knowledge or courage. They are snobs, "the true bourgeoisie" who look to upper middle-class whites for their social philosophy and are thus indifferent to social reforms and antagonistic to "liberal or even independent thought." Among one Negro college faculty the author finds no realization "that there were great issues abroad in the world" and no creative scholarship. "Mere manipulators of knowledge," they spoke of gathering data on abstruse subjects and competed for scholarships and promotions. Although supposed to be race conscious, they lacked any real pride of race and were concerned only with their individual stake in the future. Obviously, theirs was a "puerile flight from reality."

But the author sees below the surface of his own condemnation. He recognizes that their mental sterility and their sycophancy are the products of a system which holds no real opportunities for them. Those who are brilliant soon reach the limit to which they are allowed to go.

Nothing remains but to rot within the shadow of a wall. The author recalls Kagawa's statement that this wall of the white race is "higher than the old wall of China."

Much more culpable than they is the type of Negro college president who benefits from keeping his teachers and students in their places. Redding heaps his scorn on one of these Negro educators with his paternalism only partially disguising his dislike of his own racial group. The product of one of the Reconstruction-period schools, he does not believe in the vote or any political activity for the Negro. "What do Negroes know or care about isolationism, or the national debt, or breaking the third term tradition?" he demands of his visitor. Even lynching, undesirable as it is, can best be handled not by political legislation for national laws but by the common sense of the white South which is well on the way to solving the problem.

According to this president the Negroes of the South have their hands full just learning to do a creditable piece of manual labor. Therefore his function is to train them, not to educate them. "You don't talk about educating men for farming and road-making," he explains. Above all, he wants to guard against turning out gentlemen. "What good is a gentleman with a manure fork?" becomes a rhetorical question which is an automatic rationalization of his position.

Behind this policy lies a basic contention about race inferiority. He sustains the stereotypes of the white South that the Negro is ignorant and shiftless, "improvident, immoral, and generally no good." Various governmental agencies under the New Deal, specifically the W.P.A., brought out these weak racial traits by "subsidizing shiftlessness." Good, hard work under discipline offers the only hope for Negro improvement. In his theory of education his teachers are pawns over whom he enjoys ruling with an iron hand. To Redding this whole way of thinking smacks of fascism long before the power-loving yet white-fearing college president admits a political bias in that direction: " 'There's a lot of propaganda about this totalitarian business,' he said. 'All the Italians and eighty-five million Germans can't be all wrong.' "

The Negro doctor whom the author meets on the northwestern edge of the black belt states his selfish motives with more direct frankness and less concern about garbing them in elaborate rationalizations. He buys up real estate, exploits Negro workers in a mill, and uses his money as a medium of prestige. To his credulous visitor he explains good-humoredly, "I'm doing like the white folks are doing. I'm looking out for number one. That's what democracy is, son." This crass opportunism seems scarcely more palatable to Redding than that of the educator.

It is a relief to him to discover many cases of Negroes who do not fit into the pattern of inferiority set by such leadership, who are too busy about their business to be exploited unduly. One landowner in Mississippi, for example, contradicts the legend about shrewd and conciliatory Negro landowners with the right white connections. This man turns out to be self-contained. Black, "without a trace of white blood," he had refused to accept white help, and had secured his seven hundred acres with difficulty but persistence. His older sons remember the share-cropping days and feel their father's pride in his own land.

The vagabond guitar player whom Redding picks up on the road is more suave with white people than the landowner, but equally independent inside. "Colored and wrinkled like an old potato," he feels secretly superior to the white men with whom he banters to please them. "He had the complete assurance and the freedom of a man who understands his environment and has no particular wish to change either it or himself." He thinks that Negroes really have all the "good bottom gravy" because they don't get involved in the kind of troubles that disrupt white people's lives, such as "war trouble, bad-times trouble, tight-money trouble." With his musical gifts and his homespun philosophy, living is easy, a day-by-day affair culminating in the fun of Saturday evenings.

Similarly, the poolroom owner in Memphis is not intimidated by whites. He does not plan to invite conflict, but he carries "an ugly-mouthed, short-snouted automatic" around with him just in case. With all his hard-boiled profanity and gambling and his realistic view of the world, he has some bedrock conviction. Although he cannot see that the right to vote will bring in extra bread and butter for Negroes, he contends that they should have it if white folks do. He had joined the dangerous local campaign for it because colored folks must "stick together regardless." When reprisals came, when some of the leaders were driven out of town or killed and the rest were informed that President Roosevelt wasn't running Northrup County, this rotund, coffee-brown man stood his ground.

People of all shades of color, from the back county of Louisiana and Mississippi, illustrate the principle of freedom again. As they danced to the music of Louis Armstrong's band, they seemed to shake off the sterile past and breathe in the air of freedom. "It was in and of the crowd. It was that the crowd, living in the present, believed in it." Instinctively they were proclaiming the anachronism of slavery.

But perhaps the people who convey to the traveler the deepest sense of harmony and inner freedom are the farmers in the little settlement of Knob, Kentucky. Unaffected and genuine, Matt and his wife give their simple hospitality to the stranger for a week. So moved is the author by the atmosphere of the place that he captures it in particularly vivid phrases. Matt, "lean as a fence picket," liked to tell "tall tales," "liked laughter as something to live with." At the same time he had a great capacity for quiet which aroused in an observer "the same indescribable feeling of completeness and wholeness one gets in seeing an old, good dog resting." He had no desire to travel, was wedded to his small piece of land, and did not like the idea of a total stranger's possessing it some day.

His wife, "shaped like a clumsy wigwam," showed the visitor a bed "as clean as pre-dawn snow," and helped create the general mood of serenity. Husband and wife could sit for long periods without a word. "It was as if all the quiet of that golden afternoon flowed from their breathing. Behind them, their small many-windowed cottage had turned quietly and evenly from white to gray, as if the gentle wash of quiet time alone had acted upon it."

The weary guest treasured the beauty of this scarlet autumn respite, noticing when "the sun reached long fingers straight across the land and flung struck matches in the farthest field" or when later "the dark hills shoved their strength and sweetness right into the room." But the most healing quality of this experience arose from the peaceful way of life. From some inner reservoir, this unassuming farmer and his wife had the secret of contentment which was a thing in itself, regardless of the walls of white prejudice in the world outside. When friends and neighbors called, no discordant note was struck. "No one ever seemed to interrupt anyone else, and following every utterance there was a full weight of silence, the quiet recognition of each man's right to have his say considered."

Just as important as his contacts with individuals who had retained their integrity in a South hostile to Negroes is the author's discovery of social critics who could survey the scene as a whole. Although native to their regions, they are capable of joining the northern visitor in observation and analysis. Here are intellectuals of Redding's own caliber, utilizing their mental acumen not to adapt to racial mores but to attack the whole system of disparity. The author does not always find himself in agreement on all points of their thinking, but he admires their realistic awareness of Negro-white relations and their spirit of noncompromise.

First comes the communist who rides a long stretch of the road with him. Mocking hazel eyes in "crisp brown face," he expounds his views vehemently. In spite of the fact that he had come from a middle-class background and had still been "terrifically race-conscious" even when he joined a union for seamen, he soon came to feel that white and black workers should organize together for their common interests and because they were essentially alike. It was "the decency of some of these steerage bums" that had taught him finally the "humanity" of all men. As a volunteer combatant against Franco in Spain, as a union organizer, he snapped the dry twigs of his family standards into little pieces. He had a different concept of his duty to America. "I'd like to be a good American without being either middle class or Negro. You can't be a good all three. You can't be a good two."

The lawyer in the West Virginia coal mines also thinks that white and colored workers must pool their efforts if they are to survive. So sensitive to his sordid environment that he had become a heavy drinker, he has moments of lucidity when his background of wide reading and observation enables him to describe the plight of the miners. The coal companies are "machines, deliberately cruel," and "oppression is part of the system." Impatient with some of the stupid mistakes of the communists, he nevertheless approves of their teaching the Negro miners "that they were not the only victims of greed and exploitation." This lesson has "a bolstering effect upon their sense of common humanity" and proves the necessity of "collective security" against common tyranny.

The Supervisor of Negro Recreation and Education at T.V.A. turns out to be a less erratic and more solid critic. Concerned about discrimination which emanates from organized labor as well as government policy, he can document his statements from a thorough acquaintance with the findings of the sociologists and from his own statistical studies of the Negro workers. As a result of six years in this work he can claim that "democracy's taking an awful beating here on T.V.A." It is true that the whites have "a great social program." But

Negro workers are excluded from the classes which increase the skills of the white workers. The unions, with government acquiescence, protect the best jobs for white workers so that there is only one Negro skilled laborer, a Diesel engineer with pay below his rank. With no incentive or chance for promotion the unskilled Negro laborer wastes his money on alcohol and women and tries his best to live in the present.

Believing in democracy "right on down to the bricks," this Negro director is outspoken about its absence in his situation. What can he say to a slow-talking Georgia boy who wants to know why, if democracy is so good for white folks, it isn't also good for Negroes? "Maybe you know that a hundred and seventy-five years is no time in the life of a great ideal and what not. Maybe I understand it. But what do boys from Georgia know about it? They want something right now." To put it negatively, just some "plain old justice" in the question of work and wages would prevent demoralization and save future trouble in this governmental project.

The mayor of a former all-Negro town holds on to the same concept of the indivisibility of democracy. Coming at the problem from a different angle, this Howard- and Yale-trained leader shows how unnatural it was to pioneer a settlement, in the heart of the Delta region of Mississippi, based upon segregation. The founders back in 1886 were "taking flight from the real situation," were "trying to find an easy way to democracy" when there is no easy way, and no solution without the mutual efforts of both races. Even if Negro children may derive a temporary security from seeing only Negroes in all positions of authority, they are living in a fool's paradise which is threatened each day from the outside. The eventual disintegration of the town lay in the nature of things. "You don't think, do you," inquires mayor of author, "that we're really less capable than anyone else? No. River City proves nothing about the Negro. It proves plenty about humanity. Not black humanity, nor white humanity. Just humanity."

Lawyer, communist, executive, mayor, each from his particular angle, stress the common humanity of all races and the urgency of interracial solutions. With their basic diagnosis the author-investigator finds himself in agreement. Conscious that his travels have not only brought him far in space and time but also in understanding, he no longer regards the Negro as a problem "in vacuo and in toto." Rather, the Negro is "only an equation in a problem of many equations, an equally important one of which is the white man." This means that the Negro must learn to know and understand the white man as well. The author implies that the Negro-white tensions, heightened by class-caste attitudes and practices, can only be relaxed by hastening the acculturation process whereby an increasing number of individuals are accepted into the larger stream of American culture. No one-sided understanding will accomplish this feat.

The obstacles in the way can be no more evident to anyone than to Redding. He would be the first to admit to hostility of whites supported by a dozen stereotypes. Although his reason tells him that there exists no typical southern white man as well as no typical southern Negro, from childhood he had carried about with him a mental image: "He was gangling, raw-boned, pot-bellied, sandy-haired. He went about barefoot, in an undershirt and dirt-crusted blue denim breeches, without which he never slept and within which he concealed a bottle of red whisky, a horse pistol, and other lethal weapons." The childish fears centering around this bogeyman, invoked by Negro mothers to exact obedience, never quite materialize in his case. But Redding does encounter one white man in southeastern Missouri who closely corresponded to the stereotype. While ready to resist his arrogance and meet violence with violence if need be, Redding feels exhausted after the crisis. He recognizes "an almost psychopathic awareness" of his estrangement even from the two white travelers who had been decent enough to support his side of the controversy. The effect is "like a vast, steely emptiness in my stomach."

Such contacts often left him discouraged and "mired in abysmal futility." But so had his associations with many Negroes of the wrong type. What he aimed for was the ability to rise above the small-minded individuals in both racial groups who polluted the atmosphere around them with the poison of race prejudice and race consciousness. Not an out-going person by nature, the traveler rejoiced in his accelerated power to discover the best in a wide range of people and to accept these individuals easily and simply. More and more "the stuff of their lives was filling up the emptiness of my own, leaving no room for barriers."

In unexpected places and at odd moments, then, the mature man finds in the concrete those intangibles he had once sought in vain. He glimpses "integrity of spirit, love of freedom, courage, patience, hope" where there is no fertile soil to nourish them. Out of the lowest economic stratum of Negroes spring up continually these human values which form "the highest common denominator of mankind." Apparently indestructible, "quietly alive and solid," such attributes are a part of the unfinished business of democracy and thus "the bane of those who would destroy freedom."

In the author's final realization of this truth, which emerged out of "so much pain, so much groping, so much growing," lies the explanation for his title, *No Day of Triumph.* He has proved to his own satisfaction that Negroes everywhere share the universal traits. "That Negroes hold these values in common with others is America's fortune, and, in a very immediate sense, the Negro American's salvation." Certainly there is justification for a hope in America's future, if but a sober hope. With Woodrow Wilson the author can say, "This is not a day of triumph; it is a day of dedication." Victory he is entitled to feel, commensurate with the nature of his discoveries, but triumph is yet ahead, awaiting the forces of humanity.

Black Boy

RICHARD WRIGHT

ON the strength of his experience, Richard Wright belongs closer to Frederick Douglass than any of our autobiographers. A slave in deed, if not in name, trapped by a thousand cruelties and taboos, he pushes against the dead weight of his environment by virtue of the same untutored brilliance. He, too, knows the near-death of flogging, the humiliation of random blows, and the flaring resentment against an irrational violence. Born many decades after Douglass and the Abolitionists had fought the good fight, Wright is a child of the deepest South where the mores of new race relations are slow to penetrate, and where a dark skin still permits of no misstep in a white-dominated world without fear of reprisal. The fact that the boy's worst punishments were administered by his own relatives only proved the completeness of that dominance. His family, segregated from the whites, conformed to their dictates and tried to mold him into piety and subserviency. Why he rebelled and asserted his humanity while his brother, his cousins, his schoolmates fell into line remains one of the perennial miracles of personality development.

Since portions of *Black Boy* were published as early as 1937, when the author was still in his twenties, appropriately it intended to be only "a record of childhood and youth." But, in relation to the brief span of years it covers, compared to the autobiographies of Douglass, Du Bois, and James Weldon Johnson, it gives ample measure. Every facet of early experience is exposed with such clarity that the effect is startling in its illusion of reality. While a section of the general public, which has heard of *Black Boy* if of no other Negro-American autobiography, may like to explain its phenomenal sales and its many editions in terms of its "sensationalism," most literate Americans recognize that they stand in the presence of a masterpiece, that the bitterness and defeat of youth have come alive into the immortality of art. Even distortion of fact may be forgiven when it serves as handmaiden for the larger truth.

The youngest and the most famed of our autobiographers, Richard Wright is also the most generous. He approximates complete self-analysis and self-revelation. He leaves nothing to chance. The would-be discerning reader is allowed no surmises about the springs of his conduct or the state of his feelings from year to year. He even wonders why and how, under the existing conditions, the germs of higher aspiration could multiply in him; why, seething with hates and fears, he never succumbed to suggestions of inferiority. His own psychoanalyst, this brilliant writer wields the surgeon's scalpel ruthlessly and folds back layer after layer of motivation to reach the quivering reality beneath.

Yet Richard Wright never makes his diagnosis calmly. He does not utilize the detachment of a Du Bois or a Johnson in the midst of turmoil. They, too, feel the race problem at the heart of their lives, but they often approach it through tortuous intellectual channels, like scientists at work, observing even their own emotions of resentment. But Wright has a strange capacity of immediacy. He is direct, specific, personal, and of the earth. He flings himself into his analysis with an abandon which cannot be explained merely by his comparative youthfulness. He knows only what he knows and works from the bottom up, not the top down. Of our whole group, he is the most genuine representative of lower-class life and in the best position to portray its hunger, its misery, and its despair.

In an important way Wright touches the lives and writing of Langston Hughes and Saunders Redding. Each of them reacts with such acute sensitivity to people and situations that he is often on the verge of both physical and mental illness, and each is interested in explaining the process in psychological terms. But Wright goes a step further into subjectivity. We are taken into the darkest recesses of a consciousness which is cradled in conflict. Though tortured his mind is implacable in conviction, though warped his personality seeks its law of growth. The author reviews his development through the concepts of "rejection, rebellion, aggression," and relates it intimately to the "anxiety and compulsive cruelty" in the prejudice of the white South. His readiness to adopt up-to-date psychological concepts is due to the fact that they proffer the magic key to depths of maladjustment even greater than that experienced by Hughes and Redding. These two never felt the stifling grip of caste within the boundaries of the Deep South and never endured an involuntary lower-class status. By comparison, Richard Wright's heavier burdens sink him further into the morass of pain from which only prolonged psychological awareness can save him.

At first glance it might seem that Angelo Herndon offers the closest parallel to Richard Wright. He shares the fate of low-class status within the caste restrictions of the Deep South. Poverty and hunger are his familiars also. Both Herndon and Wright were deprived of the high school education which Hughes and Redding received, and which they were equally capable of absorbing to the best advantage. Both knew the anger and frustration of job discrimination because of race. But Herndon, far apart as he drew in his ideology from his family, never was subjected to the final, crushing blow of family antagonisms. His father believed in him, his mother tended him through his illnesses. As his starting point he had that stability of family loyalty which was entirely lacking in the experience of his contemporary. Child of a broken home, Richard Wright had only unpleasant memories of the father who deserted and of the mother who was too harassed or too ill to cope with his problems adequately. Prematurely, the small child sensed that he was one against the odds. While Herndon, in adolescence, was finding the outlet of cooperation with others in vigorous action, Wright was still beating against the bars of solitary confinement.

The outer events of Wright's childhood formed a crazy quilt of experience. Growing up in the region through which the lower Mississippi flows, where Tennessee, Mississippi, and Arkansas converge, he shuttled between all three states, with Memphis his northernmost point and Natchez on the River his southernmost point. After his father's desertion and his mother's failure to support her two boys in the big city he was placed in an orphanage. Then he was taken within the circumference of his maternal relatives. His maternal grandmother had had nine children who felt called upon to take a hand when misfortune fell upon one of their number. When he was eight Richard Wright lived with an aunt, when he was nearing twelve with an uncle, but his grandmother's home in Jackson, Mississippi, where his invalid mother stayed, proved to be the center of the circle to which he constantly returned, and from which the seventeen-year-old finally ran away to Memphis.

His schooling was equally erratic. Up to the time he was twelve he had never completed a single year. In Memphis he had started school later than usual because his mother could not afford to buy him the necessary clothes. Instead he roamed the streets during the day, while she worked as a cook, and frequented saloons where the men took crude delight in giving him beer or whisky and watching its effect. His first days at school taught him little more than the "four letter words" he had already picked up without understanding as a five-year-old in tenement and saloon. The orphanage added nothing to his formal education. The various schools he attended were memorable only for the progressive fights they entailed to establish the newcomer's right on the playgrounds. At twelve he had the dubious privilege of a year in a private religious school under the stern aegis of his school-teacher aunt. After taunts and physical abuse, she left her recalcitrant pupil strictly alone so that he merely occupied a seat for the remainder of the year.

Only at thirteen did the young boy have his opportunity to gain some of the knowledge he had longed for secretly since a coal deliverer had taught him to count to a hundred. By this time his personality was not only "lopsided," but his "knowledge of feeling" was far greater than his "knowledge of fact." Transferred to a public school and put into the fifth grade only because his age seemed to require it, he studied day and night for two weeks, won promotion to the sixth grade, and continued until his graduation from the ninth grade. This marked the end of his formal schooling, at sixteen years of age.

As with many boys from low-income homes, he was forced to work at odd jobs at an early age. Before he was twelve he had swept and delivered for a pressing shop, and carried food trays to trains, wood to cafes, and lunches to workers in the roundhouse. Because his grandmother was a Seventh Day Adventist who did not believe in work on Saturday he was cut off from opportunities for awhile. But by seventh grade his clothes were so ragged that he insisted he would leave home if he couldn't earn some money and began the usual routine of doing chores for white people. After eighth grade, when he weighed less than a hundred pounds, he worked as a water boy in a brickyard, after ninth grade as a porter in a cheap clothing store. The petty jobs which followed did not satisfy him. His one good opening to learn the optical trade under a "Yankee" employer was thwarted by the white workers who would not teach him the mechanics of grinding and polishing lenses and bullied him into leaving.

It was only in desperation that he entered into his single dishonest transaction in order to acquire the money to leave Jackson and make a fresh start in Memphis. Mopping at night in a hotel, and bootlegging liquor to white prostitutes depressed him. The alternative was to join the racket with the cashier of reselling movie tickets. The success of the plan enabled him to leave his old environment for good, to find a decent place to live and a steady job as errand boy of an optical company in Memphis. It was only a matter of months before he had saved enough money to send for his mother and brother and had laid definite plans toward their migrating northward to Chicago. On the verge of manhood, Richard Wright was in a position at last to shed the limitations of the Deep South and move in the direction of the creative life and work his cramped circumstances had only let him imagine faintly.

How much he had suffered under the insecurities and deprivations of his life can not be gauged by a mere summary of the events which caused them. What makes *Black Boy* distinctive as an autobiography is its running commentary of emotional response to every situation. It is only by participation in each nuance of mood and feeling that we can sense that elusive totality of personality.

To begin with, the small boy was attuned to sensation as "the moments of living slowly revealed their colored meaning." He felt wonder when he first saw "spotted black-and-white horses clopping down a dusty road through clouds of powdered clay"; delight when he looked at "long straight rows of red and green vegetables stretching away in the sun to the bright horizon"; melancholy when he caught "the tingling scent of burning hickory wood," languor when he heard "green leaves rustling with a rainlike sound." As the four-year-old gazed down on "the yellow, dreaming waters of the Mississippi River" from the bluffs above, a "vague sense of the infinite" flowed softly into his consciousness. He noticed immediately, when he was taken to Memphis, that "the absence of green, growing things made the city seem dead."

Later, in Arkansas, he welcomed again "the aura of limitless freedom distilled from the rolling sweep of tall green grass swaying and glinting in the wind and sun." Every morning he would get up early to walk barefooted in the dust, "reveling in the strange mixture of the cold dew-wet crust on top of the road and the warm, sun-baked dust beneath." He loved to play and shout in wide, green fields or watch in silence "star-heavy skies." Like a thirsty plant he absorbed all natural beauty around him.

But his starved childhood held only a small quota of such experience. The very sensitivities which made him aware of the best also made him cringe before the worst in his environment. During a moment of boredom from enforced idleness, the four-year-old experimented with burning the curtains and accidentally set the house on fire. When he was beaten into unconsciousness by his mother he was "lost in a fog of fear" and of illness for days. His imagination was no longer his friend. Exhausted, he was terrified of sleep for then he would see "huge wobbly white bags, like the full udders of cows, suspended from the ceiling," waiting to drench him with liquid.

Later, when he ran away from the orphanage, the streets seemed dangerous with buildings and trees which loomed ominously. Superstitions and fears fed his nature until he went through a period of nightmares and sleep-walking. At one time, when he learned that a boy had died in the bed he was using at his uncle's, his imagination "began to weave ghosts." Strange faces in new schools froze him into self-consciousness so that he could not recite and sat with burning neck and ears, "hating myself, hating them." His mother's sudden stroke of paralysis robbed him of any desire to play. "Within an hour the half-friendly world that I had known had turned cold and hostile." He brooded morosely, trying not to think of a "tomorrow that was neither real nor wanted," for all tomorrows held questions without answers.

Always there had been an undercurrent of hunger which sometimes swirled up around him and baffled him. It was as if a "hostile stranger" no longer waited at his elbow but stood beside his bed at night, watching gauntly, "nudging my ribs, twisting my empty guts until they ached." Often at the orphanage he would grow dizzy while working in the yard, and recover to stare "in bleak astonishment" at the grass. At his aunt's he hoarded his biscuits, afraid that "if I ate enough there would not be anything left for another time." During his grade school days he ate mush in the mornings and greens at night. At lunchtime he pretended to his schoolmates that he was never hungry at noon. "And I would swallow my saliva as I saw them split open loaves of bread and line them with juicy sardines." He knew what it was to "sway while walking," to feel his heart give "a sudden wild spurt of beating" which would leave him breathless.

By the time he was twelve, Richard Wright had already endured enough misfortune to fix his attitudes toward life. His mother's illness "grew into a symbol," and "set the emotional tone." It signified all the poverty, hunger, and dislocation he had known and cast over him "a somberness of spirit" that never left him. His innate sensitiveness had received such bruises that the dreamer had turned realist, the seeker skeptic. Circumstances demanded the cruel and violent rather than the tender, peaceful, and sympathetic side of his nature. His early sense of wonder lay buried under an accumulation of scorn and rebellion. At the start of adolescence, this boy faced more than the normal number of unresolved conflicts.

Adding to his burden of misery were some serious maladjustments in his family relationships. Worse than the shock of tenement life on his imagination or the pangs of hunger on his will to live was the fact that he seemed to be a misfit everywhere he went. He had a diabolic capacity for being misunderstood. From infancy his parents had treated him as a nuisance and a problem, to be dealt with severely. Automatically, he was the one always in the wrong.

His father assumed the role of lawgiver and became like a despised stranger, "alien and remote," in whose huge presence the small boy never ventured to laugh. The opportunity to express his resentment of this dominance came one day when he chose to take literally his father's injunction to kill the kitten disturbing his sleep. This was his first and only triumph over his father. "He could not punish me now without risking his authority . . . I had made him know that I felt he was cruel and I had done it without his punishing me." The boy's perverted happiness indicated the general unhealthiness of this father-son relationship. The image of his living with another woman and of refusing help to his wife and sons burned in the older son's memory so that in the hungry days ahead he thought of his father with "deep biological bitterness." It wasn't until years later that Richard Wright realized no basis of understanding could ever exist between them. Though tied by blood, they would always speak a different language, live "on vastly distant planes of reality."

Living with maternal relatives carried on the precedent. They regarded him as a lost soul when he unwittingly used the language picked up in his slum environment. He was beaten for trifles and blamed for his grandmother's fall when he dodged her blow one day. "I was already so conditioned toward my relatives that when I passed them I actually had a nervous tic in my muscles." Driven at last to self-defence, he threatened to use a knife or razor blade if he were touched and consequently drew down on his head the stigma of criminal. Often he asked himself what was the matter with him: "I never seemed to do things as people expected them to be done. Every word and gesture I made seemed to provoke hostility." By the time he was in ninth grade, he was treated like a pariah in the family circle: "My loneliness became organic. I felt walled in and I grew irritable."

Undoubtedly a large factor in the family antagonism was his resistance to their attempts at religious conversion. His grandmother's fanaticism connected up with her struggle from lower- to middle-class status. Her emphasis on respectability corresponded closely with her emphasis on finding God. Believing in the Second Coming of Christ, she had no intention of bringing down the wrath of God on her household because of one recalcitrant member. As a minor, an unwelcome dependent, the grandson at first "was compelled to make a pretense of worshiping her God" in return for his keep. But the imagery of burning lakes, vanishing seas, valleys of dry bones, blood red moons, fantastic beasts, and amazing miracles lost its emotional appeal whenever he stepped out of the church into the bright sunshine and world of people. He knew "that none of it was true and that nothing would happen."

Certainly his relatives did not make religion seem very attractive to him by their example. The quarreling and the violence in his grandmother's household convinced him that "the naked will to power seemed always to walk in the wake of a hymn." But an even more important inhibition lay in the power of his own reasoning. His personality had already been stamped into realism "by unchartered conditions"; his sense of living was "as deep as that which the church was trying to give." He could discover no belief in original sin. What faith he had was rooted in the "common realities of life."

The existence or non-existence of God never worried him. An all-wise, all-powerful God would laugh at his foolish denial. If no God, "then why all the commotion?" When the community joined his grandmother in pressing him towards conversion before he encountered the sins of the public school, the twelve-year-old formulated a statement which expressed his feeling about God and about his own experience of fear, hunger, and loneliness; "If laying down my life could stop the suffering in the world, I'd do it. But I don't believe anything can stop it." After this, he became "dead" to his grandmother.

During his public school days he went through a meaningless rite of baptism. Improving slightly, his mother joined the Methodist church and pleaded with him not to disgrace his "old, crippled mother." Although disgusted with the emotionalism of the revival, and adamant that he had no religious feeling or conviction, this time public opinion was too strong for him. But he recognized that he and the other boys were being "shamelessly exploited," that "this business of saving souls had no ethics." It was a tribal matter, a way of enforcing community standards by which those who would not conform changed into "moral monsters." On the whole it seemed wiser to swallow his anger and shame, to share the lot of other boys, and to agree together later that they were bored with religion, that conversion was a fraud and that playing hooky from church offered the logical solution. His backsliding from grace made his daily sins appear more scarlet to his relatives.

Against such a background the facts of race loomed all the more terribly before the eyes of the growing boy. As the vague curiosity of childhood was replaced by sharp, direct experience, he learned to hate and fear white men. By the time he stood poised in flight northward the white South aroused an almost psychopathic response.

Strangely enough, he had no early aversion to whites. Many of his relatives were as white-looking as white people. His father had Indian, white, and Negro ancestry. Although his maternal grandfather was "a tall, skinny, silent, grim, black man" who had run away from slavery to fight on the Union side, his maternal grandmother, also a former slave, came from Irish, Scotch, and French stock and bore no trace of color. In Memphis, when the small boy first heard about the beating of a "black boy" by a "white man," it was natural for him to assume a father-son relationship. White people who were not relatives existed somewhere in the background of the city but carried no emotional validity.

It was a different matter, however, when he sometimes sat in the kitchens where his mother worked, and peered at the white people eating. He grew "vaguely angry," and tried to figure out why they had enough while he went hungry. As white people became real to him, he stared at them, "wondering what they were really like," wondering about the increasing tales of violence he heard. He plied his mother with questions. Did his grandmother who seemed white become colored when she married his grandfather? Why didn't she marry a white man? But his mother turned a deaf ear or silenced him angrily. "She was not concealing facts, but feelings, attitudes, convictions which she did not want me to know." By the time the small boy left Memphis to begin the round of living with relatives, he felt a vague uneasiness but no active fear of whites.

Almost immediately disaster struck home. White men who coveted the flourishing saloon business of Richard Wright's uncle in Arkansas and who warned him to leave, shot him down in cold blood when he ignored the threat. The relatives fled for their lives. "This was as close as white terror had ever come to me and my mind reeled. Why had we not fought back, I asked my mother, and the fear that was in her made her slap me into silence." Shortly after, he saw his first chain gang, with Negro convicts watched by white guards. And this time his mother answered his questions: White men don't wear stripes because they are harder on black men than on each other. Yet all the black men don't join together and fight back for the simple reason that they have no guns.

Increasingly the child identified himself with a mistreated group. World War I contained no real meaning for him intrinsically, but the rumors of racial conflicts disturbed him deeply. Although he had not yet been directly abused by whites, the mere mention of them set off "a vast complex of emotions," involving the whole of his personality. He was as conditioned to their existence as if he had been "the victim of a thousand lynchings." By adolescence he subscribed to the racial sentiments of other boys whose "touchstone of fraternity" was how much hostility they held towards white people. Large enough now to inspire fear, these boys began to play their "traditional racial roles" with the white boys in the community as though it was in their blood.

Yet there remained a crucial difference between him and his schoolmates. He worried about the problem of race relations, trying to fathom the causes of friction. But, when he posed the larger issues to them, they were nonplussed and either met him with silence or turned the matter into a joke. "They were vocal about the petty individual wrongs they suffered, but they possessed no desire for a knowledge of the picture as a whole." They gave his restless mind as little satisfaction as his mother in childhood. Without mental companionship, he was thrown back on the need to thrash out questions for himself.

In one way affairs ran along more smoothly for the other boys. In spite of their grievances, they worked out techniques of adjustment to the white community. They observed the code of behavior with their white employers with mechanical efficiency, and sloughed it off easily after work hours. But Richard Wright operated under tension each moment he spent in the presence of whites. Because his religious grandmother, with her work prohibition on Saturdays, had postponed the age when he started doing odd jobs for white people, the process of accommodation was apparently all the more painful and labored. According to the author, with earlier experience perhaps "the tension would have become an habitual condition, contained and controlled by reflex." As it was, he "overreacted to each event" with a rush of emotion. Exhausted by conflict, he would go to bed tired and get up unrefreshed.

As he grew older, he realized that his attitude placed him in danger. He could not "grin" and seem affable and contented, he could not be subservient. He would dissemble for short periods, only to forget and "act straight and human again." When he was sixteen, a friend chided him for acting around white people as if he didn't know they were white and for letting them see it. The friend was concerned that he would forfeit his chances to eat, whereas Richard Wright was more interested in the psychology of these whites. Because he stole nothing and wanted to look them straight in the face as man to man, he seemed to make them uncomfortable. Evidently they encouraged deceit and irresponsibility in Negroes as a means of perpetuating their own "safe and superior" role. The Negro like himself who didn't conform to type was therefore an "uppity" Negro who required surveillance and might expect violence.

He was always complicating his life by this type of analysis. An inner compulsion drove him "to feel and think out each tiny item of racial experience in the light of the whole race problem." It was a much simpler matter to the whites. While he grew "conscious of the entirety" of his relations to them, they remained "conscious only of what was happening at a given moment." He could even gain a perspective on the very men who reviled and abused him, who refused him jobs or made him the butt of cruel jokes. They did not stand in his mind as individual men so much as a "part of a huge, implacable, elemental design toward which hate was futile." He longed to strike back, to assert his rights, but how, where, and at whom?

With no outlet for his aggression, his personality was shattered by each act of discrimination. Sometimes he seemed "numb," "reduced to a lumpish, loose, dissolved state," a "non-man, something that knew vaguely that it was human but felt that it was not." He was swayed by desperation, terror, and anxiety as well as by hate. At other times his reason took control. Then he would weigh his chances for continued life in the South, and conclude that he could never accept his "place" because he did not believe that he was inferior or belonged to an inferior race. This conviction gradually counteracted the negative emotional conditioning and helped him towards the decision of leaving the South.

As he studied his situation, he knew that he could not count on any "outright black rebellion" since whites outnumbered Negroes. Certainly he could never accede to the solution of transferring his hatred to other Negroes, a course of action which would be self-defeating and thus highly acceptable to whites. Neither sex nor alcohol appealed to him as escapes—a reaction which may be explainable in terms of his father's unwelcome behavior. He lacked the training and the inclination to strive towards success as a professional man. Wealthy Negroes were as alien to him as white people. Although white society had forced him outside any respect for their laws so that he no longer felt bound by them, crime held its own punishment for him. In some strange way he had acquired higher standards for himself than any of these responses to his environment implied. He still hoped that somehow, somewhere, "life could be different, could be lived in a fuller and richer manner." His star, like that of Douglass, pointed northward.

The writer can well ask himself, "From where in this southern darkness had I caught a sense of freedom?" Or again, "How dare I consider my feelings superior to the gross environment that sought to claim me?" To these we might add a question about his early childhood for which the same answer might suffice. Why did the pre-school boy thumb through the pages of stray books and burn to understand "the baffling black print?" What made him plead with his mother to tell him the meaning of every strange word he saw? In explaining that these words held no value for him in themselves but formed "the gateway to a forbidden and enchanting land," the author provides us with the clue to his survival and his hope.

Undoubtedly we have here an instance of a child who was gifted with a superior intelligence which reached out thirstily for understanding. In proportion to the thwarting effect of the real world developed the riches of the imaginative world. Family and race troubles soon deprived him of the pristine happiness in nature. But he could still endow his "bare and bleak" surroundings with "unlimited potentialities." No disciplining relatives or hostile white people could encroach. "Because I had no power to make things happen outside of me in the objective world, I made things happen within." While he always enjoyed exploring his environment and preferred going without meals at home to losing his chance to wander, his strongest curiosity was intellectual. Books thus served both as emotional outlet and mental stimulus.

In the beginning any kind of book sufficed, the more melodramatic the better. His first novel of intrigue and murder, relayed to him by an older person, filled him with sharp excitement and elicited from him his first "total emotional response." This was followed by the cheap pulp stories in a newspaper he peddled. He would lock his door at night and "revel in outlandish exploits of outlandish men in faraway, outlandish cities." But by now the appeal was more than an opportunity for vicarious violence. "For the first time in my life I became aware of the life of the modern world, of vast cities, and I was claimed by it; I loved it." He accepted these stories as true because he "hungered for a different life, for something new." His civics and English and geography books now took on fresh importance. At the beginning of each term in public school he read through them all at once and pondered over them, "weaving fantasies about cities."

But this eager mind could not content itself with mere receptivity. It had to create, in turn. Responding warmly to words and ideas, he needed to return something of himself. Even as early as twelve, during the time when his grandmother was trying to save his soul, he started to write. Closeted in his room, ostensibly for prayer, he composed a story. It had no plot or action, "nothing save atmosphere and longing and death," but it was all his own. "I had made something, no matter how bad it was; and it was mine."

Perhaps it was the community reaction to the newspaper publication of an eighth grade story which first made Richard Wright sense the full measure of his apartness from others. The Negroes who were shocked by his wasting his time and by his use of the word, *hell,* in the lurid title, as well as the whites who mocked his ambition to be a writer, forced upon him the thought of his "strange and separate road." His total environment was alien to the very notion of a Negro's desiring to express himself in writing. "I was building up in me a dream which the entire educational system of the South had been rigged to stifle." The type of consciousness such dreams presaged carried "the penalty of death."

But Richard Wright had reached the turning point where fear could no longer smother the flame within him. He realized the network of disadvantages which would entangle his efforts to write. In his "Jim Crow station in life," he would even have difficulty learning about people and places intimately enough to write truly of them. But this sobering thought quickened rather than deadened him. "I now knew what being a Negro meant. I could endure the hunger. I had learned to live with hate. But to feel that there were feelings denied me, that the very breath of life itself was beyond my reach, that more than anything else hurt, wounded me. I had a new hunger." Stubbornly, he planned to overcome his handicaps one by one. In the stirring of his own creativity lay the assurance of his rebellion as a man.

As he assumed adulthood in Memphis the reading of good books and magazines served as a means to his purpose. Reading became a drug, a dope, a sense of life itself. Although he was not allowed as a Negro to obtain books from the public library for himself, an Irish-Catholic in the optical firm secretly gave him the use of his library card. He not only ran through copies of *Harper's* and the *Atlantic Monthly,* but he read all the works he could find of modern American writers like H. L. Mencken, Theodore Dreiser, Sherwood Anderson, and Sinclair Lewis. Interested in the point of view rather than the plots, he found "new ways of looking and seeing." It was a revelation to him to discover that these men were also "defensively critical of the straitened American environment." And they had the courage to use words as weapons.

For the first time the young Negro felt an identity of mind with men whom society classified as white. "All my life had shaped me for the realism, the naturalism of the modern novel, and I could not read enough of them." He had experienced the cruelty and sordidness and stupidity these novelists portrayed at the core of American culture. Yet, because they seemed to think "that America could be shaped nearer to the hearts of those who lived in it," they held out a faint promise to readers like Richard Wright: "I felt touching my face a tinge of warmth from an unseen light." Possibly there existed, then, some "redeeming meaning" for all men who "struggled and suffered here beneath the stars."

At the end of this "record of childhood and youth" we can surmise that the north-bound traveller is awakening to a notion of collectivism. His own problems are losing their uniqueness. There must be other "black boys" who have been stunted in their development. There must be "white boys," too, young people not only in America but everywhere, at odds with their environments. Such a realization must have assuaged his loneliness and, at the same time, have laid on him the responsibility of playing spokesman for all those thousands of less articulate ones. Precipitated into manhood prematurely, the future author of *Uncle Tom's Children* and *Native Son* must have sensed at the start of his career as a writer that his work could assume symbolic importance. No one knew better than he the tale of exploitation. No one felt more strongly than he the need to exonerate its victims from moral blame.

All his life he had known what it was to suffer under false charges. Like a snowball gathering volume, his "crimes" had collected attitudes of expectation in those about him. In reality, however, as the autobiographer wishes to show, he was more sinned against than sinning, whereas society in its entity—white-instigated, white-controlled—was the master criminal. While an unfriendly milieu was forcing his personality into the mold of rebellion and rank individualism, his mind was grappling with factors in understanding. A stubborn weed, he persisted and survived until his reading and his knowledge of the wider world of men and affairs enlarged his consciousness to the point where he could pull himself out of the barrenness of his subjectivity. This process he describes minutely. The most intimate, the most emotional of all our autobiographies, *Black Boy* contains a solid nugget of social realism which weighs down its flights of feeling until they take on the importance of sober fact and interpretation for a whole culture to heed.

Summary

SEARCHLIGHT ON SOCIETY

As these last six autobiographies pass in review, we hear the militancy of a marching purpose. From North and South, with middle- and lower-class backgrounds, raised in a predominantly white or colored community, the authors lash out against the caste restrictions on Negroes in American society. Their protests, couched in different language out of differing experience and points of view, are timed to coincide with all the recent goading of the American conscience. Too modern to be moralistic, too scientific to be pamphleteers, they marshal their array of harsh fact as ammunition in the battle between reason and superstition, order and chaos, civilization and the law of the jungle.

Utilizing the data of their own lives to illustrate the forces at work in society, these thinkers evidence a deep concern for that society. Author after author refers to the friction of race relations as only one element in the dislocations of modern living. Imperialism, fascism, war, and class rivalries prevent health in the body politic. Unemployment, hunger, and want are not the monopoly of a minority group.

But what throws them back to a preoccupation with the harm done to their own racial group is not merely the nature of their personal experience but their considered judgment that the race problem is the Gordian knot of all the other problems. While acculturation proceeds for other groups in American society, caste status has been too easy to fix upon Negroes because of the circumstance of color. However much the trend of modern sociology may swing away from the whole concept of caste on the grounds that it is a misnomer in relation to the comparative mobility of American life, these authors will continue to point to its moral equivalent in their direct experience. Caste can be used as a relative term, with its rigidity less or more evident in certain periods and places, but always more evident in comparison to the open class features in American society. Consequently, "castelike" would be a minimum they would insist upon in describing the greatest forced isolation of Negroes from normal activities.

According to the data of these books, then, for all intents and purposes caste restrictions still operate as a practical deterrent to the progress of Negroes everywhere. Du Bois and Redding, northern born and educated, are just as emphatic about their existence as the others. They use the imagery of a sheet of plate glass or a high wall which separates whites and Negroes. Redding's feeling of apartness in a Northern university reaches as neurotic a pitch as Wright's in a Southern town. Thus the task of removing the initial barrier, so that normal acculturation can occur, belongs to the nation, not to a region or section of the country. It is true that Du Bois and Redding, when they visit the South, and James Weldon Johnson when he revisits his Southern home town, are struck aghast by the obvious and violent forms of discrimination they meet; that no northern-raised author can vie with Herndon and Wright in their acquaintance with brutality. But this group also hear the sleeping giant in the North. And prejudice has even greater reality for them in psychological than in physical form.

Disagreeing on specific remedies for racial tensions, these writers agree that the "superior" white man carries his complexes with him wherever he goes, and that he will continue to cause trouble for himself and others until he learns to live without the compulsive need of bullying. Meanwhile, he should not have the satisfaction of complacency in his dominance. Certainly these men are opposed to a laissez-faire attitude in this matter. Psychologically alert, they are not content with sociological investigation of the surfaces of the American way of life, but push on to probe into every corner of white behavior and motivation. Considering the caliber of their mental acumen and their wide contacts, we may safely assume that they hit the bull's-eye as often as our foreign critic, Gunnar Myrdal, in his analysis of the conflicts in the mind of the typical native white American. In fact, one only has to turn to the index of *An American Dilemma* to note how frequently Gunnar Myrdal relied on autobiographies like *Along This Way* and *Dusk of Dawn* to clarify the issue.

This last group of authors is probably more aware of complexities in Negro-white interaction than our preceding group. From Du Bois to

Wright they make greater use of the data pointing to the long-time process of curing human prejudices. Yet this knowledge seems to gird them to more determined effort rather than sending them into retreat. It is almost as if they were saying—yes, we know that we are outnumbered, we know that we have the Trojan horses of ignorance, apathy, and avarice among our own forces, we know that we may never see a day of triumph, but we cannot rest without trying to enliven and enlighten.

No given autobiographical facts can fully explain why they should enter the arena of race relations while their contemporaries in the preceding group preferred to loiter on the sidelines. Neither immediate surroundings nor family upbringing can supply the definitive answer. Du Bois and Hughes attended white schools as did Taylor Gordan, Elizabeth Adams, Era Bell Thompson, and Braithwaite. They, too, escaped any early conditioning in inferiority. They, too, had ample opportunity for accommodation on a pleasant, personal plane. Yet they showed no more inclination in this direction than did victims of early segregation like Wright and Herndon. Hughes, Redding, and Wright all had family maladjustments which may have facilitated their later rebellions to white dominance. But Zora Hurston and Elizabeth Adams also had fathers to whom they felt hostile but who evidently did not send them towards protest of white injustice.

Perhaps, in the last analysis, we should look for qualities of mind and temperament which are the result of chance combination of genes as well as of the varying impacts of a culture. If we study this last group of autobiographies as a whole, we can see that it sustains a consistently high level of penetrating thought and able expression. A majority of the group had distinguished themselves as writers prior to the publication of their autobiographies for the simple reason that they had thought through something important enough to say at an early stage in their careers. Just as their keen intelligence led them to shape their ideas in writing, so did it drive them to analyze from every angle their relation to American society.

From the untutored boy, Richard Wright, to the academic Dr. Du Bois there is a fire of intellect which consumes them with a need to understand their world. Just as the superior student in school reacts differently from the average student to the same material because he grasps further implications, meanings, and connections with other material in a never-ending cycle, so do these students of society take their personal experience as a key to unlock the larger enigma of Negro-white interaction. Secondhand answers will not suffice. They have the type of creative mentality which demands original work. This is a sobering process leaving little time for levity. Individuals who are concerned with all the whys and wherefores of life usually neglect happiness for comprehension.

Too widely informed and too observant to accept the status quos of society, these thinkers point to hypocrisies and contradictions in the social order. As a result, they show a marked tendency to be critical of both capitalism and orthodox religion. Although a majority of them have middle-class backgrounds, they feel a kinship with the masses of people who have to compete for jobs in an insecure system. In between the outright opposition of Johnson to communism and the avowed Marxism of Herndon lies a common denominator of interest in some form of collectivism, cooperative movement, or socialism which will really implement democracy. Similarly, all of them unite in a reaction to the emotionalism of any religion manipulated to soothe them into docility. In its place they put a humanitarian ideal which would make brotherhood more challenging and less speculative.

Too realistic to expect the best, they nevertheless have some philosophical basis for hope. The very fact that they never think twice about expressing their indictment of society in general, and white society in particular, proclaims their justification for hoping. While their predecessors had been conciliatory and cautious, defensive, or silent about white attitudes, these autobiographers live out their claim to the rights of man.

Their assumption is well documented that it is just as logical for one to be considered no less a Negro because he is a man as no less a man because he is a Negro. To them, the only difference between the terms is that one is specific, the other general. For white society to insist on some qualitative difference and thus force on Negroes the conflicts of a Man-Negro duality seems as absurd and suicidal as segregating all redheads, all six-footers, or all people with a Western drawl into separate categories distinct from each other and from Americans. Who are Americans then becomes a pertinent question. These thinkers would answer that accidental differences of color, stature, or speech have nothing to do with matters of superiority and inferiority as citizens and, above all, as human beings. Their realism about the present mentality of most white Americans which perpetuates castelike treatment of colored Americans does not blind them to the dynamics of social change. With them, the matter resolves itself down to a life-and-death race with time in which civilization itself is the stake.

Conclusion

VALUES FOR INTERGROUP LIVING

TAKEN as a whole, these Negro American authors illustrate the way in which human values come to outweigh mere literary values. Literary merit they possess, in good measure. As we watch the trend, especially in recent years, we can note a rapid development in the quality of their writing which augurs well for the future. Skill in joining vigor and versatility of expression to a wealth of content guarantees them an integral place in American letters. Yet they achieve final importance by their special insights into the complexities of race.

From a unique vantage point these Negro Americans penetrate a troubled area of national life with honesty and decisiveness, and leave in their wake some profitable lines of thought for all Americans. While we share their sober judgments we pass imperceptibly beyond a preoccupation with good reading to a concern for good living.

DEATH TO THE STEREOTYPE

One basic fact steps out from the pages of these autobiographies to face us squarely. In spite of the common problem which binds them together, the writers manifest more difference than similarity of attitude about race. We have found, for example, that the self-made men and women of the Booker T. Washington school who tended to believe that the right kind of virtue would be rewarded were quite out of harmony with the champions of individual pride who refused to indulge in any such optimism. Through the early years of this century apology began to make way before proof positive of Negro ability, and moral demand came to take the place of moral appeal. Or again, we have seen that the autobiography of self-expression, which purposely subordinated the race dilemma to private values, clashed with the school of social documentation in which a man's life means nothing if it cannot elucidate the muddle of human relationships. These outstanding Negro Americans, on the whole, have contrasting and even conflicting ideas about what constitutes success and happiness within the confines of a dominant white society.

This fact may or may not surprise us. In any case, it draws us to a conclusion. For if these autobiographies prove anything it is that their authors are primarily just people. Although the consciousness of race stamps their writing as surely as their lives, they formulate their reactions too variously to permit casting them into stereotypes.

Confirming Evidence of the Novel

We can easily test the validity of the case for individuality by looking beyond the Negro autobiography to the Negro novel. Here we find a parallel state of affairs. Often, it is true, Negro novelists are as preoccupied with racial problems as we would expect. But even so, they assert the same integrity of self in their variations of theme and social philosophy. Sometimes, of late, they even drop the racial subject entirely.

Negro fiction of the last generation or so has offered us not only the "hard-boiled" Harlem school of a Claude McKay, but also the "respectable" middle-class gentility of a Jessie Fauset. There was also the heavy-hitting problem novel, filled with *J'accuse* statement, as exemplified by Walter White's exposé of lynching in *The Fire in the Flint.* But that emphasis was superseded in popularity by the lightning jabs of wit and satire, at the expense of white and black alike, which Rudolph Fisher, Wallace Thurman and George Schuyler perfected. To add spice, there was even a detective story. In Rudolph Fisher's *The Conjure Man Dies,* the locale is Harlem, the cast is colored, but the dénouement revolves around murder, not race.

Then followed Richard Wright's case study of the makings of a criminal in *Native Son,* which, in turn, paved the way for the bitter realism of Chester Himes' *If He Hollers Let Him Go,* and William Attaway's *Blood on the Forge.* In these books, all three protagonists are Negro, all three are defeated by frustration and misplaced aggression. From the city street and steel mill which accentuate their tragedies we can turn back to the small midwestern town where Langston Hughes, in *Not Without Laughter,* showed the gentler yet sobering plight of a colored boy, or to the rural South and the all-Negro communities where Zora Hurston laid her regional novels.

Back and forth the shuttle weaves, between rural folk life and urban slums, from comedy of manners to satire to high tragedy. Sometimes using harsh diatribe, at other times sonorous phrases or simple, singing words, these Negro authors grope towards their various meanings. As free ranging as their choice of milieu is their style, their style as their purpose.

It is significant that an increasing number of Negro novelists are ignoring the pressures of personal experience and of public expectation by concentrating on non-Negro subject-matter and avoiding anything that might be called a "Negro" point of view. The popular success of several of these books can be gauged by their presence on best-seller lists. Yet few general readers stop to learn that Frank Yerby and Willard Motley are Negroes, since *The Foxes of Harrow* and *Knock on Any Door* bear no imprint of Negro experience or authorship. Both of these writers have thus won public acclaim on the basis of their work alone, apart from such irrelevancies as color.

It is a remarkable achievement for the Negro novelist to enter into the heart and mind of his white characters so completely. Willard Motley's *Nick,* though an Italian Catholic, is really the blood brother of Richard Wright's *Bigger,* and his disorganization is handled with as much sympathy as if he were a lower class Negro. He takes on the status of any and all mishandled children of the slums.

Nor does the boundary of color bar the promising new writer, Ann Petry, from the broader perspective. Her latest book, *Country Place,* exposes plenty of seaminess in New England small town life without recourse to racial frictions. In fact, there is only one Negro character, and she is cast in a minor role.

Perhaps at first glance we might suspect Miss Petry of an anti-white bias if judged by her host of unsavory white characters. Yet their unpleasantness is more than offset by two important exceptions, which is good measure for any realistic modern novel. First, there is the kindly druggist whom the author chooses to carry the burden of her tale. By telling the story in the first person, the druggist assumes the omniscience of a narrator, becomes identified with the humaneness and objectivity of the author, and thus exemplifies the author's "white" point of view! Then there is the hero, a returning veteran. To the problems of his marital and community readjustments Miss Petry brings the full gift of her understanding, in spite of his whiteness.

We can scotch any lingering notion we may entertain concerning

"The Negro" as novelist, in terms of a fixed common denominator, by examining in more detail some samples from the recent literary crop. Three which come to mind are George Henderson's *Jule,* Frank Yerby's *The Foxes of Harrow,* and Ann Petry's first novel, *The Street.* A thankless task awaits the critic who would classify them together under the heading of Negro literature.

Jule unfolds the simple story of a boy who has his roots deep in the good Alabama earth of an all-Negro farming colony. In contrast to that serious and factual treatment of slave insurrection which Arna Bontemps gave us earlier in *Black Thunder, The Foxes of Harrow* ranks as pseudo-historical fiction, of Civil War vintage and New Orleans flavor. Only *The Street,* from our selected samples, lives up to the raw realism so often expected of Negro writers, for here indeed we see squalor and vice aplenty in the teeming quarters of Harlem.

In *Jule* the nostalgia for land and people which breathes through the pages is more pervasive than the one sharp conflict portrayed between colored boy and white man. Here there are many dark faces for the boy, Jule, to love. Against the backdrop of sweet-gum trees and burning southern moon appears the charm of casual living and spontaneous song. Jule's forced flight to a complex Harlem existence fails to touch some inner core. The reader is not surprised to see him, urbanized as he has become, reject his two-timing Harlem girl and return home to his first sweetheart, thirsty for her unstudied devotion. Jule's boyhood has bubbled with such richness of stream and field, animals and friendly people, that no adult troubles, even those thrown up by white men against his people, can really shatter his magic circle.

With *The Foxes of Harrow* this romantic disposition in current Negro authorship burgeoned into a Hollywood contract. Irish-born, Paris-bred, and American-natured, Stephen Fox has all the appeal of a self-made man in a dangerous and glamorous setting. The turbulent Mississippi River marks symbolically his restless and unconventional progress from poor adventurer to successful plantation owner. We pass from the provincial atmosphere of *Jule* to the sweep of a saga in which Stephen's personal fortunes only serve to underline the fate of an uneasy slaveholding state, achieving forlorn glory against the odds. Ideologies of North and South acquire texture and design under the arguments of slaveholders, ex-slaves, and abolitionists, the behavior of Creole or quadroon beauties. Mr. Yerby deftly fills his canvas with at least the illusion of historical situation.

With such a broad stroke has he painted that the reader is never aware of Negro authorship as such. No bias against the white man crops out. The opportunistic hero even lives to oppose the institution of slavery. Although his stand comes only after a long evolution of ideas, after military service on the Confederate side, and along with important reservations about equality for Negroes, the writer aids even the northern-oriented reader in painless acceptance. He is less lenient with his main Negro character. When the educated and highly intelligent slave, Little Inch, faces freedom and a chance to lead in a reconstruction framework, he exhibits none of the nobility of mind and spirit so evident in Howard Fast's comparable hero in *Freedom Road.* That Mr. Yerby raises his ex-slave to higher stature in his next novel, *The Vixens,* hardly compensates for the omission in his first.

Down to his choice of emphasis in plot, Yerby ignores any possible racial claims on his talent. Even political and humanitarian issues are subordinated to the family chronicle, to the passions, feuds and pleasures of succeeding generations which spring so dramatically from the reservoir of black sweat and toil. One may well wonder what percentage of Negro spectators relishes the particular portrayal of Negroes in the screen version of *The Foxes of Harrow.*

In the last analysis, the only link which can hold Mr. Henderson and Mr. Yerby together is the negative fact that neither has produced a "sordid" book. The reader can put down each one without feeling that his need for pleasant escapes in a sorry world has been grossly neglected. The attitudes of these writers tend to confirm the view that struggle is by and large worth-while, and that decency is a basic human trait.

Miss Petry, however, gives a shake to these neat verities. Her heroine has no land to cherish, no friends to proffer helping hands. Like Jule's mother, Lutie places her small son first, but her desperate efforts to cherish and protect echo all the futility of tragic drama. Even mere survival seems beyond her grasp. Her very beauty serves as a fatal handicap, her very street functions as a menace to health and happiness. Neither janitor, lady tenant, nor boss offers respite to her problems. The dénouement is so firmly bound to violence that we are early liberated to contemplate the pathos of the stranded little son.

Yet *The Street* gains dignity by its avoidance of the overtones of hate. Although, because of her intimate grasp of Harlem material, Miss Petry, in this particular novel, might come under Negro classification more readily than Mr. Yerby, in her own way she has attained to a detachment perhaps more remarkable than his. She is dealing with modern urban life made more pitiless by forces which she could easily trace to the white man's doorstep. But no hint of bitter propaganda escapes. Villains there are. Yet the complexions are dark as well as white. Only cloaked in all its complexity is the origin of sin suggested.

At the other extreme from the glamor of *The Foxes of Harrow, The Street,* for all its sordidness, may still endure beyond the fanfare of the better-seller. Certainly it is no cardboard blood-and-thunder romance. While *The Foxes of Harrow* retrogresses to that genre of historical tale with spicy undercurrents, popularized by *Gone with the Wind* and promoted by lush technicolor, carried to the extreme in *Forever Amber* and finally burlesqued in *Grenadine Etching, The Street* tackles current issues of unemployment, juvenile delinquency and crime in a psycho-sociological framework. The more substantial fare is apt to outlive fads and become a staple in the national literary diet.

But just as individual preference of the readers enters into an appraisal of these three novels, so should the individual preference of all Negro writers in selecting their subjects be respected. This can only take place in an open and receptive atmosphere. The author who, by chance of birth, runs into the monotonous expectation from the public that he is only capable of producing problem-propaganda literature, may clutch another theme for negative reasons. He may be so anxious to circumvent expectation that he parachutes into a never-never land alien to his, and possibly everyone else's, experience. In this way he has been forced to sacrifice the free range of his talent. Or again, if he purposely chooses this same romantic material with a mercenary eye to popular taste, the least we can grant is that it is his right, as much as his white competitor's, to profit. Just as in the days of the hack writer and the literary patron, bread-and-butter motivation still wars with artistic integrity.

It is a safe assumption that these three novelists, and their fellow craftsmen, wish to be condemned or condoned only in relation to the expanded area of American letters as a whole. They do not ask for special concession as Negroes when they protest unfair bias in criticism. A single yardstick for white and dark authors will suffice for them. Each is seeking his own literary climate. Ann Petry would be far happier in the biting and bracing aura of Zola and Dreiser, Caldwell and

Hemingway, than the langorous and seductive one which Frank Yerby invokes, while George Henderson is certainly more atune to the gentle melancholy of Willa Cather's regionalism than to the shock of Ann Petry's naturalism.

The persistence of individuality against all odds makes us wonder how much less true generalizations about Negroes would be if free creative expression were encouraged by our culture. Under such circumstances, allowed a normal play of interest and ability, some of these writers would, without doubt, have turned their hand gladly to other pursuits. Others, still preferring literature, might have felt less bound by racial themes. The shunting of Negro talent towards certain grooves is one of the little known but far-reaching results of discrimination.

A Common Denominator

However, we must not bend so far towards recognizing individuality that we overlook the one point of agreement which all our autobiographers share. They unite in criticizing the "superior" white man. From the common ground of their unanimity, minimum though it be, an indictment of white behavior runs, like a scarlet thread, through all their pages.

From Booker T. Washington to Richard Wright, Negro writers subscribe to the conviction that hostility towards Negroes never does anybody any good. To those white defenders of the status quo who like to mouth the stale euphemism that hardship is good for the character, that suffering spawns genius, they would chorus the answer that their own achievements have been won at great price, in spite of, not because of white discrimination. Some of them believe in coming to terms with prejudice gracefully, while others rebel openly, but this points to tactical variations rather than to difference in principle. And tactics is always a result of environmental pressure. It stands to reason that not one of these men and women who have first-hand experience will condone exploitation even while he may refrain from condemning it.

The Non-sense of Race

What, then, is the substance of their say to white people? First of all comes the nonsense angle on race prejudice. In between the lines of recent books, especially, runs a commentary on the foolishness of mortals in clinging to outmoded theories of innate racial differences as a rationalization of white supremacy. A good many writers regard the blinders of prejudice as a public acknowledgement of ignorance and scientific illiteracy, or, even worse, as the outer props of an inner, unconscious, compulsive need to domineer. Thus what starts out as nonsense has tragic consequences for all concerned.

Latent in these books, too, lies a satirical angle. For they indicate that by means of discrimination whites thrust upon Negroes a defensive solidarity. What an ironic joke on whites if this strength of unity should develop into a threat to the "sanctity of white supremacy." Prejudice can conceivably forge a weapon which will prove a deadly boomerang. If the Ku Klux Klan-minded guarded their own interests more astutely, they would apply the Machiavellian principle of ruling by dividing, by pitting not only poor whites against Negroes, but Negroes against Negroes. Instead, they tend to force Negroes of different background, ability, and interests, religious, nonreligious, educated, noneducated, upper, lower, middle class, into one camp.

Beyond the satire we can increasingly catch a note of warning. The militancy of our last group of autobiographers is no chance occurrence. Even while they protest and protect their right to be individuals they are weighing the seriousness of the situation and choosing to focus their attention on race relations. As long as they are Negroes as well as men the Man-Negro duality does not permit them the luxury of withdrawal into their prerogative as mere men who do not have to concern themselves with social problems. Accordingly, like the old prophets, these thinkers point to danger signals on the social horizon. Let him who will not heed become chaff on the wind. For suppressed people will not remain so definitely. Exploitation is a dynamic process.

The Theory and Practice of Like-Mindedness

Yet these Negro Americans do not content themselves with condemning. On the constructive side appears a positive angle on race relations. Stemming from these autobiographies is a point of view which we might designate as a philosophy of the like-minded. The total impact of such life stories strikes home the realization that America is neglecting untapped resources of personality and human energy. It is suggested that in a disintegrating society—by general admission more in danger today under the uncertainties of an atomic age—each of us needs to feel the support of like-minded people. If value-systems remain as the only hope for the mental sanity and rational agreement which are necessary for physical survival, they should certainly be given their head over the fences of race and color.

The evidence of these autobiographies goes to show that white people, taken as individuals or groups, can indeed find common ground with darker people. Ranging from conservative to radical, from sports fans to opera lovers, from introverts to extroverts, from get-rich-quick enthusiasts to social idealists, the Negro Americans who come to life in these pages display the same variety of taste, temperament, and purpose as any other segment of the population.

These authors pose the question as to why we do not make our alignments behind logic rather than behind those arbitrary barriers of color which place the unlike-minded together and the like-minded separately. The answer to this question should particularly concern those of us who feel that civilization itself is slipping down hill. If we want one world, a people's world, we need to join hands with all of our rightful allies before it is too late. Least of any can we afford to be diverted by false gods.

It is more a matter of being sensible than being good. The closer we come to the confusion of our times the more these writers use practical rather than moralistic appeals. Prior to 1930, in the first two groups of autobiographies, there was a frequent attempt to arouse the conscience of white Americans to their own cruelty and injustice. In the 1930's and 1940's, however, appears a challenge to white commonsense and self-interest. From the scientific point of view these authors, later confirmed by the research of scholars like Gunnar Myrdal, a society which is riddled with contradictions, which divorces behavior from ideal, is an unhealthy one. In the fluid society which the American dream promises, all individuals need the freedom to seek their appropriate levels. Those who would deny others this natural growth become stunted in turn. Those, on the other hand, who are implementing the democratic process reap the benefits for themselves, too, in the long run.

Of course there is no guarantee that the majority of Americans will choose to adopt this rudimentary lesson in group relations as an alternative to disaster. As social realists, few of our latter day writers are sanguine, therefore, about the immediate future. They recognize that reason never prevails easily. In this case the fact of discrimination, whether in jobs, housing, education, or citizenship, will linger on long after the theories supporting inferiority and superiority have been exorcised. The prospects for social equality are threatened by the economic insecurity of a competitive status.

But as long as minds change facts as well as facts change minds, some of these Negro thinkers will join with like-minded whites in cultivating a "will to believe." This group can never resign itself to accepting fatalistically the entrenchment of prejudice. It has long ago countered the pseudo-science of the nineteenth century which held that prejudice was inherited, an ingrained human trait. It now goes on to oppose that school of environmentalism today which claims that early conditioning in race fear marks for life every American white child.

The emotional sets of one generation are not necessarily passed on to the next generation without alteration. The endless cycle is constantly being broken by successful reconditioning. Certainly an individual, if he bestirs himself, is not doomed to dislike through social, any more than through biological, inheritance. Thus the hope is that some day the average citizen, instead of arguing endlessly that Negroes do not deserve opportunities until they are worthy of them, may respond to the logic of the answer that no one can be worthy of any opportunity without first having it.

The final call, then, is to action. Our recent autobiographers, stressing the need of mental therapy for good health, have made a constructive and, at the same time, practical contribution. There is no point in arguing with white people about their social "sins" when they may be suffering from unconscious guilt complexes or other psychological disorders. There is more point in opening up to them a new frame of reference in which they can organize their personalities and learn to move more harmoniously with their darker fellow citizens. After all, it is the prejudiced people who must become the test-cases for an improved social order.

The Next Step

So regarded, the idea of democratic intergroup living becomes a challenge to adventure. These Negro thinkers could well be regarded as spearheads of an anti-smugness campaign. They are perfectly cognizant of the fact that there are as many different orientations on race among white people as among Negroes. They know that the indifferent, the apathetic, and the cynical can be as destructive as the hate-mongers, that the dilettantism of many liberals can be as paralyzing to progress as the outright opposition of conservatives. But they also count on the people of good-will who have stayed immobilized only through lack of information. Such people wish to widen their horizons. They may really prefer to have the comfort of their surface smugness shaken so that they can live more completely.

Once we welcome the implicit challenge of these autobiographies, we can apply it within the circle of our immediate experience. Although it is a wise reminder that each of us can take a stand against prejudice only in proportion to our capacity to do so, it is encouraging to discover that the cubic content is not only larger than we at first suspect but that it increases rapidly in direct ratio to use. A firm support of human rights in local situations, whether correcting the racial stereotypes fostered by movies or protesting restrictive covenants in residential districts, leads to a concern for legal and civil rights everywhere. It is the familiar process at work of believing through doing.

It is easier, then, than we fear. Daily we have examples from those who quietly set up new prcedents, and "call the bluff" of those who bluster. It takes the president of a major baseball league to dramatize the technique of liquidating racial antagonism. In 1947, when he issued the public statement that a qualified Negro player had as much right to play professional baseball as any other citizen of the United States of America, and when he scorned the team's threat to strike, he made social history.

How much fairer it would be to the patrons of the arts in Washington, D. C. to prove that it was not their confused whim to allow Negroes in the audience but not on the stage of Constitution Hall, on the stage but not in the audience of the National Theatre. When united action of producers and actors threatens boycott of a theatre which bans Negro patrons, it mobilizes the good will and common sense of the citizenry. The argument of owner or director, wherever he be, that he "cannot afford to oppose local custom," begins to wear threadbare.

Some day people of varying complexions will learn the relief of relaxing their guard against imaginary foes, conjured up by fear, and sustained by stereotypes. Shadow boxing is too strenuous for peace of mind, too futile for satisfaction. Some day, too, the many will weary of the hoax of hate, perpetuated in their name, but profitless to their long-run interests.

Such grasp of social sanity becomes the only tangible hope for intergroup living. And it is the same slender hope which buoys our autobiographers into perspective above the waves of despair and defeat. If they did not count on a leaven of reasonableness in human nature, they could put little heart into articulating their experience for this and the next generation.

Fortunate are those, meanwhile, who refuse to be bogged down by current prejudices. We observe increasingly in these Negro autobiographies the signs of such hard-won maturity. When a man comes to understand the meaning of his own dilemma he achieves a catharsis and a chance for personality integration even in the worst of situations. Many of our writers possess an insight into the complexities of their life-situations which raises them to a plane eclipsing the whiteness of lesser men. Such Negro Americans may well hold, with Pascal, that a "thinking reed" has the real advantage over the universe which could so easily crush it.

BIBLIOGRAPHY

The author acknowledges with gratitude the courtesy of the authors and publishers who have accorded permission for the use, in this book, of quotations from the following books.

Adams, Elizabeth Laura, *Dark Symphony*. New York, Sheed & Ward, 1942.

Braithwaite, William Stanley, "The House Under Arcturus." *Phylon*, Vol. II, 1941–1942.

Corrothers, James D., *In Spite of the Handicap*. New York, George H. Doran Company, 1916.

Douglass, Frederick, *Life and Times of Frederick Douglass*. New York, Pathway Press, 1941.

Du Bois, W. E. Burghardt, *Dusk of Dawn*. New York, Harcourt, Brace and Company, 1940.

Gordon, Taylor, *Born to Be*. New York, Covici, Friede, Inc., 1929.

Handy, W. C., *Father of the Blues*. New York, The Macmillan Company, 1941.

Harrison, Juanita, *My Great Wide Beautiful World*. New York, The Macmillan Company, 1936.

Henson, Matthew A., *A Negro Explorer at the North Pole*. New York, Frederick A. Stokes Company, 1912.

Herndon, Angelo, *Let Me Live*. New York, Random House, Inc., 1937.

Hughes, Langston, *The Big Sea*. New York, Alfred A. Knopf, 1940.

Hunter, Jane Edna, *A Nickel and a Prayer*. Cleveland, Elli Kani Publishing Co., 1940.

Hurston, Zora Neale, *Dust Tracks on a Road*. Philadelphia, J. B. Lippincott Company, 1942.

Johnson, James Weldon, *Along This Way*. New York, The Viking Press, 1933.

McKay, Claude, *A Long Way From Home*. New York, Lee Furman, Inc., 1937.

Pickens, William, *Bursting Bonds*. Boston, The Jordan and More Press, 1923.

Powell, Lieut. William J., *Black Wings*. Los Angeles, Ivan Deach, Jr., Publisher, 1934.

Redding, J. Saunders, *No Day of Triumph*. New York, Harper & Brothers, 1942.

Taylor, Marshall W. "Major," *The Fastest Bicycle Rider in the World*. Worcester, Mass., Wormley Publishing Co., 1928.

Terrell, Mary Church, *A Colored Woman in a White World*. Washington, D. C., Ransdell Inc., 1940.

Thompson, Era Bell, *American Daughter*. Chicago, University of Chicago Press, 1946.

Washington, Booker T., *Up From Slavery*. New York, Doubleday, Page and Company, 1901.

Wright, Richard, *Black Boy*. New York, Harper & Brothers, 1945.

INDEX